Ilana Bahat

The Consciousness of One

Transcending the Path of Hurt
to the Path of Heart

Ilana Bahat

The Consciousness of One

Senior Editors & Producers: Contento De Semrik

English Edition: Haim Nissim Haviv
English Edit: BookMasters Group
Graphic Design: Ivan Bogod | Contento De Semrik
Cover Design: Yael Rosen | www.yds.co.il

Copyright © 2012 by Ilana Bahat

heartpath1@gmail.com | www.lotuscenter.co.il

All rights reserved. No part of this book may be translated, reproduced, stored in a retrieval system or transmitted, in any form or by any means, electronic, photocopying, recording or otherwise, without prior permission in writing from the author and publisher.

ISBN: 978-965-550-032-5

International sole distributor:
Contento De Semrik
22 Isserles, 67014 Tel–Aviv, Israel
Semrik10@gmail.com
www.Semrik.com

Ilana Bahat

The Consciousness of One
Transcending the Path of Hurt to the Path of Heart

Contento De Semrik

Dedications

Rabbi Akiva the one and only, whose spirit still pervades the world, heralding the theory of unity for the redemption of Israel and the nations of the world. The dispenser of "The Consciousness of One" states: "Love your neighbour as yourself. Love the Lord your God with all your soul and with all your might".

My children: Omri, Yoav and Ido.
My sisters: Smadar Amit and Niva Kedar.
My nieces: Noa, Shay, Yuval Kedar and Rani Amit.
My former husband and father of my children,
Sammy Bahat.
My good friend, Liron Berger.
My beloved mother Frida Amit-Silberberg, may her memory be blessed. With great gratitude and love eternal.
My beloved father Arthur Amit–Eigenfeld, may his memory be blessed with gratitude and love eternal. I miss you both.

My beloved grandmother Carola Silberberg-Rosenzweig, may her memory be blessed. The most wonderful grandmother and a wise woman. I will honour your memory forever and I am sending you my love and undying gratitude.
To my grandfather Moshe Silberberg, may his memory be blessed.
My grandmother and grandfather who I did not get to meet, Sima and Meir Eigenfeld may their memory be blessed.

Thanks to all the people in my life, at all times and incarnations.
The people of Israel and all nations of the world.

Archangel Metatron
To all my guides
The Council of Karma
The Great White Brotherhood
The creator of the universe

Introduction
By Master Akiva

This book opens a skylight into the teachings of unity and truth. This Torah (teaching) was handed down to the Children of Israel – that unique and chosen people – during the revelation at Mount Sinai. As you know, the essence of the whole teaching is: "Love thy neighbour as thyself"; and "You shall love the Lord your God with all your heart, with all your soul and with all your will." The meaning of love, as conveyed here, is unconditional giving from the heart, an act of giving which flows, like the rays of the sun that impart their warmth and their love to all of creation, impartially and without exclusion. Such giving triggers receiving and it, too, is unconditional. Just as the earth itself and every living thing absorbs the rays of the sun, the act of receiving is done naturally and is predisposed to contain the abundance found in giving. Acceptance of what is sent, of what is bestowed, of the generous bounty, is in fact an act of giving to the one who has conferred it in the first place. When one gives to another, he receives, in turn, his own giving.

Until now, human beings have been submerged in the slumber of duality. This form of consciousness is one aspect of the perspective of opposites: day versus night, light versus darkness, good versus evil, all of which emphasize differences, the extreme separateness between an individual and his fellows, between a country and its neighbours, between one religion and another. This form of consciousness is characteristic of those who are not privy to the secret of the power of joint creation. They are unaware of their role in the process of creating reality. They are filled with internal contradictions, with inner struggles between various facets of their personality. These inner conflicts are projected into their relationships with others – be they neighbours, relatives or even other nations. Typically, this conflict is accompanied by a **course of pain**.

Many are implanted with the **victim pattern**, which twists them into duality's consciousness of separation. They relinquish responsibility for what transpires in their lives. They fail to grasp that they themselves have summoned their own karma. They tend to blame others – external agencies: other individuals, organizations, even foreign nations. At times they point a finger at God, blaming Him for events they fail to comprehend and find difficult to experience such as inexplicable death, accidents, wars of annihilation and the like.

Dear and most beloved people, it is time to awaken, to assume responsibility for creating your own reality, to open yourselves to a new awareness that is being exuded through the heavenly membrane – the "Christ Consciousness" of the Age of Aquarius.

The source of this awareness is the highest and most sublime hierarchies. This awareness is superior to and more evolved than, the consciousness of duality – the vision of separation. So say all the guides and emissaries of light who, devoid of physical form, come to light your way to: **The Consciousness of One.**

This awareness comes to teach you the highest truth, the truth at soul level, the truth that emanates directly from a God who is supremely great, high and exalted. Your source is the One.

No longer are there "others," no longer is there "separateness." "Not taking responsibility," either individually or collectively, has passed from the world.

The time has come for peace. Peace is permeating our awareness, bringing with it the benevolent, gentle fragrance of the energy of love. This love is unity. It is mutual respect among all created beings, for it is intelligence, planted and activated by a divine spark.

The time is at hand and the hour is ripe for mankind to transcend the "path of hurt" which has characterized you for so many eons and embark on the "**path of heart!**"

This course negotiates its way through compassion. It is a grand and illuminated path of recovery from every kind of conflict. It fulfils the vision of the latter days: "And the wolf shall dwell with the lamb," "neither shall they learn war anymore..." It is mankind's collective choice to go forth and develop along the evolutionary path of light.

Instead of blaming others, there is an assumption of responsibility for what is. People are taking responsibility for their innermost selves – their inner temple – in its entirety. It encompasses the entire belief–system – whether conscious or hunkering down in the recesses of the subconscious. It includes taking responsibility for all thoughts, feelings and actions. It embraces communion with the divine will. This spiritual union occurs when one is in touch with the temple of the soul. This is the exalted truth.

When you are in touch with the exalted truth, you are able to perceive the lesson mankind is being taught: Group development through drama. Drama is a form of anaesthesia.

"All the world's a stage and all the men and women merely players." This was collective dramatization, jointly planned by all human souls. Soul agreements were contracted on the high plane, in the World of Truth, which, as its name attests, facilitates union with the exalted truth of unity and co-operation, of direct linking with God. Human souls were sent to earth to reincarnate, again and again, in order to discover the truth through direct experience. Knowledge was deliberately withheld, so the souls forgot the purpose of the lessons – the "soul agreements."

All is as it should be. All is in harmony with the times. There are no errors in creation! There are no errors whatsoever.

Do you think, when following the plot of a drama with its sequence of apparent blunders, disasters, crises and even comic situations, that there is any coincidence? It is all planned by divine agencies and produced with the assistance of human actors. The guiding hand advises, navigates and provides testing grounds (which at times you may refer to as mistakes or unpleasant situations).

Evolving humanity is capable of accessing very high frequencies! Its conceptualization of truth is changing, expanding, crystallizing and ascending.

All humankind is ascending to the status of "graduates" on the planet.

There is a shift from the third and fourth dimensions to the fifth, the dimension of creativity. This is the dimension where dreams are windows, portals to the conscious creation of reality.

In order to reach this dimension, mankind must cleanse, purify, comprehend and apply the new dispensation of knowledge granted them by numerous and varied factors (which are, in fact, but one).

From time immemorial, curiosity has directed and assisted the development of mankind. Technological advances brought about co-operation and the sources and features of information have become integrated. The Internet came into existence in order to enable you to do the same. Imagine such a web in the world of ideas, of spirit – it would grant you access to all the sources of knowledge!

What you refer to today as "channeling" would be available to everyone. Telepathy is also becoming more robust.

This is not the time for harbouring secrets, for accumulating karmic debts, for lack of comprehension.

This is the time for unity!

This is the time for peace!

This is the time for in–depth insight, for comprehending, according to the mysteries of ancient mysticism previously hidden from you; the meaning of these verses:

Love thy neighbour as thyself and you shall love the Lord your God with all your heart, with all your soul and with all your will.

The time is at hand, the time is ripe and the ring of redemption is in the air! Those who are willing to open their eyes and commune with their hearts, to rise to the perception of reality through the eyes of the soul, will perceive God's light awakening unto a recognition of His divinity. They are divine sparks operated by and in unity with other divine sparks like themselves.

You are not separate from one another. That is the meaning of the verse: "What is hateful to you, do not do to your fellow men."

I bless you with a life of goodness, filled with self–fulfillment. I bless you with continued ascent up mankind's evolutionary ladder of light. I bless you with an abundance of health, a flow of creativity and copious love.

I am grateful to my dear, Ilana for facilitating passage through her, through this clean and pure channell she has within her, for which she was born and around which she has woven her life until now, as an instrument of the spirit, a trumpet for the angels and their holy purpose.

I am grateful to all those, who facilitate the passage of spiritual messages through themselves. I thank all those who read what I have communicated, who has chosen to internalize and encompass our messages within their frequencies upon this earth at this time.

I grant permission for the use and citation of these materials and ask that their sanctity be maintained and their knowledge be respected.

Here I am, Master Akiva, bearing a vision of unity and salvation, revival and the revelation of the latter days. I am dispatching to you from my frequency, infusing through words, sanctity and fusion with high truth from the plane of the soul. I serve as a mouthpiece for guides from higher hierarchies. The guides of light, whoever they may be, are ascended light entities who serve the will of God.

One is our God in the heavens and the earth. Hear O Israel the Lord our God the Lord is one!

I have concluded and opened my statement in a sentence. You should carve it into your hearts, place it in your gates and spread the message and its gospel.

Love thy neighbour as thyself!

Introduction
by the Author

This book was channelled by a great master and an emissary of the light, known in one of his incarnations as Rabbi Akiva.

Rabbi Akiva, one of the greatest sages of Israel, was a contemporary of Jesus. He was considered a great luminary, highly versed in the Torah, the occult and the Cabbala. He is characterized as having great love of his fellow man, his nation and God. He was a man of profound humility. It is said that he toiled as a shepherd for 40 years, studied for 40 years and then taught for 40 years. He left his mark on the rulings of many religions as well as the values of Jewish tradition and thought. The admiration accorded to Master Akiva the sage and authority has no parallel. According to the Talmud Moses, perceiving him in a prophetic vision, was amazed and said, "God, there is such a human being in your world and yet you chose me to receive the Torah?" Master Akiva's commentary on the verse, "Love thy neighbour as thyself" (Numbers, 19:18), is: "That is a great rule in the Torah."

He died a martyr at the age of 120. Master Akiva is regarded as the symbol of devotion and dedication to the Torah.

The book before you was written by way of channelling and out of a deep sense of mission and submission to the message of unity, the connection with the consciousness of the heart, from the vision of "Consciousness of One," which ties into the vision of world peace.

In my everyday life I am a spiritual teacher and an energetic–spiritual therapist, Reiki master and writer. I am in tune with the high light guidance and the masters and with their mission.

This book was channelled by a great master and an emissary of the light, known in one of his incarnations as Master Akiva. It was written in Hebrew, the language of holiness. According to the Cabbala, God used the 22 letters of the Hebrew alphabet to create the world. This book was written out of an understanding of my role in creation – a role I was not aware of till then.

Hebrew is my mother tongue. I was born in Israel, in the city of Haifa, at the top of Mount Carmel.

Archangel Metatron revealed himself to me and asked me to dedicate myself to important messages that are anticipated to come through me. Despite his statement, I did not apply myself to the mission until the universe sent me a sign in the form of a pigeon. It arrived in my home and settled in the centre of my living room, next to a large and heavy planter. A tarot class was scheduled to take place at my house and the ladies participating had already arrived, so I attempted to chase the pigeon away to prevent disruption. Either it did not want to fly away or it was unable to do so. We finally chased it to the balcony and shut the door. After the class ended I went to check on it. It was still there and looked swollen. By the following day it was dead. For some inexplicable reason I wrapped it in a plastic bag and asked that it would serve to expiate the whole nation of Israel.

At that time rumours were circulating that war was about to erupt, yet again, with Lebanon in the north. Because I interpret everything through its subtle meaning – for there are signs in everything – I sought to understand the message of the dead pigeon. Two interpretations came to mind: The first was personal – a pigeon symbolizes relationships and maybe a relationship had died. But I am a divorcee and was not in a relationship, so it didn't strike me as the correct interpretation. The second was on the national level: The pigeon symbolizes peace. When the pigeon dies, peace is endangered.

In order to understand the message, I summoned my spiritual teacher, Master Akiva. From the dawn of my life I have felt a psychic connection with him, identification with his life story and a profound love for him and his teachings.

He revealed himself to me and explained that is of utmost importance that I should dedicate myself to writing, because he has important messages to convey to the world during this harrowing period, the so called, "Latter Days."

When I commenced my conversation with Master Akiva on the question of love and unrequited love, I had no idea that it would open a huge portal to a whole body of knowledge about life. I have discovered that love is life itself, the connection with God and that it is expressed in every aspect of life.

Connecting with guides, including light entities and angels, has been, for many years, my way of learning. I commenced my path of awareness by studying Reiki – a wonderful form of energy I have opened up to with utter dedication. Since 1997 I have been a Reiki master and a strong believer in the pure way of Reiki, that teaches us how to be a pure channell for transmitting energies of light, love and healing. Since then I have specialized in a number of other energetic methods, including bio–energy, past–life regression, tarot and more.

In everyday life I am a spiritual teacher, Kuan Yin master, past life regression healer, karma release enabler and a developer of a healing method known as "Healing Soul Light."

Through this method of healing I actually re–build the person as a whole energy system, connected with the soul, connected with God and connected to conceptual intelligences, to life. I can examine the soul's condition from within and see if fragments are missing and then rescue and restore them. I enter the field of psychic energy and examine it at the patient's birth and at present. I do the same with all the chakra systems and tell the individual how he was born, how he developed and what is transpiring in his life right now. I also diagnose the presence of a vow to abstain, from a previous incarnation, which may be burdensome and disrupt the ability to earn a living. Numerous (past life) monks arrive at my doorstep. They have no idea of their former lives and that the vow remains in effect in their current existence. You may be surprised to know that in their current incarnations they are Jews, Christians, Muslim and Druze.

My activities were acknowledged in one of my dreams, where I met Pope John Paul II, who explained a certain spiritual rule to me and shook my hand. I interpreted it as approval of my discovery and its implementation – dissolving vows in extant incarnations. Interestingly, my father, Arthur Amit (formerly, Eigenfeld), who hailed originally from Poland, had a dream in which he was driving the Pope (John Paul II) and they travelled and held discussions. I jokingly remarked that maybe the Pope is a family friend.

The soul incarnates in different faiths in order to learn about unity. I work in full co-operation with the Angels of Karma and the Angels of the Violet Flame, who assist me in effecting karmic releases and transformations, including the energetic implantations of necessary qualities and capabilities for the individual being treated. I release blockages in all areas and help people to develop spiritually. In time I have learned that I build in the individual the ability to accommodate the "Third Temple," which is an inner temple found in the heart. It connects to the heart's consciousness, the soul's consciousness and the consciousness of one.

The system evolves continuously, with new discoveries occurring all the time. I implement them enthusiastically with wondrous results for my patients and students. I have developed sensitivity to energies and a precise diagnostic ability, something like a refined laser, scanning for energy. I teach Reiki and channelling, I conduct healing and empowering meditations; I channel angels for healing the individual and the planet alike, I write guidebooks whose purpose is ascension and enlightenment. I feel that I am on a mission of the light.

I see no coincidence in all of this – it is all happening from God. Everything is a sign sent to awaken my consciousness and open my eyes. It is all happening for my highest and best. These beliefs guide me on my path.

I wrote this book in a very short time – about two months, during 40 channelling sessions. Every day I would rise at dawn and write a chapter. It required great devotion, enlisting will power and dedication which had not been typical conduct for me before I undertook the mission.

Since completing this book, "Consciousness of the One," I embarked on a sequel, "Consciousness of the Light – Alchemy of the Soul," which was written in the state of enlightenment known as nirvana, inspired by the consciousness of seraphim, whose aim is to elevate humanity. I continue to write and receive messages for humanity.

I feel a great sense of gratitude for my purpose, my abilities, my entire life and a powerful urge to bestow, from a place of inner abundance, the light and love within me to humanity as a whole. Thank you to my beloved guides, thank you, God.

Bless you all, dear readers, who connect through your hearts to the message of unity that we are all one.

Lesson 1

What Is Love
An encounter with Master Akiva during meditation

I entered a deep meditative state during which I rose (in spirit) to the Temple of Light. I sat on a stone bench, sought to meet Master Akiva and asked him to explain the meaning of **"love thy neighbour," and the true meaning of love.**

After this experience I summarized what had transpired. It would seem that the meditation and the questions opened a portal to great knowledge and a close relationship was forged with Master Akiva.

Master Akiva introduced himself as Akiva Ben Yosef. He was clad in a white robe, his eyes were brilliant blue and he had a wide countenance with high cheekbones: An attractive entity radiating light and wisdom.

"You asked me, **'What is love?**[1]**'**" His answer was, love = giving.

Also, love = acceptance. Love includes unlimited giving and acceptance, from the heart.... There is a constant flow

---

1 I have reconstructed the beginning of the first chapter from memory. The rest is in Rabbi Akiva's own words and frequency.

between giving–receiving–giving. Mutuality is evident in the process. I see in my mind's eye a rising sun whose rays radiate toward the earth and give it life.

The opposite of boundless giving = **taking**. When you are not in love, you are in lust. You lust, instead of being in love. You try to take the love that you need by force, for you are in a state of inner want. You have barred yourself from it, you do not receive it from the other, so you attempt to compel another to give it to you. But you cannot coerce the other to give you love. Giving freely, giving that is unconditional – that is what you seek. First give it to yourself and then give it to the other, your fellow human being.

"You do not take love! Love is given and received!"

I had the idea of doing a meditation dedicated to inner and world peace. Master Akiva told me not to resort to platitudes, for they are inappropriate. "Believe me, they do not come through well. People have developed a mechanism to block clichés lacking content and inner significance and worn-out expressions."

He explained that I have to find the correct and precise words, conveyed out of pure giving of the soul and with senior guidance of the light, which desires to work through me in an energetic process of consecration. One should not sell an idea for a "pottage of lentils.[2] "We ought to relate to

---
2   Genesis 25:34.

every idea as a holy creation. Words should be treated with sanctity and treated with great respect.

Thanks to wonderful Master Akiva. I intend to dedicate time every day to learning with the guides, to summon them (actually they would be the ones to summon me, and, in fact, it would be mutual and intentional). As I was writing, the following sentence rose in my consciousness: "The time has come and the hour is at hand. You are ready to become a channell of pure and refined light **and of self-esteem**. Blessings and love. I Am Metatron, in the name of the Guidance, the Ascended Masters and the Angels."

I continue to think about love. Love is mutuality.

I think about the word: taking – to try and take **a part** of someone else, another entity (individual, nation, state). I try to comprehend and therefore I ask: Love = giving–receiving–giving. I understand. There is here a flow of mutuality. Now I would like to know: What about **falling in love**? **Unrequited love**? I ask Master Akiva to address my question.

(From this point on the messages will be brought in the language and through the energy of Master Akiva, through direct channelling.)

"Dear and beloved Ilana," says Master Akiva and his blue eyes smile and shine brightly: "If you give but do not receive, you are indeed in love, but if you expect to get something in return for the giving – that is not pure love."

ILANA: The feeling of being in love appears to be equally powerful, irrespective of whether you are in a mutual flow or not, especially in the beginning.

MASTER AKIVA: You have identified a **source** "that you delight to honour,[3]" to visit, to be near, to feel its warmth and light. You get excited, enthused, you feel the sparks of love pulsating in your chest, in your heart, causing the filaments of your soul to tremble, to resonate in your flesh... you desire to **unite** with the object of your love. Up to this point, the feelings are indeed similar, but when you cannot get close with force, it becomes a battle that leads to disintegration at the edge of the grave. That is a taking for its own sake. You accord to an external element the quality of "source," where the sun rises, radiating its light and heat on the entire world and its beauty.... The same source actually resides and pulsates in you as well. Each and every one of you is part of the same source, which is inseparable from you. That source is what you call God and designates the "divine spark."

Through intimacy with another human being, whom you identify with the source, you seek in effect to become closer to yourselves. To get near your inner source of love, buried

---

3   Esther 6:7.

deep within the cavernous furrows of your soul.

You desire to awaken and cast light upon the divine spark which is in fact pure, unconditional love.

When you bestow your love on a "source" that does not return your energy to you, it is like throwing water at a concrete wall. The water comes back dirty, stagnant and filthy with self-frustration, sadness, discontent, despair and depression.

It is a dry riverbed, a deceptive illusion, a mirage. This is why it is called unrequited love. Initially the feeling was experienced as love, but since the mutuality of giving–receiving–giving was missing, a "transgression" of taking without permission, not out of free will, was committed.

The forcefulness employed in order to **take** makes you feel that a significant **part** of you is missing. That is the lesson taking teaches.

When you are in a state of want of love, when you are not nourished because love does not flow into your being as you would have wished, you are in deficit. Your lack grows as would an overdraft in your back account, with interest. You become devoid of energy, your yearning for the source intensifies and your torment deepens.

It that love? No, in no uncertain terms, it is the lack of love.

The solution: get in tune with your inner source and replenish your emotional being. "Love is as strong as death[4]," but true love is as strong as life itself.

Life is love.

I am Master Akiva, in the name of the Guidance of Light we thank you for the question.

ILANA: I have one more question. Let's assume I have entered into a relationship of friendship with somebody. There is a flow of love and suddenly I am inflamed with the emotion of falling in love and a desire to form a romantic relationship with that friend. How would I know if that is the start of an unrequited love as opposed to true love?

MASTER AKIVA (answering patiently): Emotion is emotion. The words and definitions with which you fence in that energetic cloud, emotion – those words and definitions are the cause of your delusion. You feel a sense of desiring a particular individual. Why would you call it "love?" Be precise with your definitions and sincerely say: "I pine," "I sexually desire," "I feel a need." And so on. That is simply not love!

Perhaps the moment you precisely understand the nature of your emotions, you will cease to be confused and then

---

4   Song of Songs, 8:6.

maybe you will understand that you are severely deprived of love *for yourselves.*

Grant yourselves what you need and do not expect to receive from another what he is uninterested, unwilling or unable to give you.

Know that when you are in a state of **desiring to take** it is clearly not love. That is the underpinning of all fighting and wars. When you go to war in search of love – you get hurt.

Thank you and much love to Master Akiva.

Lesson 2

"Connection" – relationship, is it love?
Understanding truth, divinity, containment

Good morning dear and beloved guides,

I call upon Master Akiva in order to ask you about yesterday's conversation.

This is my question: **People sometimes use the terms "relationship" and "love" interchangeably. They want to form a relationship in order to experience love, in order to give and to receive. Does the existence of a relationship prove the presence of love?**

MASTER AKIVA: Good morning. I see you rose early. As you realized the moment you asked the question, the existence of a relationship does not necessarily verify the presence of love. It could indeed be a way, a conduit, through which love would freely flow in the form of giving–receiving–giving, forming an eternal cycle.

This conduit can find expression in any kind of a relationship, for instance: the connection between a mother and child, between a father and his children, between children and their parents or with their friends… it could even be felt by an animal, which is particularly sensitive and transmits the frequency of pure love, as it exists in creation. Love is present in all of nature. It is possible to connect with it in nature as one experience a sense of wonder which, in turn, is a source of joy. This experience of joy is a nourishing energy composed of pure love.

Love exists between you and yourself, when you allow it to flow without blocking it by being judgmental. The latter state is energy that does not accept and does not allow the flow, thus blocking love. The same holds true for feelings of guilt, self–anger and self–hate. All these feelings contain blocking energy that contradicts the free flowing and enabling essence of love.

ILANA: Beautiful. But, if that is so, then what is "relationship" and what is its purpose? Why do so many people desire to form such a liaison?

MASTER AKIVA: Relationship is unity, unity between a man and a woman (or those of the same sex, which is especially prevalent in your time) who wish to integrate desires, passions, fears and sexual proclivities. Furthermore, they include social conventions and the commandment to "go forth and multiply." The desire for a relationship is hardwired into human nature, due to the fear of being alone and lonely. Human beings yearn for a nearby a source of love; a source of protection and support, someone to hug and comfort them during times of trouble, someone who will warm them in the cold winter nights and play with them in the hot days of summer. Actually, humans seek a friend who will bond with them and be their partner for life.

They search for it outside of themselves. They seek union with the source of love by way of a bond of giving–receiving–giving.

It sometimes happens that a partner fails to provide the source he or she is yearning for. The reason for this failure will always be found within!!! The inner source of love is blocked, shut. Possibly, this occurred as a result of an emotional–psychic trauma. Perhaps it happens because he does not allow himself to open up within the relationship or to express himself as he really is. When communication is insincere and based in dishonesty, when it fails to respect his authentic desires and those of his companion, the natural flow of energy, which you call "love," is not viable.

The reason for this is the "taking transgression," which occurs when a person craves to take from the other without giving in return. In other circumstances the person evidently wants to give, but the partner is not interested in receiving that which the other wants to give. Accordingly, the giver is casting his hopes and desires at a barren wall. Instead of a flow, akin to a stream flowing between two people, with fresh water to slake their thirst, a dry riverbed is formed, a mirage, draining the one who vests his feelings in it. This "stream" does not flow to the partner. This is the phenomenon of unrequited love, which is not love. Instead, it is merely a desire for a relationship of taking. It is, indeed, a "thirst for love" that can never be satisfied, for there is no mutuality, no endless cyclical flow of giving–receiving–giving – which is true, natural and divine love.

ILANA: Are there true relationships and false relationships? Is there a correct liaison and an incorrect, inappropriate relationship?

MASTER AKIVA: Dear and most beloved Ilana (smiling), it is an excellent question. The answer is plain and simple: No, wherever, in **practical** terms, a couple is in a relationship. A couple is made up of one individual + another individual. One plus one equals two. That is a formula that represents a couple. The question of whether it is "true" or "false," would be determined by the internal subjective sense of the parties in any particular relationship. In a "true relationship" – as you would term it – both participants experience sensations of truthfulness, both within themselves and vis–à–vis their partner. They avoid pretense, guile and self–deceit. If they are at peace with the bond between them, then their desire for a union has turned out well. Through the union, the source of love has been opened up, for they now experience endless giving toward their chosen partner, who, in turn, receives – from the heart – their giving and channells his own giving toward them.

In a "false partnership," as you might choose to call it, there is no giving from the heart and no receiving of that which is given and there is no return. There is no true flow **beneath the surface and what we are left with are substitutes for pure love.** Above ground, the partners might demonstrate a true love bond. Possibly, they might even believe it in their hearts, for a while.

Please emphasize, **there is no "evil" or "good," there is no "right" and/or "wrong," when it comes to the relationships people opt to experience. In accord with their personal lesson plan, in relation with the will of the soul to form lessons through soul agreements, according to the universal laws of karma – a "connection" thus manifests itself.** It would serve you better to refer to such a bond as a "connection" instead of a "partnership," which has the connotation of a merger into a single aggregate.

ILANA: But, dear and honourable Master Akiva, isn't the purpose of the connection to unite and become one? Isn't there a contradiction here?

MASTER AKIVA (smiling): I have asked for precision in your definitions. A relationship does not, necessarily, equal love. Conversely, love could be part of any kind of connection, of a bond among human beings and among creatures, in general. Love can occur between a person and himself, between him and his God, between him and his fellows. That is the intent of the verse whose importance I have emphasized: "Love thy neighbour as thyself."

Notice the subtleties: Love = you will love. The emphasis is on addressing the person himself. Who will love? You.

It is an act of giving from the heart. There is no accounting involved. To give, is to give in order to bestow; to release from within yourself the feeling of being love–filled and the sense of fullness to your fellow human being, who receives from you the interchange of the energy of giving. He in turn receives it in his heart and transmits it back to you, thus performing an act of giving of his own. A cycle is formed of a flow from your heart to your fellow human being, which returns to your heart and so on.

ILANA: why isn't the saying: "Love your God as yourself?"

MASTER AKIVA (smiling widely): Dear, your question greatly pleases me regarding yourself and your learning progress! I love questions that originate from such places with you.

Well, this is my answer: Who are you? What is man, *if not God who resides in the body*? God who has multiplied Himself into parts and more parts; who has given from Himself to all of creation and who desires to return and be at one with the source, with Himself.

Therefore, it is appropriate to say: You are the loving God, who gives his love to your neighbour, who in turn is the loving God, who gives his love... and so on, ad infinitum.

ILANA: Nice. Could you please tell me about divinity, about God the creator of the universe? I still do not comprehend this business of God who apparently divides himself into His creatures. I harbour the concept of the grand old God of the Bible.

MASTER AKIVA: God is All That Is! Creation is a temple; an instrument into which divinity, as a whole, dispenses of itself yet remains whole!

Could you, using your reason, grasp all this? Your reason is the tool with which you seek to analyse, using either a very sharp scalpel or else one that is rusty and cracked. Either you perform an operation with a steady hand or you do so while your hand shakes with age and is visibly wobbly. Yet, at times, the answer is so complex that you are unable – using the blade of reason – to assimilate and accommodate such truth. At this juncture you have to extend the "bridge of faith," to open the heart's temple, to approach the soul and the other senses. To turn to subtle senses that is not your physical senses (though the latter serve you well in your earthly journey). This is about accommodating. This is why, at times, you grasp half–truths, and, using reason, magnify them into "the one nonpareil perfect truth." Truth has many facets, it is multi–layered, it has many implications and conceptualizations. **The emphasis, therefore, is on your understanding of truth, not what is *the* truth.**

ILANA: Lovely!

MASTER AKIVA: Precision is crucially important when it comes to understanding, commandments and doing. If you are imprecise, it would behove you to become aware of the fact that you hover "near" the answer, "near" the truth, "near" actualization. Comprehensive understanding requires feelings – in addition to reason. It is no coincidence that feelings and reason are interwoven with webs of energy. When there is an internal contradiction between feelings and reason, you become confused and lost. Feelings and reason go hand in hand. In the event that one pulls in one – even "contradictory" – direction from the other, you must summon the voice of your inner truth, the voice of your soul, to amalgamate the variegated types of knowledge and clear the vision for you.

You should simply declare: **"I choose to observe and contain the high truth from the plane of the soul."**

Do that about every matter that burns in your bones, about which you would seek to comprehend contradictory data or which you could not fully digest.

ILANA: Thank you dear Master Akiva. The sky is golden and bright. I hear the birds singing. The outside air is cool. I have a desire to go and take a walk along the seashore and feel the pleasant water with my bare feet. On the other hand, this is a wonderful opportunity to interact with you.

MASTER AKIVA: (smiling once more) It depends on your

ability to accommodate. Your instrument is in need of revitalizing – by instrument I mean your physical body – we can proceed with this conversation while you're walking.

ILANA: Thank you, dear and wonderful Master Akiva.

MASTER AKIVA: Thank you for summoning me and calling me hither. I would like to fill you with the knowledge available to me at present, that of being a light being who is not incarnated. I am glad and thankful that you understand and that you acknowledge your value as a special instrument of the creator. An instrument of masters, through which the enlightened masters aspire to convey a message of deliverance to the world, to ascending humanity that is being sanctified in the path of light and divine love. Continue with your blessed mission! We will meet later today, to talk about love, relationship, truth and divinity. Indeed, the conversation will expand to include surprising horizons. You will learn that it all ties together, separateness is nothing but a division for the sake of human convenience, for people cannot accommodate it all as a cohesive whole. It is like a magnificent cake you have bought or baked.. You are hungry, you love this kind of cake and you want to devour it. Could you consume the whole cake at once? Of course not (well maybe very few might actually be able to do so). You would slice it and consume it one slice at the time.

ILANA: Thanks and a great big love.

MASTER AKIVA: The ability to accommodate: That's the whole Torah (divine teaching) on one foot. That is the secret of all the interpretations. The Torah, it has justifiably been said, has seventy facets.

Lesson 3

Health, Education, Spiritual Awareness for Creating Reality

Good and blessed morning, dear guides. I call upon Master Akiva to proceed with our discussion about love and life.

MASTER AKIVA: Dear and beloved Ilana, you are invited to continue and inquire, in the name off humanity as a whole and to spread the knowledge that is conveyed through you. Whether the knowledge is considered "new" or "old," is of no consequence. Do not judge the knowledge you are receiving and do not search for additional or hidden meanings. Accept it as it comes and following its transcription you can mull it over. As you learned yesterday, words that are uttered without forming the entire concept, "do not do the job" and are therefore insufficient. People can read and learn and yet fail to have an in–depth comprehension – as you or any other person who has integrated it, has comprehended the source. Accept it patiently and without judgment. Do your best and no more. You can serve up a magnificent dish, but how others eat it, digest it and savour its scent, taste and culinary qualities is up to each and every one, individually. Many souls yearn and thirst for the light. The reason is the awakening of hidden genes in the DNA structure.

The "Messiah Gene[5]" is being activated! The activation is accomplished by frequencies of light that penetrate to your bio–molecular level. This is pre–planned and affected with precise timing.

Some people wake up earlier than others, because they were appointed to be teachers, charged with leading the awakening the consciousness of the light. These teachers experience, in their flesh, every change and transformation. These are alterations in their thinking habits and emotional formation. At the physical level, these shifts result in the renewal of body cells and blood flow. Likewise, this evolution occurs simultaneously in the individual's aura and field of energy. This is a transformation that mankind is undergoing collectively.

Some people find these changes hard to take. They develop illnesses in the joints and the bones and they develop cancer cells. The changes might manifest as intestinal infections, heart problems and inflammations of the respiratory system. There is no need to panic, however, healing will be accomplished from within. There is a need to activate the Messiah Gene and ask for complete synchronization of all the aural bodies and its layers. There is also a need to request synchronization between the biological system and all the other aspects and functions of the soul.

---

5   I have previously received material on this subject.

This development must be fully synchronized with all bodies, otherwise, short–curcuits occur and the quality of life is damaged. The "old way" – the distinct way of unawareness – includes a focus on fear and apprehension. These, in turn, lead to a physical imbalance and obstructions in the flow of energy. Those who adhere to this approach will develop various syndromes of ill–health. the ultimate purpose of which will be to awaken them from "the sleep of the unaware."

When one does not evolve naturally, when one does not develop awareness and responsibility for one's own well–being, he is destined to undergo some sort of a shakeup, in order to give him a jolt and cause him to vary his routines. He should let go of negative thought patterns and beliefs, for those create energetic formations of disease in the physical body. Human beings must understand that the condition of their health – energetic, psychological and mental – is caused by their inner content. This content includes their beliefs, thoughts and emotions. All of these are energy configurations. There is energy that flows easily throughout – "positive energy." In contrast, there is negative energy, composed of negative beliefs, thoughts and emotions. These are damaging to the physical body and form obstructions in the energy passageways. These energy impediments affect the person's overall condition. You can be certain of the truth of the saying: "A healthy mind in a healthy body."

Holistic medicine is at the threshold of unprecedented success. Many will be drawn to study the holistic arts, as they encounter the ineffectiveness of 'modern medicine'." (We put the term in quotation marks, for this type of medicine is somewhat obsolete). Truly modern medicine has to incorporate man's body and soul in one harmonious whole. Physicians have always been aware of this, although the knowledge was not publicized by those in the know for fear of being ridiculed by their colleagues and in order not to risk their reputation and professional standing. Moreover, even they regarded the knowledge as experimental and conjectural.

Sometimes, when people come before a physician to complain about what ails them, they need a heart–to–heart discussion that addresses their soul and even if only a placebo is prescribed, their disease will pass, because they trust the doctor.

When practitioners prescribe, instead of chemical therapy: "rest and recreation," "patient needs to listen to particular music" (frequencies in music are valuable for healing), "specific nutrition and special food supplements," "must avoid daily attention to news broadcasts," and the like, there will be a great awakening to the presence of inner awareness.

Large places of work will organize directed imagery days, yoga happenings and holistic experiences of various kinds, which will improve the quality of their products, because they will be manufactured by more satisfied workers. "Those working with joy bring in the harvest singing."

ILANA: Thank you; very interesting. Please continue this elucidation about health.

MASTER AKIVA: With your permission, I would veer into what is seemingly a different subject: **Educational institutions. There is a need for a shift in the understanding of the purpose of educational institutions. There is a need to re-examine and redefine the central goal that guides the system.** It is very important for the development of an enlightened, educated population, endowed with survival skills for modern society.

In the past, during the period when I lived, acquisition of knowledge was less important. A person was simply required to be a decent human being: to love the Torah and the Commandments and earn a living to sustain his family. Knowledge was conveyed through oral tradition, by the head of the family. Life was simpler and more natural. Today, an uneducated person who cannot read or write, cannot properly integrate himself within society. He may turn to paths of unnecessary misery and even crime, which would disrupt his and his environment's karmic balance.

Basic literacy, as well as the rest of the learning conveyed at schools, colleges and universities, is important.

Nevertheless, there is a certain deviation and loss of direction in the definition of the main purpose. This applies equally to kindergartens, elementary, junior and senior high schools. The Matriculation Certificate, as it exists today, does not really testify to maturity in thinking. It is a symbol of societal competitiveness and the process of compressing data into pupils' heads. That is not an educational goal!

The proper purpose of education is to unchain the fetters encumbering logic, speech and philosophical insight. The true aim of education is the development of the heart – sensitivity, good manners, love of your fellow human being: "love thy neighbour as thyself." The task of education is **to develop consciousness.** This avenue has been almost completely abandoned and certainly has not been sufficiently developed in your times, in this era. By consciousness I refer to the integration of diverse elements. You, diffuse all the "courses of study," disengaging each from the others and thus you fail to see that which ties them together.

Would you like to know the fundamental theme that ties them all together? It is: **human development in all possible directions.** Man retells his chronicles in various ways: through history, Bible stories, literature, civics studies, biology, chemistry, the knowledge of numbers, i.e., mathematics, handicrafts, the arts, i.e., painting, photography and the like. If that is so, there is a need for a subject that will combine them all these in a holistic vision:

Spiritual awareness for the creation of reality.

Such a course of study should include the following: Spiritual understanding – the origin of souls and their purpose (people should not be afraid of the so-called "mystical" aura of the subject); comprehension of aural energy; understanding of chakras (energy focal points); learning about aural bodies and bodies of light. This course should also include dispensation of knowledge about these issues: What are thoughts? What is the source of thoughts? What is the relationship between energetic balance or imbalance and thought reception (i.e., telepathy)?

Such a course of study would be augmented by various types of music, conducting students with guided imagery and more. Do not worry about either imparting the knowledge or withholding it from the souls of the great teachers (the children) who are destined to guide humanity in the near future and pave its way to the stars.

This knowledge, if it were to be transmitted and grasped at an earlier age, would facilitate an increased assumption of responsibility among those participating in planet Earth's "drama." Likewise, the much anticipated messianic world peace could reign here. It is difficult to effect progress without knowledge,. If the requisite knowledge is not passed on, every person has to reinvent the wheel and thus much valuable time is lost.

People are afraid to know the quintessential purpose of life. They are afraid to understand how they create every dimension of reality. They are not afraid to listen to broadcasts by the mass media, watch horror movies, tune into horrifying newscasts that generate fear and anxiety, such as alarming economic forecasts. Why? Only because of faulty education.

Mankind must aspire to a true "graduation certificate." This implies comprehension of every facet and aspect of the process of reality formation, both its material and its spiritual characteristics. The focus of history and civics courses must shift to "how beliefs form the ambiance that leads to action." Belief lies at the root of any act, whether it is a war instigated by an individual or a nation or the choice of comprehensive peace and forgiveness.

If we now return to the subject of love with which we commenced our prolific discourse (Master Akiva is smiling and his eyes sparkle with humour, joy and mischievous delight), then you can see that love is consciousness. It would be more accurate to say: **There is a consciousness of love that is natural for all of creation.**

When a segment of love is removed and thus becomes deficient, consciousness of un–love forms, accompanied by a desire to seize it at all costs, legitimate or otherwise. That is consciousness of war and fear. Human beings then seek, as forcefully as they can, to secure influence, wealth and social standing. They also erect defences of force and fear, lest they are robbed of the hallmarks of their aggrandizement and in order for them to feel "whole" – a feeling real love imparts spontaneously. Needless to say, they do not acquire love and settle for substitutes. Instead of the pure love of God, which is a fusion with all that is and all the bounty they could ever need for their existence – they search for a physical–emotional indicator that represents love for them and which forever remains outside themselves.

They do not say to themselves: "Let me be happy and I will accord myself more love." Instead, they face outward and say: "Let me find for myself a person who will bestow love on me, who will accept me as I am who will fortify my weak and deficient self–image, who will, in effect, fuse me to the source of love – to myself." And the thought ensues, even if unawares: "I will give that person the role of loving me, so that I might recognise that I am worthy of love and that I may love myself." Notice that now you have formed a dependency on another person as an exterior source of love in your life, one who is expected to afford you the regular nourishment you are in need of – love.

But, it is difficult to find individuals who have the capacity to be connected with the sources of love. Every person has his own inner need, which he wants to embrace, to fill and to extract from someone outside himself.

Love is not physical attraction. It is not lust or the heartache attendant on falling in love. Love is not sexual interaction, as wonderful and delightful to the senses as it may be. Love does not entail encumbering another with the yoke of your desire or taking possession of him, his time, his deepest thoughts, his free will, his entire being. Love is not external beauty – purportedly the indication that you are qualified to search and find love.

Love – people are confused about its definition and search for it everywhere and in every way, especially in relationships. In relationships you do seek to utterly own your partner. The partners acknowledge that they are committed and bound to each other. At times, this will create friction, dissatisfaction and difficulties. Often, this path is tolerated because of a belief that, "that's how it is." Folks bend themselves to societal norms as they comprehend them and do not dare to think differently. "What would the others say," is a common hallmark of earthbound humans.

"What would they think," "what would they say," "to blend in with the others" – these are entirely twisted values with which the educational establishments fill the minds of those they instruct.

Due to the "education" you were fed, an urge has materialized, pushing you to compete for grades, for social status, for achievement of external appearances. The latter are fostered by plastic surgeons and beauty parlours and the cosmetics industry. This need to impress others in order to foster one's sense of self-worth exists in most people. In fact, among all, save for a few outstanding individuals.

Your failure to meet the goal of being comparable to others causes you to punish yourselves. You judge, criticize, develop a lack of self-esteem and values and in extreme cases, you judge and criticize others harshly, within your family or social circle and even when you are not personally acquainted with them. This phenomenon is the result of the influence of mass media that, for the sake of ratings, spreads ill-willed gossip to serve their narrow economic interests. Since you are captives of the external and the material, you move further and further away from the true source of love. Conversely, you are close to that source of love when you stride toward a spiritual bearing, by linking up with your heart and through your heart to the soul, which is tied by bonds of love to eternity, to creation in its entirety, to God, the source of all life. Entering in, within your own selves, brings you back to the source of love.

When you lust – know that you do not love. When you truly love, you do not lust. The difference between lust of the flesh and true love is great indeed, although you confuse the two. Some of you say you are "searching for love," when in fact you are looking for sex, which you call "making love." Dear, beloved and exalted friends, you do not "make" love. Love is neither "acquired" nor "lost." You *connect* with love. The connection is accomplished by way of awareness, by opening the gates of your heart, by affirming your presence under the light of your soul.

Be blessed in your eternal existence. This is our lesson for today. Light, love and joy upon our joint enterprise, I am Master Akiva, in the name of the Guidance of Light and the Ascended Masters of the Great White Brotherhood, who is dedicated to humanity in its path to ascension.

Questions to Master Akiva about Reiki Treatments.

ILANA: Michele is asking, may one use Reiki on individuals who are treated with psychotropic medication? Some Reiki practitioners claim that it is dangerous and should be avoided. Specifically, she wants to treat a woman who has been suffering for the last 16 years from post–partum depression, who is taking psychotropic medication. I would like to add that Reiki energy is divine intelligence, love–based energy, whose purpose is healing.

MASTER AKIVA: Dear and wonderful and beloved Ilana and Michelle. It is in the question, so well–defined by Ilana, that the seeds of the answer are found. Is it not so?

Do you think that Reiki energy is intended for a healthy subject, who is worry–free, devoid of any anxiety or stress and under no medication? Do we not observe here hints of consciousness of fear that seeks to avoid all responsibility for po-

tential consequences? You'll do best – in finding the answer – by asking two questions in this formula. Ask yourselves:
a. Is this love consciousness talking?
b. Or might it be the consciousness of fear in that is being expressed?

Do you think, dear and enchanting Michelle, exalted and wonderful readers, that you should avoid any doubtful subject for healing and only treat the healthy and the balanced who would assure you that no worrisome syndromes would appear? Do you think you can promise immediate success, by way of the miracle of healing, to anyone whom you wish to heal? Naturally, I am asking with the expectation that you will respond, "No and no."

You should treat those who need divine energy, whether for physical, emotional or spiritual reasons; anyone who thirsts for support in any area of life. Those who ingest medications are not barred, God forbid, in any way. They are not guilty of any transgression; they are without sin, for they are abiding by the treatment prescribed by a physician who is familiar with the symptom–masking qualities of the chemicals and preparations.

Did the woman who for the last 16 years has been suffering from depression, suddenly – following consuming the psychotropic medication – become a vital person, filled with *joi de vivre*? Of course not, for if she were, you would not have mentioned her medical history.

Reiki energy is the path of compassion, the path of love; it is contrary to and neutralizes releases and heals the way of fear, which harks from the shadow region where the delusion of fear, various illnesses and horrific nightmares reign.

"Depart from fear,
Acquiesce with responsibility
And become a channell of light
Clean, pure,
Through whom God's healing
Shall stream,
Then every human being
Shall part with darkness
And emerge from the pit
Unto the innocence of light
To freedom
To liberty."

Carefully notice and observe your feelings. Take note of your suppressed emotions and ask yourselves: Am I really the right person to treat this patient?

It is possible that one could receive Reiki treatment or treatment of any other school of medicine, but due to lack of energetic harmony or because of your own deep fears or your own lack of basic balance – it may not be proper for you to be the one to administer treatment. Therefore, use your intuition and heart wisdom well and ask yourselves:

Is it right for me to treat this person? Am I the right person to help him?

Perhaps you will feel that you are not the right person to provide healing in that specific case. Accept and honour that feeling! It is not because the patient is undeserving of treatment or because Reiki is an inappropriate method, but because you are not supposed to undertake the responsibility of helping him.

Always remember – you attract those who complement you, who reverberate in frequencies that you can accommodate, who have experienced what you have experienced in your own life. Accordingly, you are familiar with the appropriate "escape route," the proper exit strategy from difficulty to ease, from darkness to bright light.

In summary I would say: Be generous with yourselves and with your fellow man. Understand that you are a pipeline and you should not discriminate between cases. That having been said, sense whether you are capable of resolving the "predicament" of the treatment's subject, as well as the results of the therapy provided.

And leave the outcome to God.

Not every person who seeks your assistance and comes for treatment, even for payment, truly desires to be healed. And furthermore, he may have the will, but if a different soul choice has been made and there is a contradiction between the two, he may still have a long road ahead of him before his soul's passageways and experiences open up, in accord with the options made by his soul.

I am Master Akiva who conveys to you the message: Carve upon your heart and in your consciousness the following verse: "Love thy neighbour as thyself."

ILANA: Thank you and much love. I would like to add, from my own insight as a therapist, that it is important for the therapist to maintain neutrality, as you said, "a clean pipeline;" and that he must be sincere when he inwardly examines his own suitability for providing a particular treatment. Not because "he may not," or because in some cases treatment would be ruled out, but because he is afraid or because he is not whole–heartedly in accord with the matter or because he is experiencing imbalance and a lack of ability to accommodate the treatment.

MASTER AKIVA: I agree and accept this important addition and would like to clarify and refine it: Every person should know his boundaries and limitations and act according to his character, according to his inner truth. Without any need to please and without any fear, but simply out of a sense of mission that springs from pure and true love. "Love thy neighbour as thyself," as you see fit. Dear and beloved readers that is the whole, all–encompassing teaching of life.

Lesson 4

From Toil and Trouble to Treasure Trove

ILANA: Good morning, wonderful and beloved guides. I call Master Akiva to proceed with our conversation.

MASTER AKIVA: Dear and beloved Ilana. Your likability and nobility have touched my heart. Yes, we entities of light have a heart and preferences and choices. We love and it is pleasant for us to glide into communication with entities whose frequency reverberates with ours. Your frequency is now more uplifted and clearer than ever. You are becoming more and more sanctified, truly a light entity in human form. It is a great privilege for me, us and you, to communicate among ourselves.

At any rate, I would like to remind you of the dream you had last night, where you saw yourself in a library of children's books. You found no books for adults. You knew they had been borrowed and they were being read, but some books were missing. You considered loaning your own books to the library so that the empty shelves would be filled.

The purpose of the dream was to imply that your books are vital and much space is still available on the shelf. People thirst for the knowledge yet to be conveyed through your scepter. In the past you doubted your skillfulness. You doubted and minimized your importance as a channeller with unique messages to impart. You thought it enough, in the presence of channelling authors Sanaya Roman, Deepak Chopra, Lee Carroll and maybe a few others. You thought that your materials are redundant and would be channelled through many others, right?

ILANA: Every word you utter, esteemed master, is true – of course.

MASTER AKIVA: Accordingly, we sent you lessons about acknowledging your self–value. You followed them well, as evinced by the fact that you present yourself faithfully day after day , as the venerated Metatron and his emissaries requested. And ever since – for such a long time – you have devotedly served the Source, the Light and God.

One should not belittle his own worth, though I do understand it; sometimes it is a function of modesty. Still, **one must distinguish between humility, true modesty and lack of self-esteem.** Think of Moses, the principal spiritual leader of humanity in his time. When God bestowed his mission upon him, he tried to evade it by claiming that he is "slow of speech and of a slow tongue."[6] In effect he was saying that he was unworthy of the mission. But it is God who examines man's kidneys[7] and sees what man can

---

6   Exodus 4:10.
7   This is reference to the original Hebrew text in Jeremiah 11:20: "But,

and cannot do; for man emphasizes the exterior, the skills and superficial accomplishments. The quintessence is the soul. The essence is the calling. A human being who is not connected to the guidance from his soul – thus removed from the manifestation of his calling and from a suitable course for apposite choices – is suffering and can never feel contentment.

One should find purpose and reason for his life beyond material exploits, which are so typical of your time and culture.

Truly it can be said that material achievements are expressions of the beliefs and determination of the individual. They should not be undervalued, of course, but neither should they be glorified or idolized. Spiritual undertaking – being a good person who walks the path of righteousness and frequents the company of the righteous, of angels and who is under the direct guidance of God – is sevenfold better, bringing immense satisfaction in its wake.

Certainly some people have the wisdom to amalgamate spirit and matter, with no artificial division between them. They would do well to understand that giving willingly and expecting nothing in return will bring them to a natural cycle of abundance, of the flow of love: giving–receiving–giving. They would do well to realize that taking does not draw them near to the spiritual dimension of their being.

O Lord of hosts, that judgest righteously, that triest the kidneys and the heart...."

Ideally, when you are close to the spiritual dimension, you are immersed in material economic security. Nevertheless, know that there are diverse lessons for different individuals. There are those who will only get close to the spiritual through trouble and economic hardship and first, they will get close to themselves. There are those who need spurring and challenging, which they will encounter as they engage in solving their material difficulties. This circumstance – on its face far removed from spirit – is what will bring them close to their calling. That is because they will be required to generate ingenuity, courage, detailed and precise self-examination, revision of their beliefs and inner approach, modification of reality perception, change of priorities and acceptance of what is.

When I say, "acceptance of what is" when facing a difficult economic situation I do not mean that you should give up, feel helpless, prepared to give up on the spark of life. Not at all! What I mean is, that first you accept the existing condition without anxiety.
Tell yourselves:

"Well, I have created this distress and I – on my own power, combined with my utter faith in God Almighty the creator of the world – will emerge from these straits and create a treasure."

I am speaking of feelings and a way of thinking. First you have to be grateful for what is, that which exists, then focus on your will, with a determination to receive whatever is necessary.

First give yourselves the peace of mind that you need. Accord yourselves self-worth and accept yourselves as you are, without criticism, judgment, fear or guilt.

Say: "**I accept my condition.**"

Now the universe has an opening to help you emerge from your difficulty and discomfort.

Remove the fear-based motive from the script. Know that you have the ability to change your circumstances. How? Take action! Think of someone, a friend for example, who is close to you. Take yourself for a moment out of the drama you have created and in which you are wallowing. Try to advise yourself as if you were that close friend. For you would not fall prey to the trap of his emotional fear; no doubt you would be able to advise him how to act with a cool head. **Think of practical solutions for an exit strategy from the undesirable circumstances you find yourself in.**

Think about a second job or a loan; think about cutting down on expenses and increasing your revenue. Think about moving to an area where the cost of living is lower; think about changing the type of employment you are in at the moment. Think about extending your faith, hand in hand with expanding your income.

Know, that every situation, every crisis – has a solution. You can consult professionals to emerge from the hardship.

Self–pity is, in effect, inner floundering in the drama, while depriving yourself of the ability to understand the power of creating your own reality. Self–pity fogs up your ability to understand and blurs your awareness of responsibility for the choices you have made – leading to the problem you find yourself mired in – in order to learn and grow from it. Fear is magnetic energy. Let go of the fear, if you want to effect a change in your condition. Realize that the present is formed by your past beliefs.

To sum up: Defuse fear and fill yourselves with faith and inner knowing. Amplify your appreciation of your own worth and the feeling that that you deserve prosperity. Breath and affirm that you will contain the bounty. Ask to grow and evolve not through hardship but by way of spiritual insight, with ease and joy – which are byproducts of positive beliefs.

Remember, that there is a solution to each and every problem – and tell yourself that. The fact that you cannot put your finger on it – that you do not know what it might be – does not mean that it will not be found.

Stop your survival anxiety. Instead, ask to increase your ability to accommodate your own life. Ask to strengthen and reinforce the faith in abundance, which you deserve

as part and parcel of your existence. Increase your desire to live with great potency and full self-actualization. Choose to be in communion with your soul. Through its light and guidance you will learn to overcome hardship and suffering, which stand before you as a signal and a presager of personal growth.

The way to get in touch with the highest assistance you could avail yourself of, would be by expressing inner and deep intention, from the heart. An intention that you declare in words:

"I opt to accept assistance and express gratitude for it.
I choose to be in touch with my soul's full measure of guidance.
I elect to be a soul in a physical body.
I accept the way of light, love, compassion and ease."
And, to be sure, so it is.

Well, as much as it might amaze some of you, the way to end economic adversity is through getting in tune with the spiritual and enhancing the reservoir of faith. Doubt is the main cause of cessation of faith. Doubt reduces your spiritual understanding and your capacity to contain your spirituality. It accelerates the rate of diminishment of self-esteem and engenders lack of spiritual understanding. Doubt is the energy that halts the flow of prosperity into your life. The opposite of doubt is faith. Affirm that your faith shall grow.

You can help yourselves with the power of your imagination, which is a great gift bestowed on you. Creation is preceded by envisioning and visualization. You are great experts in doing this through fear. Why not try it the other way – the way of love? Instead of generating anxiety and imagining fear-based scripts, create scripts of abundance and profusion.

To minimize doubt try to imagine: That at the centre of your throat, the area of the energetic centre known as the throat chakra, whose colour is light blue, sits a mass of doubt. Imagine it in any colour, size and texture you like. Now, imagine rays of light descending from your crown (the top of your head), penetrating your throat, dissolving and eliminating the clump of doubt. Know that these rays of light are augmenting your inner reservoir of faith. And so it is. That which you believe, you shall create and experience!

ILANA: Dear Master Akiva, people complain about the lack in their lives – lack of love, of a relationship, of money, employment, even entertainment. What would you say to them?

MASTER AKIVA: Dear Ilana, thank you for being creation's mouthpiece. I would tell these people to look inside themselves, inside their hearts and begin by filling that void – their inner spiritual need. Focusing on the material instead of the spiritual will not advance their goals. Whatever they request, it really all comes down to happiness and security, right? When they seek a relationship with another, they want to experience happiness and security. When they are on a quest for money, they are hunting for financial security, which then would bring them happiness. When looking for employment, they are aiming for a sense of security that would bring them peace of mind, on the way to the happiness they yearn for. When entertainment is the desired goal, they are in fact searching for meaning and significance that would bring them happiness. In other words, looking at it from every possible angle, you discover that they are looking for security that will bring them happiness. They could secure it swiftly and easily, depending on their choice and the inner connection between themselves and the point of divinity within them.

I am not preaching for anyone to be "born again," as conventional religious interpretation would put it. What I mean is that every person should take it upon himself to understand that he is a divine spark in a physical body. Each individual should comprehend that he is spirit encased in a material sheath; that the physical and the spiritual, the emotional and the intellectual are all one, each with its slightly diverging aspects and interpretations.

First of all, bestow upon yourselves that which you seek to draw from without and which, consequently, is causing you stress. Avoid the stress by working inwardly, coupled with rofound soul–searching.. Be determined to be connected. Declare your intention loudly.

Declare: **"I choose to connect with the centre point in my heart. I choose to connect with the divine spark and to re-activate it here and now!"**

Carry out this process as a holy ritual and repeat it three times. After each repetition take a deep breath and contain the light and energy of the holy connection. You may feel the resulting energy as currents, as excitement or as a sense of peace. Maybe you will simply be aware that the connection was made in the best possible manner.

The results will not be immediate. Sometimes a long process of assimilation is required – internalizing, growth, insight and finally accommodation. Know that you have taken the first step toward ensuring your continued existence and finding the highest meaning and significance – a connection with your calling and its actualization in the best possible way.

In order to amplify the flow of prosperity for which you are aiming, tell yourself: **"I am grateful for my happiness. I choose to be unconditionally happy. I am joyful. Thank you. I am thankful for my security. I am always totally secure in my existence. Security and plenty are increasing in my life. Thank you."**

Know that money alone will not provide you with security or happiness. Know that the same holds true for everything you sought for yourself when you were in need and focused on the "external achievements" in your life.

ILANA: if I understood correctly, dear and wonderful Master Akiva, it would seem that people do not always know what they lack. They simply feel want. They point at the first item that comes to mind and then they place a checkmark to indicate that they have met their goal.

MASTER AKIVA: You understood well, my talented student. Be accurate with your requests, be exact with what you desire for yourselves.

For example: A person is unemployed and that threatens his survival. He needs the money that work would bring him. Meanwhile he is scared, lacking self–worth, very miserable. He is unhappy that his stature has diminished, he may even experience despair and depression. Then his luck changes and he secures employment again. At first he is glad, believing that a solution has been found. But after a while he starts to find fault with his new workplace. He grumbles: The pay is inadequate, the work is too hard, his boss irritates him, his co–workers are obnoxious and so on. Once again he is focused on hardship and anguish and he fails to be grateful for the money he is earning.

Did he secure his survival? Apparently he did and indeed he thinks he did, but his emotions tell him otherwise. Soon he will manifest some new kind of trouble, maybe health–related, maybe psychological. In the fullness of time, the need will, like a magnet, attract to itself the next trial.

Does a man who find a mate and marries automatically become happy? The answer is, by and large, negative. Everything that you search for externally is potentially disappointing and liable not to attain what is expected of it: To provide happiness and security.

ILANA: This very minute the doorbell rang and the maid arrived. I asked her about her suitor and whether they have met yet – it's like a serial suspense story. She said they haven't yet. I told her they are afraid. She claims they are not. They haven't met because his vehicle is uninsured, etc. To make a long story short – it seems to me that they are making excuses in order not to meet. They are Druze and, therefore, are talking about marriage before they even get to know each other. Suddenly she declared that she wants to be happy. But she added that she is afraid if she gets married she may not be happy, because her husband may be unfaithful and cheat on her or he will abuse her. However, remaining single does not make her happy either. I explained that happiness is an inner experience and she should choose the road of love, not the path of fear. She should affirm, verbally and in writing, what she wants in a relationship, not what she does not want. I suggested she talk to God and communicate her wishes to him. Isn't it nice how this ties in with our discussion?

MASTER AKIVA (smiling): In fact, there is no separation. All of creation is talking to you all the time. Open the channells of the heart, the inner ear and the soul and perceive. Every person you encounter brings a message from the interior of your world. Everyone is an aspect of the whole. You can see your beliefs reflected through the words and the eyes of others.

You, too, desire a mate to fill–up the empty space and the lack in the field of male–female balance. On the other hand, you tend to think about a fear–based relationship and what it might rob you of – your freedom and your extensive and sanctified living space, which contains clear, holy and even divine frequencies.

It is true that you have all the right answers. You express love and focus on what you desire. But at the same time you cannot deny that you have a side – an incomplete side – that is very afraid to get hurt, to be burned by an unsuitable relationship.

In order to receive what you desire and yearn for, you have to depart from the path that is aggravating your condition – the path of fear. In order to receive all that "is" you must transport yourselves to the path of love and focus on what you feel you deserve. Yes, you deserve to be happy. It is natural and easy for you to be happy. Just tune into the sensation that you are connected with God, which will bring you happiness. It will let you create, from the point of happiness, which you are expanding to all the planes of your existence and your universe – the byproducts of the grand ecstasy that enfolds and inundates you.

What I am saying is: first choose to live in happiness and security and out of this psycho-emotional experience, which floods and fills you, create the treasure, instead of creating problems.

ILANA: Dear and wonderful Master Akiva, are you saying that people can feel happy and fulfiled even without having all the things they "need"? Without being in a relationship, having an assured income, money, material accomplishments and the like?

MASTER AKIVA: Yes, it is so my beloved and wonderful student. Human beings are actually required to get in touch with their true essence – to remember and commune with God day and night. That is the simplistic answer, yet it is in fact the proper and complete response to all requests addressed to God and the universe.

ILANA: And what about health? A person who gets sick and suffers, all he wants is to be healthy. That is what his relatives wish for him, as well. What can you advise us on the subject?

MASTER AKIVA: Health is an aspect of creation. All is caused by God. Nothing occurs without a reason. Every sick person should seek to understand the inner purpose of his illness, which precedes its physical manifestation. Why did he let go of his healthy condition? Did he constrict his ability to contain life? Did he lose his sense of meaning and purpose in life? Have despair, guilt, anger and fear grabbed him – as an octopus would – and squeezed (distorted?) his inner balance? One should observe, learn and comprehend the relationship between inner and outer, spiritual and biological, emotional and intellectual. One should assume responsibility for his beliefs.

He can opt, first of all, to heal himself from within. He can accept what he is going through on the paramount level; i.e., that it is he who created it for his soul's benefit, because the time was ripe to alter patterns that were lodged within him, causing a considerable imbalance. He should forgive himself and the body that has "betrayed" him. He should know that, with the strength of his faith alone, he can move mountains.[8] Thus certainly he can remove the "bad microbes" inside his body. The body's wondrous natural mechanism has the ability to restore itself, regardless of its state of health.

ILANA: And what about a baby or a little child or a person who is incapable of comprehending what is stated here?

MASTER AKIVA: Learn to accept a disease not as a war, despite its threatening attitude toward the plane of life, but as a way of mending something that was distorted within and became loose, It is time to rid the self of it.

---

8   "If ye have faith and doubt not,... if ye shall say unto this mountain, be thou removed and be thou cast into the sea; it shall be done." Matthew 21:21. See also, Mark 11:23.

When a baby or a little child is at issue, it is the duty of his parents to comprehend this. They should pray from the depths of their heart to rid their child of whatever afflicts him.

You need to understand that what is done is what is supposed to happen. It is possible to alter the outcome and cancel a soul agreement. However, if things do not proceed in an orderly fashion and according to expectations, if the sick person's condition deteriorates and even if a patient is in extremis, close to death – there is, of course, a need to grieve, but also to know, deep inside, that things happened as they should. There are no mistakes. There is no coincidence. There is meaning and purpose. The parents of a baby who has passed away should mend their own minds. They should tune into spiritual knowledge, to the Creator of the universe. They need to learn and accept their mourning lesson, by declaring and reinforcing their own will to live: to fall in order to get up.

Never, ever lose hope or faith or the ability to recover and stand again on your own two feet – no matter how hard the fall may have been, in every aspect of life, be it bereavement, mourning, financial collapse, war, etc.

ILANA: Is potent faith a cure–all? Is it the solution for every misfortune in life? That is what I understand from your statements.

MASTER AKIVA (with satisfaction): Indeed, faith and acceptance. To accept with love, as is written: "**Love the Lord, thy God, with all with all your heart, with all your soul and with all your will; meditate upon him day and night, when you go to sleep and when you rise.**" Accept with love as it is said, "**love thy neighbour as thyself.**" Stay on the path of love, which is giving from the heart and acceptance of all that is.

Honor yourselves, in that you are a divine spark in flesh, spirit in matter. honour your fellowmen, who are made as you are, each a divine spark manifesting in matter. honour your enemies, who fulfil their role in the common drama you all have created in order that you would learn through peace, through the path of love or even through the path of fear.

Two paths – fear and/or love – both come to teach you the same lessons. The path of love – is called "light," while the way of fear is called "darkness." You need to understand that light and darkness, too, co-operate in the drama of life's journey on Earth, which is also called: "the Planet of Choice," and "the Region of Duality."

The path of fear, which we will call "darkness," is rooted in the sense of survival and existential fears. These fears are sourced in the red chakra, an energetic region of the base of the spine, the root.

The path of love, which is the consciousness of, "light" – is based on giving–receiving–giving. It is about enabling, about the "is." This road is linked with the heart chakra – *sephirat tif'eret*. The path of love befits your era, the era of the Messiah, of salvation, that which you call, "the New Age" (though "there is nothing new under the sun," as King Solomon said [9]).

You can ask to be driven by love and its urges, instead of fear and its horrors.

Decree hereby, if you so choose, of course:

"**I now choose to be on the path of love and all that is implied thereby.**
"**I request the annulment of all my soul agreements that are tied with the way of fear.**
"**I request karmic release of all my fears.**
"**I choose to be centreed on love and compassion.**
"**I am grateful for every possible help that comes my way.**
"**I am that I am. This is my choice in life.**"

This is a renewed contract of the soul. Invite the angels of karma to sign it and assist you in its execution. Actions taken between you and yourself are honoured by Spirit and, thus, are implemented in the corporeal world.

---

9   See, Ecclesiastes 1:9.

These are my words for today. I am Master Akiva who respects your free will and commends to you the path of love. As is written and stated again and again: "Love thy neighbour as thyself."

With much love and gratitude to you dear, Ilana, the emissary of Spirit, beloved by God.

And here I am, Metatron, exalting you for the serious approach and dedication you have finally enlisted for the mission.

Lesson 5

On love, War and Peace, Fear, Truth, Accommodation

ILANA: Good morning to all my wonderful and beloved guides. I would like to proceed with my discussion with Master Akiva.

MASTER AKIVA: Dear and beloved Ilana, you and I have been assigned the task of writing together the next book to enlighten humanity, a book that will open a window into the expanding consciousness and into new empowerment and strength.

We commenced our conversation with the subject of love, but it is becoming clear as we proceed that everything is love. There are aspects that obscure love, love cannot be discerned in them. Yet, even in these circumstances – love seeks to be perceived. When there is no will for giving, while there is demand from a certain party for love, the latter is attempting to effect a taking, which is a forceful act. Taking generates defensiveness, aggressive reaction and loss of energy by both sides involved in the drama of taking. Both come to the situation to learn a lesson and develop the insight that to take something, piece by piece, to slice the whole into segments, will not accord them the result they desire.

ILANA: Behind your words I sense that we are discussing **war and peace**. Is it so? What can you tell us about the subject?

MASTER AKIVA: War come into existence due to dearth of love. When love is present, giving is done willingly and there is acceptance from the heart, both of which activate and perpetuate the cycle of abundance. When people find themselves – due to a perceived lack – in lust to seize for themselves the estates of another, be it an individual or a nation, when people try to take the property of others by force – be it a woman, an estate, status or land – they are not in a state of wholeness with love. They are in want, in fear of scarcity. They are in a state of envy or jealousy, they want to fight and grab for themselves. It may be clandestine, experienced in a hidden chamber of the heart and never executed, but whether it is merely a plan or the actual materialization of the plot; in every scenario there is a taking, because they do not feel giving and receiving in their hearts.

When people are truly in tune with their hearts there will be a paradigm shift in mass consciousness. The **collective heart** will be activated and it will influence reality. At present collective fear, pulsating and active, is weaving the tapestry of reality. The personal fears of individuals on both sides of the fence, across borders, feed the collective fear. It, in turn, augments individual fears. However, a symbiosis of giving–receiving–giving takes shape on the plane of fear.

ILANA: Dear Master Akiva, I find a contradiction here. If love is giving–receiving–giving, where the emphasis is on giving willingly – unconditional giving, how does it tie in with the fear–energy that generates wars? You are speaking about a cycle of giving–receiving–giving, which I understood to be love. Please clarify your statements. Thank you.

MASTER AKIVA: Dear Ilana, the universe revolves in circles of reciprocal influence. In its essence love cannot at present be comprehended by you,. Love contains everything that is. Everything that exists is love. So you see even fear is part of love. Fear is love hidden from itself. It does not contradict love. Even fear, it can be said, is searching for love in its own way. Not everything can be comprehended by the mind, by logic. Thus, I suggest that you simply write and open your heart. Let it come inside of you and ask for an enhancement of your capacity to accommodate cosmic truth. Are you ready for it?

ILANA: Gladly. Energetically, through my hands, , I am exploring my ability to accommodate cosmic truth. It is scant. Therefore, I choose to expand it. I already understand something – that is arising with my request: Truth does not come in colours of black/white, good/evil, not even war/peace, right?

MASTER AKIVA: True!

ILANA: I breathe and expand the breathing capacity in my lungs as I affirm: "I expand my capacity to accommodate cosmic truth!" Now I again measure my ability to accommodate cosmic truth. I observe that I have opened up for infinite accommodation. I understand that as human beings, we tend to colour reality and divide it into black and white. It is the world of duality. Love appears in shades of pink in the whitest portion of the map.

MASTER AKIVA: People like to think in terms of "simple" – "good"/"evil," "black"/"white," "master"/"servant"... and, indeed, love is considered a good thing, white and desired.

Love is indeed a good thing, just as life is a good thing, just as God is a good thing. This great good contains everything and by "everything" is meant the infinite wealth of what is. Even what isn't is part of that which is – only veiled. All of creation has this characteristic: It is always seeking its balance. That which isn't is searching for what would make it whole and the whole provides of itself in every way. All is. There is no "light" and "darkness" opposing and contradicting each other. Instead, they are participants in the grand game called, "life on earth." The light is the (+) end while darkness embodies the (–) charge. Together, like batteries whose purpose is to generate activity, the two create one whole.

People should stop being afraid of the "dark," They should focus on what is desired for them, which is light. When people are immersed in fear, they feed on and are nurtured by the collective fear, which becomes kinetically energized and affects the feel of reality, influencing the formation of events and scenarios of war, crime, poverty, suffering and of pain.

When people focus on the light – where love is present and revealed in its entirety, they contribute to the collective heart.

ILANA: I received a call from someone who is attending a Reiki Master Level course with me. She wants her father to take the Level One Reiki course and then join the Master course. She asked me if she is inconveniencing me. I told her she was not, for there are no disruptions and everything happens according to plan. I wonder, what I should derive from that conversation, in relation to our conversation about the collective heart. Incidentally, I did not give her an answer, I asked the father to give me a call, so that I could sense whether he would be suitable for the current course.

MASTER AKIVA: Your heart was closed by the fear (smiling), that one more person might "spoil" the wholeness of the wonderful circle that has formed. The truth, however, is that you can open your heart and include one more superb Reiki master. It is often a question of the capacity to accommodate. Can you, are you able to, do you want to include one more human being in your life? It may be in a relationship, an intimate liaison, a social association, as a patient or as a student in a course of study. Examine your ability to accommodate new students.

ILANA: Indeed, it is limited. Accordingly, I am now expanding my capacity to accommodate patients and students. I breathe deeply and tell myself the following sentences: "I accommodate more and more new people in my life, I accommodate many easily, with love, with joy, with pleasure." And so it is! I continue to breathe, until I feel comfortable with these statements.

My capacity to accommodate has grown and expanded. I like that. Clearly that phone call was not coincidental.

MASTER AKIVA: Accommodating is a key concept in your world, in relation to all relevant subjects for you. You are searching and asking for love. Ask yourselves: Can I accommodate love? The ability to accommodate love is related to the degree that your heart is open. Am I the owner of an open heart? Am I in tune with myself? Do I possess positive self–esteem?

Do I own a capacity for giving and receiving what I expect to find?

You are on a quest for material wealth, money and good income – ask yourselves: what is my capacity for accommodating what I seek? Am I truly capable of accepting and giving money? Am I afraid of being a proprietor of many assets? ("He who has much property has much to worry about.")

Are you looking for many new friends? If so, then ask yourselves whether you have sufficient emotional capacity to accommodate them: Will you be able to open your life pages without fear or apprehension?

Health. You seek good health – **do you have the capacity for accommodating life?**

Examine your capacity to contain life. When a person lacks this capacity, he is in the process of crumbling, of depleting his reservoir of energy. He is becoming empty, first, of the joy of life. He loses his sense of meaning. He sinks into a monotonous routine that taunts him to stop and express gratitude for what he has. He finds himself sliding down the slippery slope of a growing lack that steadily expands, manifesting itself in his spiritual, mental, emotional and eventually, physical body.

People are seeking happiness – but can they contain it? Do they feel, deep inside, that they deserve it? Can they grant themselves moments of unconditional happiness in their present state, no matter what? Check your ability to accommodate happiness.

Some people can accommodate a great deal of knowledge. Others, less. There are those who contain knowledge at high frequencies, others at lower ones (which are not less "good" – there is no judgment involved here). Some are wide and tall. Others are narrow and long. Some resemble a small utensil, some are even cracked, others broken and there are those who have particularly thick and strong sides. Imagine a receptacle – containers of different types and various forms. There are vessels that contain wine. Others are designed to hold water. Some are intended for vinegar, others for oil. Note that food fried in oil cannot be fried in vinegar or water. Thirst can be quenched with water or wine, but not with oil or vinegar. You can only wash with water, not with oil, vinegar or wine. Each one of these liquids has its own definition. There are containers for all these liquids, but you could not use them concurrently.

People are like containers with differing capacities and purposes. There are those who accommodate knowledge only for themselves – those who are larger in size have a task to contain knowledge for others. And even that knowledge comes in different frequencies and types and is designed for several ends.

Each container has its own capacity.

Some individuals hold a great measure of grace, love and mercy. Some are the seat of precepts, justice and judgment. There are people who hold magnificence within – which is the heart: They can accommodate, in moderation, both grace and law and apply them compassionately, as needed.

The measure of compassion is not the measure of pity, even though, at times, their end–product appears similar: taking a considerate stand, with the intent of helping one's fellow. Compassion allows you to observe the "drama" from a perspective – through the soul's eyes – employing the understanding that the object, be it a person or a nation, has created his/its reality, which it now finds difficult to digest, for one reason or another. The reason, is always spiritual and its purpose is to provide evolutionary lessons. The final outcome is the end result of processes evoked by inner beliefs related to the specific lesson being learned in the journey of life.

Pity is empathy interwoven with judgment. It takes the form of assuming a judgmental position. There is neither acceptance nor accommodation of the higher and fuller cosmic truth, which is: There is no coincidence, everything has a high purpose and goal.

Those who identify with and enter the frequency of pity are, in fact, drawn into the "victim drama" in the role of "saviour, rescuer, redeemer." That is a role that the ego, the personality, loves to fill, for it empowers, aggrandizes and enlarges it – in its own eyes! Also, sometimes in the eyes of others. This role serves as a tool to augment the sense of self–esteem. I would like to clarify, that there is nothing wrong, evil or inappropriate about it. It is splendid that people can "come out of themselves" to lend a hand and help others. It would behoove them, however, to understand why they are acting that way, so they can understand why they sometimes feel depleted energetically or alternatively, why are they brimful of energy. Identifying with a "victim" can drain you out of energy, thus, depleting your energy reserves. To ascertain, if that is the case, notice whether you have suddenly become tired, exhausted and impatient. These feelings indicate loss of energy.

Since the universe does not admit of coincidence, even the role of a person who pities – to serve as a saviour, redeemer and liberator, even if temporarily – is necessary.

Know nevertheless that when you find yourself in frequencies of compassion, you are beyond being judgmental and past the place of pity. At times, you'd feel – from within, through the guidance of your soul – that you should assist another, one who is subjected to suffering. It is our intent to demonstrate here that the final outcome is the same as if you were moved by pity.

At other times, you may feel that a person ought to struggle with repeated challenges. If he does not learn how to emerge from difficult circumstances on his own, the lessons will recur and be progressively more difficult. The Butterfly Allegory tells of a man who observed a butterfly trying to emerge from his cocoon. The man saw it was struggling and that it was taking a long time. He pitied the creature so, using a pair of scissors, he cut an opening for the creature. Indeed, the butterfly emerged quickly. But, since it had not yet developed wings or lungs, it was destined to struggle weakly all its life, The end.

Note, when you help another – what are your true inner motives? Is it because you cannot bear another's suffering? Is it done for your own ends? For your conscience? Do you lend a hand in order to gain your own peace of mind?

Be totally honest with yourselves and do not delude yourselves about your hidden motives. The truth is crucial to your own development. Can you contain the truth about yourselves?

Can you accept the parts of yourselves that are less evolved? Can you accommodate a truthful self–image, without aggrandizement, cheating, suppressing or painting the truth with bright ego colours?

And now dear Ilana, due to the limits of your capacity to accommodate this channelling, we will take a break. This way, the readers will be able to absorb the information, to breathe it in and to ask for accommodation of the knowledge.

Thank you, a blessing and much love, from the Heavenly Temple, Here I am, Master Akiva, in the service of the Great God.

Lesson 6

More about War, Peace, Karma, Forgiveness

ILANA: Good and blessed morning to all my wonderful guides. I turn to Master Akiva and ask for our discussion to continue.

MASTER AKIVA: Dear and beloved Ilana, it is an honour for me and I am glad to respond to your call and request.

ILANA: I am wondering what to ask you. Can you convey messages even if I do not ask you specifically about a given issue?

MASTER AKIVA: Yes. Let's return to a subject we have addressed since the commencement of our conversation, which by now has been lasting a few days: "Love thy neighbour as thyself."

People wonder how they can love their enemies, how they can forgive individuals, nations, who "stuck a knife in their backs." How can the anger, the froth of hatred, metamorphose into love? There are those who would not even address the matter. For them, an enemy is an enemy for eternity, just as a loved one will forever remain beloved.

If you look at the historical map of the nations of the world, along the wheel turn of time and its events, you will surely see how nations who once engaged in wars of bloodshed and annihilation entered into peace treaties after the warring ended, some years later or maybe it took a few generations. Eventually the reasons for the last war are forgotten, peace is now at their doorsteps. They forge diplomatic, economic, commercial, even social ties in that region which once was considered "enemy territory that must be destroyed." A few good examples are England and France, Britain and Germany, the U.S. and Japan, the U.S. and Germany and more. The same kind of relationship can be the reality for Israel and its neighbours – the Arab countries. What is needed, is a transformation of the perception of truth by both peoples: The Hebrew nation and the Arab nation. They need to recall their common ancestry – Abraham our forefather, the ancient common and admired father of both Isaac and Ishmael.

Often a bloody war, harsh and economically draining, combined with the loss of hope and bitter despair, are needed to convert the defeat of one side into a peace treaty. This is universally understood – when there is no choice, a new and different alternative is devised, in order to survive. When human beings gain the insight that through battlefields they will not get any closer to their purpose, only then will they agree to undergo a paradigm shift in their understanding.

When people understand the essence of love, which is willingly giving from the heart and acceptance from the heart of what is provided without lust or greed, without taking what has not been given – even if it is desired, wanted or yearned for – then they will cease the covetous exploitation of others, be it an individual: a fellow man, a friend, a neighbour; or a national entity: a people, a country, a continent.

Now, I would like to steer the subject of the discussion to the individual and karma, whose importance is great, yet little understood you have seen that nations who once lived in a state of war, fear and hate, now live in peace. Why, then, can't you understand it on a personal level?

Well dear, know that all human beings are actors in The Game of Life on Earth. All human beings, at the soul's plane, have devised and entered into soul agreements among themselves, designed to effect personal and national growth and global evolution for the entire planet, which is approaching its intended ascension.

To ascend is to be past judgment, past the level of truth seen from the altitude of the drama. To ascend means to accept the errors of the other, as well as your own. To ascend is to give up the need to be right at any cost. (Each side has its own subjective truth. Each is convinced that that its position is righteous and justified.) To ascend is to let go of anger, fear and hatred and the need to punish and avenge. It also means releasing the need for self–pity or the necessity to feel guilty about what has or hasn't transpired in the past, based on what you wanted and believed. To ascend is to understand that your beliefs are just *your* beliefs – not some immutable universal law – thus there is no compulsion for any other person or nation to believe in them.

Your beliefs are the course, the path along which your soul wanders, out of its own free will, based on the awareness that these are your rules of the game. **Belief, dear friends, is not carved in stone and believing in it is not compulsive. It is a privilege, a right, a choice you are free to either believe or discard.**

It is within your power, for example, to choose and believe in the path of suffering, the path of poverty, self–abnegation and austerity – and even sanctify such beliefs. You can develop anger and jealousy toward those who deviate from the narrow confines of your belief and even dare to live in utter contradiction thereof. They "dare" to live in affluence, with ease, self–fulfilled in the material plane.

People are not required to believe in the same set of laws or religious edicts, which have been invented and interpreted by parties with a vested interest. This does not mean that I judge whether they are good or bad. It is simply a statement of fact. From one's understanding of a given belief, a perception of reality is formed which is actually a subjective interpretation. It inclines one to lead a group of people who share a joint frequency. That is all.

People call others "interested," "agenda holders," "commercial," with a tone of disparagement, resentment and judgment. However, it should behoove them to gaze inwards, checking to see whether they are blameless of the same indictment. Everyone, every individual, every nation and people has its own existential interest.

Now, people must understand that they operate out of their beliefs – a private, inner codex which is theirs alone. They should not expect others to operate according to the codes by which they themselves are guided. People have diverse behavioural norms and different moral codes. You must learn and comprehend this paradigm; coming to grips with the notion that what you think is the absolute truth, is but your perception of truth at that immediate instance. It is possible that in your past you interpreted that very same reality differently. It is equally possible that in the future the dynamics of your insight will rotate 180 degrees. Regard yourselves as beings created by the Divine with varying perceptions of reality and different belief systems. Respect the beliefs of others, but do not regard them as the source of transcendent truth, something you may not veer from. Observe your beliefs and ask yourselves: "Does this belief serve me well right now?" "Is this belief positive and empowering?" "Does it reflect a part of me that is not yet aware of the general direction of my personal evolution, which might be out of tune with light and love?" Know how to release vacuous, limiting beliefs which engender doubt in yourself, in the beauty of the world, in its innate bounty and in your fellow human being.

When you are in total agreement with each other about a given assertion, for instance, "the world is becoming more and more corrupt," or "it is impossible to trust individuals and leaders anymore" – I beg you: Stop! Do not believe your own statements! Realize that you can interpret reality in a different and more constructive fashion. Remember that you validate a declaration until it becomes a "knowing," since you install it in your reality. You constantly recycle the belief. Consequently you encounter others who prove themselves unworthy of your trust. You feel you are "being stabbed in the back" in various aspects of your life. On a personal level –in your relationship with a mate, family, among friends and acquaintances and even among politician and statesmen whom you have elected and who represent your beliefs. It may also find expression in economic or national security and the existence of the nation as a whole.

Let us remind you, **beliefs create reality** and you must take responsibility for the kinds of beliefs you agree to have and which you reinforce by reaffirming them publicly. Beliefs which you gladly bestow on others, so that you have a common denominator and a basis for agreement.

Every drama, every reality is subject to interpretation. You can use it for constructive inspiration, vision and mental strength. Or you can trash it, malign it and use it as an instrument to sow fear and despair. It can be read it in a way that improves, as an attempt at finding a compromise. Or it can be explained in a way that causes withdrawal and helplessness. There are myriad ways to interpret reality.

Since, in its essence, interpretation is subjective, even when one is more "popular" and accepted than another, know to relate to it not as truth but as a construction of truth from a specific bent, based on particular interests. Note whether it is painted with the colours of love: abundance, light, equal measure of giving and receiving – or whether it surfaces from a place of great fear, from a "dark place" of want and disparagement; in order to cast shadows and doubt.

I am asking you to notice energies. Everything is built on the flow and mutual effect of energies. There are numerous forms of energy that do you good. We call them "energies of light," energies from the province of love. Conversely, there are energies that rob you of your peace of mind and plant the seeds of fear in you. We call these "darkness," they arrive from the province of fear – they are love that hides from itself and becomes unseen.

Interpretation that gives you inspiration, vision, enthusiasm and strengthens you from within – is desired for you. Interpretation that reduces you from within, shrinks, frightens and effects despondency – is desired for those who want to control you and rule your minds. Know, that to believe a particular interpretation, is a choice you are making. Do not pursue apocalyptic prophesies, battles of Gog and Magog and wars of annihilation. Be courageous and choose the way of peace, the approach that paves a road of hope, of dialogue between two nations – erstwhile enemies who nevertheless at their core are close to each other and love one another.

Do not doubt your ability to influence reality. True, you are now experiencing a reality that was forced on you and which is influencing the individual and national choices you are making, but nevertheless, each one of you can take a small step – open his or her heart and choose to traverse the path of love. This path ties in with understanding, for you have witnessed the drama that has manifested in your reality, in order to teach you to overcome it you must learn to utter complete forgiveness and absolution. To know how to ask for forgiveness, to know how to forgive an enemy – within or without. And to figure out how to forgive yourselves and let go of feelings of guilt and victimhood.

By way of forgiveness comes the elimination of the drama and its consequences – which spread as a ripple in the river of karma, of life on earth.

Karma, which was created by God, started its course in the Garden of Eden. When God created the world, he planted the perfect garden, with two trees: The Tree of Life and the Tree of Knowledge of Good and Evil. He created

Adam and Eve and commanded them to be the keepers of the garden. He allowed them to eat of all of earth's fruits, but he totally and strictly prohibited them from tasting the fruits of these two trees.

When there is a prohibition, when a restriction is in place, when a boundary is erected – the person whose freedom of choice was narrowed feels a need to breach the barrier, to acquire, if not by giving and receiving, then by taking. It is clear that the story is about karma. Accordingly, Adam, Eve, even the serpent (whom we love to blame and hate), are not really guilty – they are merely actors in a preordained drama, whose purpose was to test the concept of freedom of choice.

Human karma emerged, in its entirety, from the passions pulsating through the story of the Garden of Eden: Forcible taking, disobedience of an express decree, denial, casting blame on another, guilt, cover up, punishment and banishment. That is how mankind's course of karma commenced in earnest.

If you were to interpret the story in a different way, without blaming the woman, the serpent or even ancient Adam – how would your lives be perceived nowadays? If you interpreted the story not simplistically but with insight into its inner dimensions, you would perceive that it is the path of karma that was paved for you, as the chosen species created in the image of God.

Now you can transcend the story. You can go back in time and shift to a different path, in which the negative karma no longer holds sway. You can do that with the intention to ascend by expressing a wish for comprehensive forgiveness, which is a complete karmic release for yourselves, your people, your world.

Energetic channels, opened in dimensional portals, are aimed at this goal of allocating ascension frequencies to all of humanity. But, since this is a course of free choice and an apportionment of karma to negative (–) and positive (+), it falls upon each one of you to make his or her choices.

You are invited to choose between two distinct options. One, we will simply call: "the Path of Peace." The other, "the Path of War." Only through forgiveness and compassion is it possible to heal the Path of War and transform it into the Path of Peace. You must open up "the lanes of imagination," the bridge through which manifestation shifts from the plane of vision of the soul to implementation and creation in the physical dimension, the earthly domain of Kingdom (*sephirath malchuth*).

The path of imagination open up when you intend it to take place. Open up your inner channels and envision peace with your mind's eye: Peace within yourselves – see yourselves whole and accepting of who you are, as you are right now. Without criticizing or doubting your actions or being. Be at peace with your fellows and accept them as they are, without the need to change them or to preach at them, without negative residue and feelings of anger, sadness, apprehension, self–pity, hate or revenge. When you agree to accept the existing situation with your cross–border neighbours and release your resentment toward the "enemy" and toward yourselves and your leaders, whom you have chosen and who reflect your beliefs, you actually accept responsibility for the situation and truly decide to transform it. After you have accepted it, you are invited to extend a hand of peace. Look into the eyes of other humans like you, good souls such as yourselves, immersed in the game of life – and understand that the similarity and commonality between you is much greater that the difference. If you but learn how to respect every human being, with all his beliefs, without forcibly imposing your beliefs on him, without fighting for your beliefs, then the prophecy – "the just shall live by his faith"[10] – will come to pass.

ILANA: thank you dear Master Akiva, a wonderful presentation. I have a question. It is about peace in the Middle East, between Israel and the Arabs. Islam speaks of jihad, holy war, hate and annihilation of the Jews, or, at least these are the current interpretations of its messengers. How is peace possible in the face of such beliefs, which utterly lack love and light?

---

10 Habakkuk, 2:4.

MASTER AKIVA: Beneath the beliefs are human beings. In their chests beat hearts like yours. They are flesh and blood like you. They have parents, children, families. They, too, are home–dwellers who desire to live quietly and peacefully, make an honest living and bring home a loaf of bread.

People have to understand that we are all human beings. Each has an energetic system of chakras, thought–forms, beliefs, karma. You operate very similarly. What motivates you, at this juncture of your human evolution, is the existential need to survive. Your survival blueprint has been imprinted in your DNA since prehistory. This blueprint articulates in terms of life and death, decided by physical force and personal power. It generates taking, on the one hand – warring and aggression. On the other – defensiveness and flight. These are universally shared instincts.

However, in this new age, the emphasis is on opening the heart essence – glory and wisdom. Bereaved mothers on both sides of the fence can lead the campaign to influence public opinion, beginning with the opinions of the family.

Compassion constitutes understanding at a higher level. There is no longer any need to forcibly take, to coerce, to acquire lands and to superimpose your fears on other people. There is a need for compromise, sharing and most of all – mutual respect.

There is a need for national absolution. Shimon Peres, the current president of Israel, can certainly lead a respectable, supra–religious move, together with a Muslim cadi and Druze, Circassian and Catholic priests. It is no coincidence that Israel is home for the scatterings of the world. All the nations of the world raise their eyes to your centre: Jerusalem. A city that was reunited, a city that is holy to three faiths: Judaism, Christianity, Islam. Remember that Christianity and Islam's origins are in Judaism. Both Jesus and Mohamed were influenced by the Old Testament, by Abraham, by Moses and by all the prophets.

You can create a public campaign of the Tree of Faiths, where the origin of the religions is seen and the common beliefs and customs of all three religions are emphasized. **Remember, these three religions were created as gates, as paths for interpretation with a single purpose: to unite people with their spiritual source – Faith in God, one God, the God who is the Creator of the world.**

Every religion is a portal. Every religion contains knowledge. The faith of the future will comprise the essence of the three religions in symbiosis. It will not even be regarded as a religion. It is more accurate to say that the knowledge of the future will embrace an understanding of mutual respect, "and the wolf shall also dwell with the lamb,[11]" as is written in the Vision of the End of Days:

---
[11] Isaiah 11:6.

The word that Isaiah the son of Amotz saw concerning Judah and Jerusalem:

"And it shall come to pass in the last days, that the mountain of the Lord's house shall be established in the top of the mountains and shall be exalted above the hills and all nations shall flow unto it.

"And many people shall go and say, Come ye and let us go up to the mountain of the Lord, to the house of the God of Jacob; and he will teach us of his ways and we will walk in his paths: for out of Zion shall go forth the law and the word of the Lord from Jerusalem.

"And he shall judge among the nations and shall rebuke many people: and they shall beat their swords into plowshares and their spears into pruning hooks: nation shall not lift up sword against nation, neither shall they learn war any more.

"O house of Jacob, come ye and let us walk in the light of the Lord."[12]

And,
But in the last days it shall come to pass, that the mountain of the house of the Lord shall be established in the top of the mountains and it shall be exalted above the hills and people shall flow unto it.

---

12   Isaiah 2:1–5.

And many nations shall come and say, Come and let us go up to the mountain of the Lord and to the house of the God of Jacob and he will teach us of his ways and we will walk in his paths: for the law shall go forth of Zion and the word of the Lord from Jerusalem.

And he shall judge among many people and rebuke strong nations afar off and they shall beat their swords into plowshares and their spears into pruninghooks: nation shall not lift up a sword against nation, neither shall they learn war any more.

But they shall sit every man under his vine and under his fig tree and none shall make [them] afraid: for the mouth of the Lord of hosts hath spoken it.

For all people will walk everyone in the name of his god and we will walk in the name of the Lord our God forever and ever.[13]

Now, please understand, dear ones, that things do not occur of their own accord and there is a need to focus upon them in order to accomplish them, even if they are written in the prophecies. An excellent example is the establishment of the State of Israel on 14 May 1948. First there was the vision, which pre-dated its actualization through all the generations of the Diaspora. Then there was the belief that the vision could become reality, followed by the understanding that

---

13   Micah 4:1–5.

the state will not be given to the Jewish people on a tray of silver and gold. There was a burning faith in the right to live in the land granted to Abraham by the Lord, Creator of the world. There was a belief that the children of Abraham have the right to live in an independent country, free of the Ottoman and British regimes. There was also a belief in the urgency to struggle for this right, even to fight fiercely to acquire the desired goal.

People cannot remain complacent and do nothing. They must take a stand. They can bring themselves to a renewed vision of the latter days and the establishment of God's temple as a light unto the nations. They can navigate their choices to a path of peace, prosperity, brotherhood and mutual respect among all the nations of the world.

"The end result comes, first, from a thought." And we say to you (here the group of senior guides, of which Master Akiva is a spokesman , joins in): **Choose your thoughts! Choose and hold them, refresh them; alter your beliefs! Choose your desired path again: War or compassion - war or peace.**

"He who makes peace in the heavens, will bestow peace upon us and upon the entire nation of Israel and we'll say, Amen!"

Wishing you a great day, the day you celebrate Pentecost, may it be a happy day for all the people of Israel.

I, Master Akiva, am pleased to be at your service for the sake of the people of Israel and the nations of the world, who are tied together in ties of karma and the threads of divine destiny.

"Holy, holy, holy, is the Lord of hosts: the whole earth is filled with his glory.[14]" I Metatron, am here, supporting and inspiring the process with my light and authority. I thank you for understanding your mission and for your willing participation in the communication with us day in and day out. Blessed be, you and your entire family forever and ever. Amen, Sela.

---

14 Isaiah 6:3.

Lesson 7

The Circle of Creation and Creativity
Self–Image and its Importance

ILANA: Dear and beloved guides. I would like to summon Master Akiva, in order to proceed with our discussion. Thank you.

MASTER AKIVA: Gladly. I am here, ready to be of service to you and to continue with our fascinating and fruitful exchange. We will talk, as per your request, about your self–image and ways to improve it.

Your self-image sits at the core of your inner identity, within the creation and formation circle of your trials and experiences (indeed, a new function). See this circle as a pool of materials you maintain for creation. It includes imagination, memories imprinted in your DNA, different beliefs found in various layers, from parallel and other incarnations. This circle is the heart and the core of your creation, it and none other.

For precisely this reason, you should not disregard or belittle the value of your self–image, thus damaging it. This self–image forms your relation to all issues at all levels: Do you really and truly believe you are entitled to plenty, to love, to good health, to success in your career, to prosperity and to your relationships, first and foremost your relationship with yourself.

This relationship also manifests externally – in the manner and quality of the relationships you would weave for yourselves. For example: A man, who criticizes and disparages his own body and is displeased with it, will attract to himself others who will be critical toward the definition of his physical exterior. They will look down at him, causing him to depreciate his own self–esteem. They may even humiliate him. If the same person criticizes his personality and considers himself to be stupid, useless, etc., that is how he will endure his external experience. Your external experience always reflects your inner beliefs, to which you have given weight, validity and substance till they materialize in the physical at the plane of reality of your lives on earth.

If an individual is displeased with his body, but loves and is at peace with his personality – he will experience relationships where his character will be acknowledged and appreciated, while his body will be rejected. If a man is pleased and at ease with his body and his personality, the relationship he would attract – that would be attracted to him is a more precise term – will reflect this appreciation and love of himself.

When people experience financial want, they in fact

externalize an inner belief of scarcity, of a feeling of being unworthy of financial abundance. When they examine themselves, they will discover beliefs of worthlessness which find expression in their emotional and material existence.

Every problem, every trouble, every difficulty reflects a failure to consider an inner interaction with the issue. Your self-image is at the heart of the matter. Only by dealing with it can you, once and for all, solve the impeding factor.

How can you enhance your self–image, which is so deeply imprinted in you?

You do it by reprogramming your experiences. You do it by aiming energy at the symbol of your self–image, as it is presented to you by your higher self and the consciousness of the cells of your body. This can be achieved by way of affirmations – which are positive declarations uttered in the present tense. The declarations are then expanded into emotional awareness. It is not enough to – robot–like – make an affirmation, if you do not believe your own statement.

ILANA: Dear and wonderful Master Akiva, for all I know and in the way I use it, I have never heard that emotional current should be added. So far as I know, those who need positive declarations usually do not believe in themselves and their words, at least not from the outset. Nevertheless, I know that is a way of creating reality: To link faith to thought, emotion and imagination.

MASTER AKIVA: Indeed. When people do not add the elements of imagination and emotional current, the declarations have little effect. Some, add them intuitively, thus it works for them. You intuitively connect emotion to thought and they are fully integrated. That is the secret of self–programming.

ILANA: Some people are horrified when I ask them to say, "I love myself." They do not actually believe it and some find it difficult to even utter the words. I tell them to take a step back and declare a preference, "I choose to love myself," and with that statement they do not, for the most part, seem to have a problem.

How is it possible to help such people? Those who do not know how to use imagination and through it feel the words they are saying, which otherwise would be devoid of any meaning?

MASTER AKIVA: These people should use their bodies to reshape their self–image. They need to act in the physical. I will expound on my statement: Individual reality is the product of a joint experience of all bodies – the physical, energetic, emotional, intellectual and spiritual. It is not an experience that is limited to one body. All bodies participate jointly in creating the experience, the experience of forming reality, which takes effect in the personal experience of a human being.

A person is shaped by his past, by his memories – both his successes, as he defines them and his subjectively defined failures.

The memories are of "real" experiences. Why were they real? Because they contained an experience that is common to all the bodies. As a rule, one would not remember a thought that passed through his mind a year ago. Nor would he attach any importance to a non–physical emotion. Experience is the materialization of what you feel, think, act upon, behave in relation to and, especially, what affects you directly. Sometimes, it affects you indirectly, when your subconscious assimilates an experience you prefer to suppress or even "forget." The subconscious forgets nothing. Everything registers and therefore affects your self–image and consequently your experience. Accordingly, in reshaping your self–image you cannot settle for just a mental statement in present tense. With all due respect, it is but one element of a continuum and a whole and since only one element would not take you very far forward, clearly it is insufficient.

The course of action should therefore include: Specific intent to own a particular quality or to have a specific experience; the desire will shape you into a channell through which to direct imagination, thought–forms, emotion and action. For instance, if you aspire to be financially wealthy in order to realize your material wishes, you must imagine it, to see in your mind's eye your riches or the assets you desire to amass, your bank account, etc. Now, after envisioning it, tune into the emotional aspect, experience how it feels to be rich... stay there, emotionally. Now add the thoughts of a rich person. Imagine: now I am a very rich person, what would I be thinking about as I get up in the morning, what do I think about during the day. You might be surprised by new worries, even more burdensome than those you are presently experiencing. Perhaps you would enjoy your imaginary wealth. Now get in touch with creative and generous thoughts. Finally, you need to effect an action that would prove to you that it is a memory and not solely an imaginary event. How? Buy yourself something that you desire, even something very small like a snack, ice cream, a book, a bunch of flowers; give a beggar some money or put it in a donation box. Feel rich and generous. The following day remember the experience and repeat it. Now say to yourselves: "**I am rich. I have plenty of money.**"

The longer you affirm, imagine and feel this way, the more generously you will part with your money and the aspiration will then be transmitted, as electrical pulses, into your knowledge and self–image memory reservoirs. Your self–image will change if, until now, you imagined yourself a pauper.

To clarify: I do not suggest that you suddenly make yourselves over into a wastrel, constantly buying luxury items and accessories. But I recommend that when paying for service, you expand your heart instead of contracting your belly. Know how to give generously and lovingly, out of a clear awareness that your money will always return and, for the moment, it serves you by being bestowed on someone else. Connect yourself to the circle of abundance, of giving–receiving–giving. Do not resent paying bills for which you have received a full return. Be thankful for your ability to receive and to give.

ILANA: If I understood you correctly, dear Master Akiva, if we translate our desire into an actual experience in which all bodies participate, we create for ourselves the reality which our self–image will project into our life experience. In other words, we will then create for ourselves that particular reality – our self–image will project it into our life; that is, even by self–imaging we are actually creating reality – a popular issue nowadays.

MASTER AKIVA: That is true. Ask to receive a symbol of your self–image. Do it by taking a deep breath through the nose and slowly exhaling through the mouth. Do it three times. Imagine that a beam of light descends through your crown, connecting you to large bright star. The star is your soul and the beam of light descends from your higher self. Now close your eyes and ask to receive a symbol of your self–image. Accept any image that comes up. Open your eyes. Imagine and feel how the beam of light appears out of the palms of your hand. Project the light onto the symbol you have received and see how the light penetrates and empowers it. Place the symbol inside your heart. Care for and attend to it daily, by making positive affirmations accompanied by feelings and imagination.

Always start with the understanding that you are entitled to whatever you ask for. Start with the understanding that you must grant yourself love, that you must enable yourself to be in a state of acceptance of whatever you ask for. Know that occasionally a request might contradict the lessons and express desire of your soul and therefore you will not always be granted that which you desire and imagine.

However, it is crucial that, regardless of all else, you heal and revamp your self-image, which creates your experiences and trials in life, some of which are threatening and even undesired and burdensome.

Your self–image will be healed by love, which you give yourself. It will be healed by forgiveness, which will release all your feelings of guilt, whether or not you are aware of them. It will continue to receive healing by way of forgiveness and acceptance of all factors that hurt and traumatized you in your past, leaving an imprint of negative and even dangerous beliefs.

Your self–image will be restored by focusing on gratitude toward all that is. Likewise, removal of the "victim pattern," which manifests itself as self–pity, anger, hatred and a desire to hurt yourself or others – the self–destruction urge.

Invent positive experiences and understand that they are imprinting new memories in your subconscious – which does not distinguish between "real" or "unreal" programming. An experience is an experience. This should help you understand the value of guided imagery as a tool of healing; you could even term it, "healing imagery." **There is no limit to what you can accomplish with the power of the imagination. It is a powerful tool of creation, with tremendous value.**

Imagine yourself looking and feeling good, doing what feels pleasant, living in opulence and harmony. Act in accord with this new image and see slow changes in the reality you are currently experiencing.

Expand the experience to all your senses, by connecting it to all your bodies. For example: when you tell yourself, "I am attractive the way I am," know not to fall in the trap of comparing yourself to others. Know that the beauty and light of your soul is very great. The moment you stop covering it with exterior layers, piled on top of more such layers, of negative images of the personality (ego), then it is revealed for all to see, influencing you to feel beautiful and causing your environment to relate to you accordingly.

Get in touch with the emotional aspect of your being. Ask

to feel true beauty radiating from within, from your soul and to feel it permeating through all the layers of your being – ethereal, emotional, intellectual and physical. See yourselves in motion, radiating the beauty outwardly. Feel surrounded by pure soul beauty… beauty that is nonpareil and can never be compared to anything external, such as other people. God created you unique, each with his or her own special beauty. Sometimes, the beauty is hidden in the eyes alone, which hold the secret of one's charm and magic. When the eyes are clouded with negative self–images, immersed in stress and worries, they will not project the beauty that radiates from within.

People these days undergo a lot of cosmetic surgery, even if they appear attractive, out of a desire to improve themselves, because they are self–critical and they are not at–one with what is. This is not to say that it is a negative phenomenon, It is extant and subject to freedom of choice. But I would like you to know that makeup and plastic surgery notwithstanding, the source of the greatest beauty you could acquire – for free, for no money at all – is love. Love of the soul that is fused with God and ennobles the physical body that transports it like a chariot (merkaba). Surely you have encountered people who are less than perfect, yet noble character emanates from them. They might be too skinny for your taste or too fat, according to your rigid criteria, too old or any other shortcoming you might imagine. Nevertheless, their loveliness radiates from them. You feel their inner beauty and it affects you, whether you are aware of it or not. You have felt the beauty of their soul beaming at you, gently touching your soul, which yearns to beam forth its light – on wings of love.

Your self–image has several territories. It is like a multifaceted diamond. At its core lies a divine spark that is entirely light and love. Its facets contain these images: exterior self–image, economic self–image, self–image in a relationship, health self–image, spiritual self–image.

These self–images include many visions, holograms of inner scenarios, continuously projected from your subconscious. Holograms that are dramatized and broadcast, attracting all the materials that make up the inner picture. These might include extremely positive and pleasant thoughts and emotions or, conversely, negative and unpleasant thoughts and emotions.

ILANA: Dear Master Akiva, if I have a negative inner image in one of the areas you mentioned, would it necessarily create an experience that I would consider "negative" in that particular area?

Let's presume I have difficult inner experiences, even traumas in the area of relationships, would they affect the formation of my next relationship? After all, there is no doubt in my mind that people who experience negative relationships and get divorced nevertheless subsequently succeed in forming a successful partnership. Please explain.

MASTER AKIVA: Dear Ilana, you understood this correctly. There is no way you could assess "success" in a relationship in which you are not directly involved. You do not really know what transpires in such a relationship and the nature of its inner dynamics. Certainly it is possible to transform from a negative to a positive experience, depending on the inner images of both partners.

The prevalence of past negative experiences is not, necessarily, a reason for them to recur in the future. The determining factor is the inner processing of the past experience. Did you 'take it hard,' and consequently develop negative beliefs, as opposed to one who 'took it easy,' learned its lessons and opted for positive beliefs? What matters in the end is the emotional and mental processing of the experience.

In your particular case, intellectually you have managed to overcome a difficult – even traumatic – experience, which has re–invigorated beliefs held since your childhood and in previous incarnations. You arrived with them and were further influenced by your parents and grandparents. However, there is a gap between your wonderful intellectual and spiritual insight and the emotional experience you underwent, which has left scars on your physical body. There is a scar in your aura caused by the trauma you experienced. You can ask to feel it and to heal it. You have to form an intent, then request and believe. And so it will be, of course.

ILANA: I request to feel the energy of my marriage trauma or – it would be more accurate to term it – the traumas caused by infidelity. I feel a very strong energetic lump, with weak radiation between my hands. I think I should send it love and light and see what will happen. I am affirming healing to this scar! My stomach is contracting. I feel it physically in my solar plexus. I even feel a bit nauseated.

I radiate light from my hands and breathe deeply. [A few minutes later] I am flooded with calm stillness; I am feeling lightness and an inner expanse. The contraction has been loosened. When I ask to feel the trauma between my hands, I feel nothing. My hands remain together. There is no energy of trauma or deposits from the divorce, at least not energetically.

I understand that this is a way to heal every trauma in every field. Every person can use his imagination to see and/ or to feel. We must understand that everything is visible, palpable energy.

Now I would like to accommodate all that was said and done and am asking, with your permission dear Master Akiva, for a short break.

MASTER AKIVA: Mental knowledge requires time and a measure of internalization.. Therefore, we will end our discussion for today at this juncture. We may reconvene later today for a further co-operative effort. I thank you very much for having summoned me and, again, for the great dedication with which you undertake your mission as the mouthpiece of creation, which contains and heralds the intelligence of light and the essence of love. Be blessed in your eternal being.

Thank you and all my love.

Lesson 8

Childhood Diseases, the Ego

ILANA: Dear Master Akiva, I would like to address to you a question I was asked by Margaret, who is herself an alternative therapist. She writes:

I was most interested in the part about sick or dead babies. This is a *tikkun* (a process of soul mending, repairing). Could you please ask to enlarge on the subject; for we really learn and teach, all the time, about the soul's choices and about lessons and that disease is a choice – whether conscious or unconscious. So what really happens to children and babies, who have not yet developed awareness or awareness of choice?

Also, a subject that interests me: How can one feel happy when there is a sick or dying child in one's experience? Does it occur in order to teach the parents something?

MASTER AKIVA: Dear Ilana, dear Margaret, dear readers. You are regarding the baby and the child in an overly emotional, uncomprehending manner. You fail to notice that it is a soul that has chosen to come to this world. The soul arrives with "baggage," with deposits, with scars, with choices it has made, with karmic debts, with lessons it needs to experience and complete. You observe the exterior and see a cute baby, an innocent toddler, right?

Well, to be in sickness is no crime, dear. A disease is not a punishment one "deserves" and must suffer. That is an obsolete and erroneous perception, more suited to the Middle Ages. In those days the sick, the leprous and the crippled were shunned. They were feared, the objects of anger and pity. They harboured the "knowledge" that theirs was a time of vengeance and retribution,[15] and they were being punished for a sin they committed.

To be sick is not a punishment! Being sick is not evidence that you have committed a transgression! Being sick means that the balance of your biological system has broken down!

Soul choices do not refer to conscious selections of the personality, whatever its biological age. Why do you think that the agony of a sick and suffering baby is greater than that of a child of five? Of 10? A teen? An adult? Or even an elderly person? Torment is torment and the experience is hard on anyone. Your emotional outlook and your lack of understanding that each is a veteran soul in a physical body, causes you to artificially distinguish between the sickness and death of a baby, a child and an adult.

---

15 Accord, Deuteronomy 32:35.

As I have already stated, the soul has certain lessons to undergo, karmic debts to pay, things to learn – even to teach. The effect of karma is that of cause and effect. There is an affecting factor and one that is affected and there is a symbiotic relation between them. Accordingly, every human being, regardless of age, including newborns, is a factor that influences and is influenced. The baby comes into this world to experience the choices his soul has made and, contemporaneously, to impart an instructing experience, not necessarily a light and pleasant one, to his parents and immediate family.

The question expands and raises the following issue: Is it possible to be happy when undergoing trials and tribulations, when your child is sick or dying, even in the event of death? The answer in one word, is a clear and simple: "No!"

You need to understand the meaning of happiness and divide it into its constituent emotional elements. What is happiness? Happiness is an amalgam of several dominant emotions, including a flood of joy, of love, of feeling light, of deep gratitude and possibly great inner peace and calm. That is the range of happiness, which can vary from very small to grand, from light to heavy, from a few fleeting moments to an extensive existential experience.

You can certainly define yourself as a happy person, who validates his life experience and fully accommodates,

the entire array of "negative" emotions that traverses the range of your soul.

When a person is immersed in anguish, due to illness of a dear one or himself, he is not expected to hold happiness – a state of validation of his condition, acceptance thereof and joy. You will never hear a person saying joyously, "I am so sick and it makes me so happy!"

Nevertheless, when one opts for an existential experience of happiness, continuous communion with the soul and a sense of attainment of a desired goal, he can alleviate the most difficult feelings into greater ease. If he does not choose to experience deep agony and sink into bleak depression, torment and self–pity, maybe even loss of faith in the Creator of the world, in physicians and in himself, he can request spiritual assistance from his soul. He would then better contend with his condition, from a position of greater mental strength. It does not mean that he would feel cheerful and joyous, yet he would experience greater strength and confidence. The factor that will help the most is faith.

A man goes to war, withstanding what befalls him and his dear ones. By so doing, he only enhances the suffering, the mental stress, the hardship. He could be at peace with it, accepting his situation. This does not mean he sits idly by, doing nothing to ameliorate his condition. What it means is that he seeks to do his utmost for those who are sick, for example, yet maintains his own balance to the greatest possible extent.

When one is very ill and suffering, it is highly recommended that both the patient and his relatives, instead of generating worry and fear, increase their faith and pray. This is not a suggestion for religious conversion. It is meant to increase the awareness that God is accessible to all – not just to "religious" individuals.

The power of prayer is that it eases the situation, it lessens the "verdict," it creates hope; it has the effect of summoning the angels and healing energy. It opens the door for miracles. Scientific studies have ascertained the power and importance of prayer, both as a cause and a catalyst of faith and hope – which facilitate recovery.

People must understand that death is not the end of the soul's journey. When they internalize the knowledge that souls are eternal and the world is but a corridor, a narrow bridge, leading to the next world – the World of Truth, of souls, then they will no longer fear death. Those who have experienced clinical death and remember the event, are powerfully affected, their faith is augmented and their life gains meaning.

Yes, you find it hard to lose a person who is close to you. You suffer from abandonment anxiety; you have an enormous fear of death, which threatens and robs you of freedom and choice in life. You are very afraid of bereavement and loss. However, **you can transcend the fear** and overcome your feelings of torment. The transformation will be realized if you form a bond with the experience of the soul, rather than the limiting and fear–haunted experience of the tormented personality.

How does one accomplish it? You do it by declaring an intent, with declarations and deep breaths. Say:

**"I choose to be connected with my entire soul now.
"I choose to transform my current experience and witness it through the eyes of my soul."**

Feel how the light of your soul penetrates your head, your brain, your eyes, ears, lungs, kidneys, your abdomen... the light of the soul enters and floods your emotional and mental bodies, together with the physical, connecting them with the spiritual body. From here you can experience silence. Peace. Transcend the stress, the pain, the sorrow, the fears. **As a matter of fact, it is possible to accurately say that you will move past the experience of contraction and apprehension to the experience of fullness, which is love.** You will experience love and compassion through inner silence and peace, endowing you with the mental power you need, a precious resource of fuel for your machine. You will certainly not experience love as a revelry, joy or happiness. This is not the time for such an experience. Know to accommodate sadness and joy, but silence and energetic vitality as well.

Now, know that there is no coincidence, no errors, no guilt whatsoever. There is conscious creation by the soul together with unconscious participation by the personality. There is a supreme goal to all that happens, including illness, dying, death and suffering. Accept your situation and the event, the "drama," you are submerged in, as a trial and a lesson. Do your best to maintain a state of faith, of hope, of compassion and love. To the best of your ability, help those in need of your assistance. Give all you can, but know, whatever happens, God Is and the situation you are in did not manifest in your life because you are being punished or because you are guilty of anything; neither you nor your sick relative.

It is okay to cry, to weep, to ask for help; to break down. It does not mean you are acting inappropriately. All emotional experiences are natural. However, know how to accept help at the level of spiritual understanding, as we have delineated for you. Even as you are falling, choose to ascend. Remember the wise saying: "After the darkest moments, in the darkest tunnel, the opening and the light will come." Choose the light, choose hope, choose to reinforce faith, choose to contain the drama, choose all these by connecting with the temple of your soul, which is at–one with the source – with God.

Let it be the will of the divine that you shall know no

suffering, that you will not experience sorrow anymore than the requisite minimum and that complete and utter healing will be granted unto you and your dear ones and all the people of the world, let us say amen, so be it.

Thank you for the excellent question, I am Master Akiva in the service of the light, conveying to you the essence of the Book of Utterances – Love as Creator of the world.

"Love thy neighbour as thyself."

ILANA: Thanks to the wonderful Master Akiva and to Margaret for the fascinating question, with utmost love, Ilana.

Questions to Master Akiva about the Ego[16]

ILANA: Dear and wonderful Master Akiva, the question arises: What actually is the ego? Is it good, is it bad? Should we do battle with it and how? There are those who claim not to have one. Is that possible? Is that a worthy goal? If the ego is eliminated, what replaces it?

MASTER AKIVA: Dear Ilana, dear and beloved students, the ego – I have defined as the physical body's personality – is a key part of you. Imprinted in it are development plans and

---

16 Additional materials on the ego can be found in Chapter 10.

your soul's choices. The ego has a perception of separation and a worldly illusion of self–identity. It includes character traits such as mental abilities and shortcomings, distinctive emotional reactions within a pre–selected and definite range. There is the truth of the ego, which is the perception of the reality through its own unique interpretation. The interpretation of one who carries the victim pattern differs from the interpretation of one who has strength and conscious insight into reality creation. Some individuals are characterized by specific personality patterns, defined as sensitivity or excessive sensitivity, a tendency to be argumentative – quarrelsome and angry – and then there are those who are peacemakers and lovers of harmony, even appeasing others at the expense of what they themselves really want. There are people of many types, with differing perceptions of reality, each perception a programme impressed into the ego.

Such programming may be defined as soul lessons, karmic deposits, soul agreements or choices of life experiences. The programme is made up of separate identities, aspects of shadow (unconscious but controlling and affecting reactions), who are stirred by negative thought patterns, which in turn are composed of fears and limiting and reductive elements. They are tied to either a comprehensive negative self–image or a specific one in a particular area of experience, as explained in the relevant chapter.

In an entertaining and paradoxical way, the ego's solution

in order to rise above itself, because it is combative by nature, is prescribed in its own devices: "Fight the ego!" is the ego's solution. But this is impossible. In effect, it creates a split identity. A part of the self that is at war with itself – what else could it engender?

Some people claim to be without ego, but they are merely boasting from within the ego that has diluted itself into believing it has been done away with, while merely masking itself as something else. That something else is "an egoless ego."

The ego, which is characterized by action arising from the three energy centres in the "lower," more earthly frequency, cannot make itself disappear, nor does it wish to do so. You have to be precise with definitions. You could define your query as follows: Is the ego in need of healing? In other words, is there a need to heal its content – basic beliefs, thought patterns, memories, karma? The answer will be positive: Yes and yes! Of course, not every ego needs healing.

The best way to refine, reconcile and improve the ego is through convergence at the highest centres, especially the spot at the heart – the unconditional love chakra, the heart chakra. Love is the cure for all the negative patterns that afflict the ego. Since love in its essence and substance is the inverse of war, it is unnecessary, in fact it is harmful, to fight or invalidate the ego. The better approach would be **to** embrace love in the ego. Love that will keep on growing, softening, enlightening and restoring the interior. All parts of the shadow will be healed and transformed into a single whole. The ego will experience love and unity and then it will no longer be defined as such. Body–personality will become soul–personality. Such a personality will not define itself as owning – or being devoid – of an ego. It will accept with compassion and understanding the term "ego," with all that entails.

To sum up: Ego is separation, reduction, taking, having only for oneself. It causes distancing from unity, from the circle of plenty, giving–receiving–giving, which is love. Furthermore, it effects distancing from the source to the cold regions.

Thank you for your excellent question, my dear and talented students. Thank you dear and beloved Ilana, for your dedication to writing and for allowing the flow of knowledge to come through. Blessed be in your eternal being. I am Master Akiva, joyfully conveying my words and proceeding with my study: "Love thy neighbour as thyself."

ILANA: Thank you dear Master Akiva for your wonderful and clear words, which elucidate our soul's purpose. After incorporating the idea I understood that the ego is the wish to accept for itself. Above the ego is love, that is, the wish to receive in order to give and inspire.

Lesson 9

Masada will not Fall Again[17]
About the Sanctity of Life

ILANA: Good and blessed morning to all my guides. Good morning to you Master Akiva. I call you, please, to proceed with our discussion.

MASTER AKIVA: I am happy to continue with our joint project, dear Ilana. Before waking up, the sentence, "Masada will not fall again" rose in your awareness. With your permission and agreement, I have planted it in your mind, to provide a header and stimulate our conversation this morning, this habitual, enjoyable and desired activity of ours, whose flavour is improving by the day. I am grateful to you for allowing my energy and words to come through you, as creation's mouthpiece.

---

17 During the first Jewish–Roman War (66–70 AD) a group of rebels occupied a fortress – till then held by a Roman garrison – on top of Mount Masada near the Dead Sea. In 72 A.D. the Roman legion X laid siege to Masada. The Romans breached the wall of the fortress in April 73. When they entered the fortress they discovered that its 960 inhabitants had set all the buildings (except the food storerooms) ablaze and committed mass suicide. The account of the siege of Masada was related by two women who survived the suicide by hiding inside a cistern with five children.

ILANA: Thank you, dear Master Akiva. I am very happy to write down your words. I will be glad to discuss the subject you have raised. I remember that I found the subject fascinating and submitted a major paper on it in high school. The period of the Second Temple, including the times during which you were incarnated, always riveted and excited me, It was the focus of my academic studies (History of the Jewish People) in college. The subject has always touched my heart.

MASTER AKIVA (with extraordinary softness): You – your soul, your heart – have always been in harmony with your roots; you have walked in step with your enlightened and wondrous soul – which is a sister soul of mine.

What is the meaning of the quoted saying? Why did I plant it in your mouth and in your heart, especially today? What is the deep import veiled in the idea? I speak to all human hearts, in every faith, for the verse, "Love thy neighbour as thyself," speaks of the unity of creation. It speaks about the unity of mankind, who were all created in the image of God. I speak about life, not about death. Indeed, I have mentioned, when discussing the sick children, that you do not understand what death really is – a passage to the World of Truth, a world where the righteous gather together with the best of souls that emerge above duality's drama. It is the world of unity and light.

The world, as you experience it, is a gateway to life. It is the gateway to great holiness; a gateway to the training ground for fulfiling the commandments and responsibilities and integrating them with faith and ideas at the plane of creativity and inspiration.

The sanctity of life is of paramount importance. In the Ten Commandments that God handed down to his messenger, Moses, it is written: "Thou shall not murder." (Exodus, 20:13). The Ten Commandments are strict dictates, instructing us not to trespass the holy utterance. Of course, beneath the negative lies the affirmative. When people were unable to accommodate that which is, they were given the commandments in the form of "do not" and "thou shall not." In actuality, the commandment, "thou shalt not murder" means: honour the sanctity of life, for it is God's creation.

"Life" refers to the life of all souls in all bodies, including nations, people, tribes, societies or political parties. Life also includes the myriad fauna on the planet. Life is all flora planted by God in the Garden of Eden for man to minister. All Earth's resources are the same life.

"Thou shall not murder" applies not only to the extinction of the life of a human being, so that his heart stops beating and his physical body expires. Since humans live simultaneously in several bodies, all united in a single temple called the "human body," the intent has been to sanctify them all. "Bodies" refers to the aura, which contains the emotional, ethereal, intellectual and spiritual bodies. Man is not a biological machine in a physical clay vessel, it is an amalgam of spirit, of the divine spark that powers the "machine." The spark is the soul, which God breathed into the nostrils of the first man.

"Thou shalt not kill" also means "do not murder hope, faith, love and trust," the intellectual, emotional and spiritual underpinnings of the soul.

ILANA: Thank you, brilliant Master Akiva. With your permission I would like to take a short break, in order to accommodate and meditate on what was just said.

MASTER AKIVA: Granted and you have passed your test well.

ILANA: Thank you. (It was a test of faith and truth.)

MASTER AKIVA: Dear Ilana. We are discussing the sanctity of life; the ability to accommodate life, honouring life wherever it may be, transcending to the level of the soul and perceiving it above the ego's interpretation. The term, from now on, will be: ego, the body's personality, in contrast with the soul – the divine within you. The latter, is aware, filled with the light of creation, with holy and pure love, which, indeed, is unconditional.

People operate through the personality of their physical body. This personality is prompted by the survival urge that is immersed at the base, the root – the red – chakra that links one to life and movement, execution and activity, to *sephirath malchuth* (Kingdom level of attainment, in Cabbala). The personality feels very threatened, thus, it is found at the opposite behavioural ends, thought of as preserving what exists: On one hand defenciveness, on the other aggression – a whole world of warfare – initially, internal; within you. A war between the conscience, on one side and the "devil within," on the other. A battle between lust and what is forbidden. A confrontation between polar opposites.

This conflict is external, for you are the Minister of Foreign Affairs in your inner world. You attempt to secure for yourself more than the other has, whether it is a person or a nation, which you would designate as 'an enemy state'. In fact, you are the one adopting the role of enemy instead of that of lover. You do so because you believe the planet's resources are limited and must be defended at all costs, in fact you strive to increase your share at the expense of another. Accordingly, you are in survival and hostility mode. Peace is only the means to the end of amassing gains at the other's expense. Otherwise it is merely a compromise, when the warring parties estimate that they cannot defeat the enemy.

ILANA: Dear Master Akiva, most wonderful being, if I understood correctly, the source of warfare, which is the antithesis of the sanctity of life, lies in the transgression of taking by force. It stems from the craving to obtain at the expense of another, in order to increase wealth, whether it be material or spiritual (faith and religion). This instinct is deeply planted in the ego personality of all humans. What happens if we ascend and function from the level of the soul? How can we accomplish it? What would happen to the physical body's personality, the ego, in this case?

MASTER AKIVA: You have understood and internalized my teachings well. The solution to finding peace, in order to accommodate the essence of love and to fulfil the divine decree, "Thou shall love the Lord thy God with all thy heart, with all thy soul, with all thy mind and with all thy strength," and, "Thou shall love thy neighbour as thyself," will soar, from the body's personality level under the control of the following chakras (chakras are energetic centres responsible for all functions in all walks of life):

The first: The survival chakra, as it is written, "He who comes to kill you, arise earlier and do away with him."

The second: The sex chakra, as was said, "Go forth and multiply." (But then came the injunction, "Thou shalt not commit adultery," and, "Thou shalt not covet your neighbour's wife.")

The third: The solar plexus chakra, where the base emotions in the personality level reside. They are the lust to take for myself, to seize and hold, even by force and through war.

These three pivotal centres are responsible for running the world and they are the reason why the Temple was destroyed.[18] Rising above them, in the direction of the high spheres (also present in the human body at every level), are the three centres on which the world stands:

The Heart Centre: The splendor of kindness, charity, benevolence and freely given unconditional love. Love that is in communion with the circle of divine love: giving–receiving–giving. That is the fourth centre.

The Centre of Truth: It is located in the throat. The whole Torah was given from truth. This centre is responsible for personal communication with one's own self, with God and with one's fellow human, be it friend or foe. It makes absolutely no difference, for a man is a man, no matter which side of the fence he chooses to be at in order to fulfil his role in the "drama of life" enacted by souls incarnated in body personalities. This is the fifth centre.

The Faith Centre: It is located in a place you refer to as the "third eye," meaning super–natural vision, inner vision, utilization of the power of imagination and intuition and the wisdom of the ancients. This centre is at the front of the head, in the forehead, as is written, "… that they may be as

---

18 A reference to the second Jewish temple in Jerusalem, destroyed by the Romans in 70 AD.

frontlets between your eyes.[19]" It serves as a bridge to faith and insight into the occult (which underlies the obvious level of manifestation). It grants the ability to delve deep into the exegesis layer of insight.

Above these three spiritual centres is a **portal to the temple of the soul and to God.** It is customary in some religions to cover this portal with a skullcap. It is the "crown," the seat of the corona of wisdom, of the spirit that enters through various apertures of the body.

It is the seventh centre. God created the world in six days and on the seventh He rested "from all the work which He had made.[20]" The holiness of the Sabbath and the Holy Spirit enter from here. When it is blocked the connection to God and to inspiration from the soul is blocked. It then becomes necessary to unclog this centre and all those below it.

I am not, God forbid, trying to imply that the energy centres below the heart are less important that those above, for the latter are portals to the world of action – *sephirath*

---

19   The entire verse reads: "Therefore shall ye lay up these my words in your heart and in your soul and bind them for a sign upon your hand, *that they shall be as frontlets between your eyes*." (Italics added.) Deuteronomy, 11:18.

From this passage came to pass the ancient Jewish custom of wearing phylacteries (*tefillin*) which are two strips of parchment inscribed with passages from Exodus 13 and Deuteronomy 6, enclosed in a black calfskin case and fastened by thongs to the forehead and the left forearm and hand.

20   See, Genesis 2:2.

malchuth. However, I would like to emphasize that true peace can only come to pass with the total accommodation of divine love energy. Strengthening, transforming, healing – elevated frequencies are required in the lower centres in order to unite the dimension of matter with the dimension of spirit.

"Lower" does not connote criticism. It refers to the rungs of a ladder. You must ensure that the legs of the ladder are securely planted on the ground before commencing to climb and every rung must be strong and stable so your foot does not slip. All rungs are equally important. You must start on the bottom rung because your legs cannot reach the middle of the ladder, first and certainly you would never reach the top that way. Every step is crucial for your development. Every step advances you to the next, on the ladder of spirit.

Mankind has arrived at the Messianic Age, as this New Age is called (although, in the words of Ecclesiastics, "there is nothing new under the sun"). This is the Heart Point. It is a spiritual stage that allows understanding, insight, incorporation and the initiation of "love thy neighbour as thyself."

ILANA: I would like to take a short break to assimilate and digest this knowledge, with your permission, dear and wonderful Master Akiva.

MASTER AKIVA: you are accorded as much as you can assimilate and accommodate. Your instrument is expanding and stabilizing. You need a break and so do our readers, so they can absorb the knowledge. We will resume during the day. Thank you and much love.

Lesson 10

Ego Transcendence
The Awareness of Unity

ILANA: Wonderful morning to all my beloved guides, wonderful morning to you, dear and beloved Master Akiva. I call on you to arrive and please continue our discussion.

MASTER AKIVA: Good morning to you Ilana, my dear and beloved student. You rose very early; in fact, you hardly slept. Do not feel sad, as if an experience has been taken from you, for the biological body is now being synchronized with the gentle light body at very high frequencies. That is why you could accommodate my frequency. Sleep hours change, habits change; do not stick to your old identity at all costs.

Habits are what keep you attached to the body personality (as we now call the ego). They flow from your pool of memories and experiences, scattered through countless dimensions and incarnations. But most of these habits have been developed in your current body, in this incarnation. This is because from early childhood you invented an identity (which nonetheless is very real in your mind), into which you cast traits and habits. First comes the form, the vessel into which you place the ingredients you choose and mix together. The dish is then placed in the oven and comes out in the form you opted to create – a cake for example. Since you have formed particular patterns: thinking habits, emotional habits, addictions, obsessions and habitual fears, they all now accompany you loyally, as ingredients of the dish you have baked (i.e., defined as yourselves). If you are released from the bonds of ego and succeed in unraveling the invented – but ever so real in your perception – identity you have adopted, without which you think you would cease being human, you will change. You will no longer be addicted to the habits that fuse you with the same old personality patterns. You will need to redefine your identity, your goals and your course of action in every aspect of your life, be it intellectual, emotional, spiritual and especially, physical.

We are dealing with identity re–formation, based on the lofty goal of soaring to the spiritual and refined energy centres that connect you directly to the full guidance and light of your soul. This overhaul can be compared to baking a cake: First, choose the goal. What kind of cake do you want? How large? What flavour? Is it going to be decorated with fruits, candy, some sort of frosting? Is it a mixed cake? Is it a cake made of dough that needs to be rolled out? Does the dough have to be chilled first? Is it made with yeast and should it be allowed to rise? Similarly, your ego requires a stable framework, a shape and materials for you to choose freely.

But take heed of the trap laid by the ego. Where would you find the knowledge to transform the ego, if not from the ego itself? From a desire for self-aggrandizement? That is indeed one possibility, that the definition will come from the ego's own limited understanding. Perhaps you will seek the definition externally, by seeking inspiration from role models. Either way, you have defined your goal of transforming and refining your ego.

The best way to commence the modification is by connecting to the level of your soul and accepting its guidance, light and inspiration. This path will be taken by choice, which is your true creative ability, because you are a divine spark and the knowledge of creation in its entirety is incorporated in your DNA. Eden is a gene in your DNA, enabling creation. You can set a goal for yourself and even choose to create from light:
"I choose to grow from my soul level!
"I choose to refine my ego and to contain in it my soul."

The latter choice will transform your ego into a transparent liquid material, expanding and absorbing the essence and quality of your soul. Being connected and containing your soul powerfully within your personality blurs the separation and isolation characteristics of the ego, which is its goal as an ego: to secure for itself, to obtain and even to take by force for its survival and empowerment. On the level of the soul there is no such conscious separation. The soul lives in true, pure love. It is love that asks for nothing, it requires no quid pro quo, it just is – a great, ever-growing expansion, unity, harmony and joy. This can be experienced while you are still in your physical body. It is an empowering experience, one that expands your horizons and awareness, attained when your soul dynamically expands its function and meaning, becoming a significant facet of your identity. *This is the beginning of your I Am awareness.*

Naturally, the personality of the body, with its habits, fears and beliefs, could opt for separateness, which would limit the opportunity to ameliorate the deficiency of the existing experience. The soul has its own choices and preferences and these might be different and even diametrically opposed to the personality's choices. The soul experiences differently and interprets differently from the higher truth of unity. Conversely, the truth of the personality is experienced from the perspective of separateness and from the need to defend its distinct and familiar identity. The truth of the personality differs from the higher truth of unity, which is present at the soul level.

With your permission, I will clarify the matter and provide you with an example that will make it easier for your eyes to see and your hearts to understand. Imagine that someone who has experienced an emotional upheaval is telling you about it. He tells you that someone shamed and insulted him in public without any apparent reason. This person has experienced pain, hurt and even humiliation. These feelings rose from his emotional body, which faithfully recapitulated other experiences from the distant past, that have flooded his emotional body. He associates them with the statements made by the one insulting him at present. After passing through the stage of anguish, he may interpret the experience from a place of haughtiness. He may respond by insulting the one who hurt him; certainly he will feel more righteous and correct, more innocent, as the one who was deliberately or accidentally wounded by a malicious scoundrel.

Another possibility is that he would become angry, overtly or covertly, at the person who attacked him (ironically, not only did the latter attack, he indeed hit the target – causing the recipient to regurgitate memories of that which needs healing, change and transformation in his psyche). He may want revenge, to publicly shame the offender or he may wallow in self–pity and depression. In all likelihood, after a while he would forget the incident, in effect repressing the memory by burying it in the memory box of the subconscious which stockpiles information about various experiences along with their attendant emotions.

The question then is: Where does the truth lie? Isn't the injured one in the right? Of course he is – from his point of view, by way of ego detachment: The truth is as he sees and feels it, as it translates for him. But wouldn't the soul's recognition and translation of the experience be different? And, if so, wouldn't the truth be different?

The soul perceives everything in the form of unity, not division. The soul does not experience life as either victim or victimizer. It does not see reality in terms of duality: black vs. white, good vs. evil. It sees the ultimate goal for whose ends the drama was experienced in the way it was experienced.

The ultimate purpose is the insight that everything is interconnected. The whole is a universal amalgamation of divine creation that comes into being through the mutual interplay of love, which, in turn, materializes – or, alternatively, is in search of itself – through a circle of giving–receiving–giving. Mutuality and reciprocal stimulation is omnipresent in all of existence.

The paramount truth is perceived as harmony among souls, whose purpose is to elucidate the substance of their inner creativity. What does this mean? Creativity encompasses emotions, thoughts, beliefs and the entire inner world, which is creativity's treasure box. The resulting creations could be experienced as "trouble," as "being between a rock and a hard place;" it could be an evil inclination. Conversely, it could be a good proclivity – the conscience.

Because this treasure box is hidden from humanity's ability to perceive, only through its external reflection (the mirror theory – every person is your mirror) will you be able to know what it contains. Naturally, if you do not know what this box – which holds materials for creation – contains, it will be difficult for you to use it in accordance with your conscious will. Matter from your subconscious, such as your fears, will rise, surface and take charge of the process through which you create your reality.

Were you to discover within yourself creation material having negative characteristics, you could negate their effectiveness and defuse them by choosing diametrically opposite beliefs.

Now, with your permission, I will return to the example of the person who was insulted, either intentionally or inadvertently. When a person opts to observe and understand, from within his soul, what has happened in his "creativity workshop" – that dramatic (hologramic) stage known as reality – he will perceive something very different. He will realize that something positive has taken place. He will understand that the other person reflected a belief he holds that he lacks self–value. He will notice a vulnerability that can be traced to his childhood or even "previous" incarnations. (The quotation marks are there because all lives occur simultaneously.) Once he has recognised something he did not know about himself, he can shed light on the source, to send it healing; to understand that he must strengthen his self–image in the very area where he felt insulted; that he needs to change his perception.

Since the person who purportedly insulted him played the

role of the "bad guy" in this mirror–play, the insulted one should cherish him and express his gratitude for the service he rendered him. Naturally, the understanding that he should forgive everyone is a prerequisite even when severe hurts were inflicted. He should also forgive himself, especially when he realizes that his reaction did not originate from unity with the soul. When he truly comprehends the favour, he will be able to express his gratitude sincerely and even feel a flow of love on the soul level, toward the person who was previously the object of his rage. That is the high truth.

You can apply this truth not only on the individual, micro level, but at the macro level as well. Wars erupt between tribes, nations and cultures against a backdrop of the personality's ego tendency to exclude and separate, its instinctive inclination to defend itself, to seize territories, to react to national insults and to prove the justness of its beliefs and the rightness of its path.

Without a doubt, wars occur because of ego attachment and actions based on the energy of three lower chakras: survival, the sex drive emanating from the urge to "go forth and multiply," and the solar plexus, i.e., the wish to be right, strong and conquering. The emerging formula will lead us, surely and step by step, to a far–reaching understanding about peace among nations, cultures, religions and opposing factions.

Connect to the point in the heart which opens a window into

the soul, allowing for the accommodation of the soul and transformation of the ego, based on the energy of the higher chakras: love, truth, faith, unity (heart, throat, third eye and crown chakras), which, in turn, would metamorphose the perception of reality and the national will of all nations.

Do away with the desire to get, the act of taking, which has the effect of splitting and forming parts that, in turn, rob the whole of its unity, be it jointure with love or with the high truth of souls; unity, a circle of giving-receiving-giving. Thus, harmony will be established between man and himself, between woman and her God; between the individual and his family, his tribe, his people. Peace will grow to encompass other individuals and nations, who currently create the perception of reality of ego, exclusivity and enact the truth based on their interpretations of separateness.

ILANA: Dear Master Akiva, you have wisely shown me how we can walk toward inner and world peace. But what is the requisite first step? After all, you cannot just advertise in the newspaper: "Today (or at such and such date), everyone is called upon to open his heart and declare that he desires to connect with his soul and his higher truth." Not only that, but also to ensure that the same ad is published in the newspapers in enemy states (though it is not such a bad idea after all).

MASTER AKIVA (smiling): Indeed my dear, it is not a bad idea at all. Even though you are amused by the idea, the power of imagination can actually influence public opinion and create unity in consciousness, by changing individual and national goals. Instead of the need to survive and the desire to defend yourselves by developing so many weapons, instead of engaging in preemptive war (as is written, "He who comes to kill you pre–empt him and kill him first"), there will be a change in the will of the nation. Understanding the higher truth will create trust and mend the distrust that land disputes and bloody wars have brought about. The karma of war will then make room for joint creativity, centreed on peace and based on a real desire for harmonious co–existence.

Know dear, that if even one person arrives at an existential solution through the web of consciousness shared by all the seed of the First Human, by way of telepathic waves sent to all of humanity, it will be possible to convey the solution and endow all with the transmitted knowledge. This does not mean that everyone can, in any given situation, compel others to succumb to his will. I am simply speaking about the **developmental evolution**[21] **of the soul.**

---

21 Evolution (from Latin, *evolvere* – development) is a process through which genetic changes occur in organisms, gradually and over time, coming into effect in their morphological, physiological and their qualities and behavioural traits. Evolution occurs along the axis of time and is the result of choices brought by pressure and random processes, which give an advantage to certain qualities from an extant variety in the general population. (Translated from an excerpt from Wikipedia, in Hebrew.)

Humanity is rising through the rungs of consciousness, ascending the centres of information of the chakras, which include their perceptions and beliefs about reality. The path ascends to a link with the source of all souls, All There Is, divinity.

As said previously, comprehension and creation of reality stem from the truth of the ego's three lower chakras. Humanity is rising to the heart centre, which is in tune with eternal love. This love contains the soul and its higher truth, which is unity and means giving–receiving–giving. It was given by the Torah and the commandments: "Thou shall love the Lord thy God with all thy heart, with all thy soul, with all thy mind and with all thy strength," and, "Thou shall love thy neighbour as thyself."

This process is already occurring in your world, propelled by the reverberations of the New Age. The knowledge is transferred through pure light channells of messengers – chosen by angels, light entities, the righteous ones, all the divine hierarchies – the high kingdoms, all the way up to the high and exalted throne of God. The path is Jacob's Ladder of wisdom transmitted from the higher rungs, to the lower ones, knowledge that is transformed and rises to the topmost rungs.

People of flesh and blood, who contain their soul in its entirety, who contain the truth and purity of unity and love, become God's angels on earth. They embody the verse about the latter days, in the words of the prophets Isaiah and Micah: "In the latter days... nation shall not lift up sword against nation nor shall they learn war anymore... and the wolf also shall dwell with the lamb....."

In fact, the wolf and the lamb are the outer trappings, the rind, of victim and victimizer, carnivore and prey, innocent and cunning. This is but a separate identity of ego. The inner essence is one: God's creations containing the holy essence of life.

I urge you to contain the **knowledge of unity**. Please, make room in your hearts, in the temple of your emotions and ask to internalize that energy and transform it in your entire being. The insight conveyed here is beyond the logical but limiting perception of your mind and your intellect, that eagerly analyses everything, dressing each experience in words and labels from what is familiar and remembered.

Blessed be those who climb up the rungs of the Ladder and link their ego, the body personality, to the plateaus of unity and the soul. Here I am Master Akiva, on the path of love. I thank you dear and beloved Ilana.

ILANA: Thank you dear and wonderful Master Akiva, for the way you weave your message with wisdom and love for all humanity and thank you for the verse, "Love thy neighbour as thyself – that is a great principle of the Torah," which, as you have shown, is, in a nutshell, the whole Torah.

Your great spirit shines upon humanity, teaching and affecting the formation of its consciousness. From here I can see that every death is but an illusion of separateness and the divide between the World of Truth and the illusory world (our so–called reality), is in fact imaginary and can be removed by intent and faith.

Thank you to whoever reads, accommodates and re-conveys the knowing of love and unity to all humankind. Thank you for the opportunity to transmit this holiness.

Metatron: Thank you Ilana, dear emissary of the light, for your service, your dedication and your contribution to the whole temple of creation. Blessed be in your eternal being and may you be privileged to do only good. "Holy, Holy, Holy is the Lord of Hosts and we are his angels," says the choir of angels accompanying him.

Lesson 11

The Supreme Will, the Supreme Purpose, defence Mechanisms
Healing through the "Light of Consciousness"

Good morning to all my wonderful guides. Good morning to you dear and illustrious Master Akiva. With your permission, I would like to proceed with our conversation. I said to myself, maybe on a Saturday you would not come, you might be busy. However, I understand that I am projecting from a human stance.

MASTER AKIVA: Dear Ilana, a blessed Sabbath to you and yours and the whole Nation of Israel. Writing on the Sabbath, especially when it entails holiness designed to be transmitted through the mouthpiece of creation,, spreading the awareness of "love thy neighbour as thyself" to all of creation, does not constitute a desecration of that which is holy.

The Sabbath was created for you[22] so that you will honour creation, respect the Creator of the Universe and all His creatures and congregate in the halls of holiness, whether they be synagogues, churches, the enclosure formed by

---

22 "And he said unto them, 'The Sabbath was made for man and not man for the Sabbath.' " Mark 2:27

the walls of your dwelling places or your hearts. You are not enslaved to the Sabbath. In this regard some of the Commandments have been taken out of their original context. I have no desire to preach in favour of or against following the commandments, in order to avoid fomenting strife. My words are addressed to everyone, whether they are religious or secular. Some of whom have fervent faith, while others have no faith at all. I am not here to discriminate, because each person takes the road that fits his purpose, the path his soul has woven and paved for him. There is no "better" way, just as one experience is not "preferable" to another.

Your entire life substance is expressed in your interpretation of your experience. This interpretation can be literal, based on implied reference or it could be based on intellectual delineation or on a metaphysical mystery. An interpretation could add impetus to a material manifestation, an emotional experience, a mental articulation or a spiritual activity. No one interpretation is better than another, since an interpretation is just that – an interpretation. It is a way of comprehending issues in a subjective fashion. Sometimes you draw insight from a certain experience, thus ensuring that your method of interpretation is subsequently transformed. At other times you do not draw any conclusions and even repeatedly re–enact the substance of the experience, in different forms, with the other participants in your drama.

You may interpret from your perception of love or alternatively from your fear–generated vision. Every interpretation adjusts in consonance with the viewer's outlook and his notion of truth, as he is experiencing it at that moment in time. If you focus your awareness on the subject, you may notice that in the distance of the future, you will interpret the experience differently than you did when it occurred. You may even regard an experience that was difficult, painful and seemingly negative as something that in a future moment you will interpret as having been "positive" when it occurred. The sayings that support this insight are: "In anything bad there is something good;" "Whatever happens it is for your ultimate good;" and, "out of the strong came forth sweetness" (Judges 14:14). During the experience you may have cried, complained and fought within or without yourself. You may have opposed the experience with all your might. However, with hindsight, if you have grasped the high purpose of your soul, you may understand how the experience served to empower you and enrich every aspect of your personality.

As a metaphor, a difficult experience is a crucible. The pain strips away layer after layer, so that the light of the true diamond of your soul can emerge and be intensified. It is your hidden, true identity, the divine spark. This divine spark conceals its identity from itself. It comes to the world replete with layers upon layers that obscure its astounding glow. Your goal in the journey of life is to shed the layers; there are physical layers, emotional and psychological layers, intellectual and even spiritual layers. The polishing of the diamond is effected by replacing your beliefs.

Let me elucidate: If you or a close family member experiences a difficult episode such as ill health, you are likely to find yourself in the crucible of hurt and torment. Were you to hang onto your beliefs, for example, failure to allow hope to fill you or to renew and empower your faith or to seek enlightenment about the sanctity of life and its purpose, i.e., unconditional love that includes acceptance of All That Is, then your outer layer would remain unchanged, assailed by more challenges in the spheres of income, relationship, family, career, health, personal safety and so on.

I want you to know that you can produce pearls from your experience. You can dredge up the treasure your experience was designed to confer upon you. Self–learning will allow you to cast off the outer layers that cloak love and light and prevent you from shedding fears and ridding yourself of low and negative self–images. You can learn about the sanctity of life, how to cherish what is and how not to take anything for granted.

Every moment is holy and valuable and it would behoove you to notice it and learn to be grateful.

You set targets for yourself; you mark goals and seek to accomplish them. Be aware of the manner in which you conduct yourself. Are you aiming at the right objective? Is this really what your higher self desires? Is it your final destination or does it merely advance you to the next target?

Ask to sharpen your will. Ask to be in tune with your soul's highest truth. Ask to be one with the Supreme Will, which includes your soul's highest purposes, the designs of your higher self for advancement, connected to the highest hierarchies of creation.

Affirm: **"I choose to be in unity with the Supreme Will!"**

Intend it, if that is your choice. Declare it three times (three times is the number of commitments to the personality, the higher self and the soul). Then breathe deeply and take the request's energy into your centres of energy and into every cell of your body. Thereafter, you may experience a shift in the aims and objectives you previously set for yourself. Desires will either increase or diminish and your overall intention may even change completely. You may not feel the shift in the short run, because the goal you have set parallels the new direction you have taken.

Agree to relinquish the goals your ego has set for itself, which it did in order to fill up the absence and emptiness within. For instance, when a person aims to acquire wealth, he should honestly ask himself: Why is it his goal? What is he trying to accomplish with his financial status? Is it power? Is he seeking to impress others? Is he looking for influence, security, faith or is he on a quest for love? Or, are his reasons altogether different?

I emphasize that no reason is "incorrect" or "wrong," except when it is deliberately intended to injure and hurt others or to exploit the weak and subjugate them to one's lusts.

After you have communed with the Divine Will, it may be that your personal will survives and the target of amassing riches remains attached, but it will shift to the side, transposed by a new desire. The target may be transformed into something more substantive, such as a state of unconditional love, a state of generous giving or a desire to give, in order to make a difference. If so, the material component will, of its own accord, manifest itself after you have stabilized in relation to your new goal. Maybe you will no longer have any need for it, since your original request for material wealth stems from a sense of inner want that no longer exists.

It is possible for a person to seek wealth simply to have peace and quiet and be happy. When you are in tune with the Supreme Will, with the truth of the bright light of your soul, your fundamental goal instantaneously becomes actualized of its own accord. Money will not necessarily buy you the inner peace and happiness you seek.

Material goals actually reflect spiritual wishes!

This holds true for every target and objective you set yourself. I invite you to ponder the subject and ask yourself: What is the spiritual purpose underlying the material goal I have set for myself? Once you have identified the intended spiritual purpose, I suggest that you sanctify it and make it your guiding light. Invest it with the power to lead you in every path you undertake, in every byway you consider right for yourself.

This concept may appear too abstract to be easily understood. If so, breathe in the written material and ask for it to be internalized and accommodated. Do it right now.

Declare: "**I request and choose to assimilate and accommodate the knowledge about superior goals!**"

Repeat the process three times, as described above.

ILANA: I understand that our conversation today revolves around the will of the ego and its goals, as opposed to the soul and its superior purpose. I can see the connection to my own life and understand why certain things do not happen the way I expect, in the manner in which I attempt to create reality based on familiar knowhow.

If, for example, I seek to find myself in a relationship, I have to ask myself – who is the "self" that has formed the desire? Do I not possess other aspects of "self," higher and better endowed with consciousness, an "I Am" that sees the superior purpose of my soul and, therefore, blocks the creation of that particular reality? The question then becomes, do I see it as an edict or a superior purpose, and, can I fuse the Supreme Will to the will of the personality and reach the Superior Goal in a different way? To my mind, it connects with free will: everything is foreseen, but we have the license to choose. But is it really so? And how does it relate to consciously creating one's own reality?

I'll be grateful for insight and clarification and even novel ideas on the subject.

MASTER AKIVA: Dear and beloved Ilana. I embrace your pain and envelop your contradictory desires. I understand you. First, accept that there is no coincidence. Everything happens for your higher benefit. Second, hold onto what your personality truly desires. Do not disregard it. Do not make light of it and do not consider it unworthy, lowly, unenlightened or even a weak part or a dependency. honour your femininity. Respect your very natural desire to share your life with a partner. God made you male and female so you would cleave together and become one flesh (accord, Genesis 2:24). Understand that the side of you that desires to fill the emptiness is the same side that was badly hurt, in this life and others. It requires reinforcement and healing, which **must** emerge from within you! It is you who must forcefully request, nay demand to enable healing for these open wounds. Every so often, certainly during your incarnations, these injuries attract experiences that match and are synchronised to their plot and their energy.

The experience of pain results in the fear of getting hurt and the fear of betrayal. This leads to a desire for introversion, for escape from the experience of life, escape from emotional experiences and the fear of falling in love that you associate with suicide. The experience of pain creates fear of rejection. It causes you to shut yourself up within your four walls in order to avoid further rejection. It causes you to reject others and prevent them from getting too close to you. Many who fear being hurt terminate ties with others even when they feel love and desire toward them. It all stems from defensiveness. It relates to the saying, "He who comes to kill you, kill him first." You are afraid of getting hurt and so you become the one to inflict the hurt, to reject, to let go. You are the one who terminates ties and relationships.

There is within you a highly protective element, an independent mechanism. It protects you from painful experiences; it also allows you to become stronger and improve your self-image. It empowers you and gives you the opportunity to become independent. It renews your reservoirs of love.

These vast reservoirs contain all of humanity, the host of heaven and God himself. But when you are in a constricting love relationship, the love creates dependency and you internalize and direct it (its interpretation of love in the narrow sense) toward one person only (though sometimes you also direct some feeling toward yourself and others), it actually manifests as what we have previously termed false infatuation.

In order to penetrate this mechanism, you have to explore and understand its function and importance, but first you must alter the reservoir of beliefs that create and even reinforce its automatic function. (Incidentally, this mechanism exists in all of mankind).

You ask about **free will**. Well dear, you do have the right to choose – receive a lesson and learn it or oppose it. By doing so you may intensify its effect on the inner cycle of want, which in turn creates pain and torment.

You do indeed create reality. At times you rapidly reach the goal you have set, provided that it does not conflict with your superior goal, that your beliefs are positive and that it is right for your highest good.

Conversely, it is sometimes important for you to fail to fulfil a goal you have set for yourself. This apparent failure actually serves as a portal, enabling you to go deep within and ask: What are your true beliefs? What is actually blocking you? What are you afraid of? What are you defending yourself from? Failure will occur even though your desire is apparently instructing you to choose to proceed in a particular direction.

Dear Ilana, you can add to the treatments you provide a new function called **defence mechanism**. You will be able to look into it, observe its activity and energy and the beliefs it contains. You can ask for its operating code and use it to reprogramme the mechanism. Any reader who is in need of such treatment will then be able to ask to see the mechanism, internalize the knowledge and figure out how to utilize it correctly. Please understand that under no circumstance should you disable the mechanism completely. It is of inestimable value for your soul. It is highly valuable and, in effect, it protects your life.

ILANA: Wonderful. I understand from your words that I should accept my condition as is. That it is the same for all human beings. However, if I believe that I create reality and yet, although I proceed along the known courses over a considerable time period and the intended creation does not come into fruition, I then must understand that the defence mechanism in me is blocking the manifestation and I should look into the mechanism to see what fear–based beliefs are limiting me.

Now, let's say that I have ascertained the clockwork of my mechanism and I have fished out all sorts of negative beliefs, traumas and fears. What should I do with them? How do I heal and extricate them?

MASTER AKIVA: here we focus on the task of your unconscious, the repository of your memories and beliefs. I would like to address Yuval's question:

Yuval asks: **"Why are so many dreams unclear, requiring intellectual analysis, which at times is forced, in order** to reach the meaning? At other times, it is not possible to logically analyse a dream. All in all, I'd be happy to receive more information about deciphering dreams."

You (Ilana) wonder how this question tie in with your inquiry (smiling). Well, the tie is both direct and indirect. The defence mechanism resides in the unconscious. It releases to you your poisons as well as the good drugs, your medication, through your dreams.

Dreams are true tests of the soul at different levels. Some are portals to previous (actually parallel) incarnations. Some are your soul's yearning and longing, while others are future lessons. Dreams are not limited by the analysis and interpretation wielded by the scalpel of your logic. They have their own dynamics and integrity.

At times you dream about a particular event and suddenly you get a flashback showing how the event commenced and how it is destined to end. Sometimes you experience the dream as a disinterested observer from the sidelines. You may experience a dream through someone else's eyes. You can also dream of yourself with your current awareness, but as a different character or at different ages.

When you attempt to catalogue and define an emotional experience through reason or logic, you may miss its essence and the truth of its message. Some people translate the excitement of an experience as fear and they are therefore unable to contain it. Others translate fear-based experiences as excitement and joy. They may convert it into adrenalin and yearn for such experiences. Some develop an addiction to fear or an addiction to thrills and through them, an addiction to drama. This responds to their inner need to increase the quantum of feelings that are so fulfiling to them.

Ilana (after a two hours break designed to digest previously dispensed knowledge): Can a defence mechanism be antagonistic to life? In other words, can people sicken and even die as the result of fear, of emotional or intellectual experiences? What are the effects of the mechanism, what makes it tick and how is it possible to neutralize its effect?

MASTER AKIVA: The defence mechanism, as its name implies, is designed to protect you from experiences that are difficult to adjust to. Some people develop emotional protection in the form of a sheath that covers the emotional body. They appear nonchalant, insouciant, in control of their emotions (which, actually, do not exist) and they may convey the misleading impression that they are in a state of constant balance. Others develop a mental defence for fear of confronting certain experiences. They put up a screen of forgetfulness, suppression, mental retardation, dullness and even various afflictions of senility. Others are frightened of physical pain, so they develop a defence mechanism to avoid the experience. They may lose consciousness and pass out. Others develop an array of diseases in their endeavour to avoid physical pain, such as pulmonary disorders, heart trouble and the like. They may even go into a coma and become vegetables. They may develop personality types which would result in habitual long stays indoors, avoidance of physical activity, any effort, adventure or travel. The defence mechanism develops habits and shapes the personality so that it can avoid the factor of which it is so afraid and anxious.

Sometimes the defence mechanism is the cause of difficult and chronic illnesses, so that the person will not have to confront emotional or mental fear. The mechanism can even arouse an impulse towards self–destruction. This operates like a delayed time–bomb, every so often exuding poisonous substances. This system emerges in those who cannot contain the potency of their life, preferring to end in a form of death, of which their personality is unaware.

No medication or treatment can help in such cases, for the self–destruct mechanism has been activated to protect its owner from an intolerable experience which is causing him tremendous anxiety.

It can definitely be said that forms of senility such as Alzheimer's disease are intended to protect their sufferers from mental and emotional confrontation. Their consciousness tells them that what they do not know or remember does not exist. In fact, it is suppressed into the reservoirs of the unconscious and finds its expression in dreams.

Some people fear life no less or even more than they fear death. Not all are aware that they harbour such fear. Others are equally afraid of life and death. They experience a paralysis of activity. They develop diseases and habits that conform to their fears and their personalities are formed accordingly. It is crucial to identify the fear of life and likewise the fear of death and disable them both.

ILANA: How do you counteract existential and other fears?

MASTER AKIVA: By acknowledging their existence, first of all; by accepting their presence, understanding that they have value and serve a purpose. By understanding that fear creates experiences in one's journey, until the fear peels off from the self. It is necessary to respect the fear and then direct consciousness, light and love towards it.

The *light of consciousness* will release the fear. Try it, please.

ILANA: I identify within myself fear of over–exertion, fear of exhaustion. I examine the energy level in my hands and it is infinite. I attempt to figure it out: is it a fear of mental over–exertion? I get a positive answer. Is it a fear of emotional effort? Again, I get a positive response. Does it include fear of a spiritual exertion? Yes. A sigh of relief.

Well, I knew about my disinclination to overexert myself, my reluctance to travel away from home, to work too many hours and to stay up late at night. But I was unaware of emotional, mental and spiritual fears.

MASTER AKIVA: In that case, let me introduce something new to you and through you to your readers. Every fear has four aspects: Physical, emotional, mental and spiritual, in the same way that every material goal has a spiritual aspect – the spirit enmeshed in matter.

ILANA: Okay. For the first time in my life I acknowledge the presence of fear as a formative dynamic of my experience. It is fear of over–exertion. I now have an entertaining thought rising to my consciousness, really funny. Most of my school report cards contained the comment: "Ilana can make more of an effort." It's really funny... and indeed I did not see fit to make an effort. Whatever came easy – wonderful! Whatever entailed an effort was superfluous. Now I acknowledge this fear, without shame, excuses or guilt. I smile at the fear and send it love. I hug it. I feel serene. I feel that its energy has effervesced.

Until now I have worked with the Angels of Karma to release fears. Another way is to utilize the violet flame and its angels and command it to transform fear. The new way proposed by Master Akiva is simple. It is linked to love and inclusion.

MASTER AKIVA: It is indeed so. There are many ways to relinquish fears. They include repeatedly experiencing that which caused the fear in the first place. Someone who falls off a horse is always advised to remount and ride again, for example. This is called a mending experience. It imprints itself in the unconscious memory, filed under "success" instead of "failure." A "failure" tag causes the defence mechanism to throw up barriers to forestall a repetition of the same experience. In the case of the person who fell off a horse and did not undergo a mending experience, not only is it possible that he will never again ride a horse, his mobility may become restricted. He may develop acrophobia, the fear of losing control, which will affect his life.

The therapeutic process can be divided into the following stages:
a. First stage: Identification and acknowledgement of the fear.
b. Second stage: Acceptance and respect of the fear as a creative force of experiences and lessons in life.
c. Third stage: Appreciation (gratefulness), light and love.

We will call this therapy "**Light of Consciousness**."

Now, let's return to the subject of dreams and the unconscious. When you are unaware of motivating factors in your life, such as fears, beliefs and memories, they then take control of your life, utilizing the concealed mechanism known as your defence mechanism.

It is within your power to heal the conscious but not

the unconscious aspect of your psyche. If dreams of fears surface (in conscious memory) or nightmares of persecution, crises, lack of safety and the like, look for evidence of their existence in your life. Ask to go through the suppressed issues you have opened up, which are part and parcel of the defence mechanism. Recognize them as an inner truth of yourself and heal them with the Light of Consciousness.

The purpose of dreams that you remember, is to agitate the suppressed memory and direct awareness to inner experiences that might not have been processed emotionally at the time they were occurring or when aroused again, later.

For example, you will recall the story of the divorcee who had experienced great suffering. As a result of her predicament she discovered her emotional strength, which served as a powerful impetus for spiritual growth. As a result she developed tools of self–healing, restoration of her self–image, indeed she was even able to lend a helping hand to others. Since she has spiritual expertise, she understands the importance of forgiveness and the role drama plays in one's life; she is convinced that she is back on track. She does not think she still bears deposits from her past and is convinced that she is wholly and exclusively present in the light of consciousness. And yet, she dreams time and again of loss, the breakup of her family and pain. When she separates the dream substance from the totality of her life, she is actually suppressing the fact that, emotionally, she has not yet assimilated or healed the traumatic event she has experienced.

If she were to opt for these dream materials as a means of releasing the defence mechanism (from having to protect her from that particular trauma), in accordance with her ability to hold and retain, she would really be able to heal inwardly. Only then, would she learn to progress to a new and meaningful rung in her journey toward the comprehensive healing and consequent defusing of her defence mechanism, which at present inhibits her ability to create and affects every aspect of her life.

I do not underestimate the value and importance of the defence mechanism, quite to the contrary. Without it, you cannot survive. Similarly, the mechanism occasionally releases materials for processing, precisely measured against the person's ability to process them and make a difference in his life.

ILANA: Some people, notably Holocaust survivors and war veterans, experience nightmares and memories of long-ago events. Does this indicate that they have actually not overcome the trauma or have they repressed it?

MASTER AKIVA: This is an excellent example, because it is a testament to human nature, the ability to fall and rise, resurrection and redemption, despair and hope. People persevere despite the painful and traumatic episodes they may have experienced. But the dreams you have referred to indicate that they have developed strong defence mechanisms and that it has affected their lives. It is worth identifying the mechanism and its activation modalities. Sometimes it is preferable to suppress a trauma until one finds the mental strength to cope with it, which is actually how the defence mechanism operates.

ILANA: Is it possible that various crises such as financial collapse or the breakdown of a relationship and disasters are correlated with the defence mechanism? Or maybe there is no connection and the defence mechanism will just endeavour to cope with them somehow? In other words, is the mechanism simply reactive or does it produce events?

MASTER AKIVA: an excellent question, dear and beloved Ilana. Contrary to the connotation of passivity entailed in the word, defence is often active and assertive, as evinced in the saying: "He who comes to kill you, kill him first." Sometimes the best defence is offense. Sometimes people resort to a verbal offensive in order to defend themselves. A defence mechanism is thus a very active apparatus, creating an array of experiences to suit the character and belief system of its owner. If someone, on his soul level, fears spirituality and believes spiritual endeavours are an idle waste of life, his defence mechanism would create a dynamic to spur him, in the form of lifelong crisis, which, according to his beliefs, would prompt him in the best possible way.

ILANA: I have reread the material in this chapter, but I feel a message has been left unsaid. Dear Master Akiva, would you like to conclude the subject at hand?

MASTER AKIVA: Thank you dear, Ilana. This lesson speaks about the unity between matter and spirit, pointing out that all is planned well in advance and that there is a supreme spiritual purpose to everything. In every apparently material goal dwells a spiritual essence, which preceded the creation of the material goal. Mankind should probe deep into their will and learn to deactivate motives that stem from fear and lack. When the essence of the soul is understood, the goals can change, becoming more accessible and more manifested. By tuning into the desired essence within, the Supreme Will of the soul becomes crystal clear. Man will be able to live in harmony with his soul and experience that which he yearns for: Love, acceptance, security and unity.

It may be that his interpretation will differ after he redefines the needs of his personality and sets them as his goals, but the combined essence of the personality and the soul is immediately attainable. All you have to do is *intend, choose, declare and breathe...* and contentment will emerge.

Know: the universe is love. You are created from love. All the affluence you seek is in fact a materialization of love. Tune into the following verses: "Thou shall love the Lord thy God with all thy heart, with all thy soul, with all thy mind and with all thy strength," and, "Thou shall love thy neighbour as thyself." And, of course, love yourself, – as the materialization of a divine spark, as spirit in flesh, which is what you are.

Blessed be in your eternal being.

I am, Master Akiva, dispenser of love, compassion, acceptance, light and the unity of all creation. "How beautiful are your deeds O God." And thank you, Ilana, for your tenacity and dedication to the supreme purpose of the soul, that has become a clearly understood and important goal of the personality. Your investment and perseverance have borne fruit and the whole world will savour its nectar and flavour. A blessing to you and yours. Amen.

Lesson 12

Precision in Definition, Messiah Consciousness

ILANA: Dear and wonderful Master Akiva, I want to thank you. During the treatment today, I felt you had joined me and advised my patient through me. I have implemented the ideas I received from you about the defence mechanism and the ultimate goal. I also used your emphasis on precision in definitions. Also coincidentally, (which, of course, is not a random occurrence but the universe's way of bringing my attention to a particular matter), two individuals wanted to know what is exactly my method of treatment. I understood that I should give my method a name. It is a channelling-based method that constantly evolves, amalgamating my ability to sense through energy, channelling and angel therapy.

I called it, **Soul Light Healing.** What do you think?

MASTER AKIVA: My opinion is the same as yours and that of the people who contacted you (and who have emphasised my words). It is important at this stage of your development, that you should know precisely who you are channelling and the manner of your activity. Precision in definition is very important, because the word is the power of creation. Intent and association, found in every word, can activate it in a manner that is not clean, not the way it is supposed to work.

For example, your patient seeks permanent work, in order to have stability in her life. She has been looking for work as an independent contractor for more than a year, to no avail. With my guidance you explained that she should note what she associates with the word "routine." Since she is addicted to excitement, as you told her (and she admitted), the idea of routine is associated in her mind with dreariness, inertia and boredom, quite the reverse direction of the adrenalin thrill that makes her feel at her best. She even interprets "quiet" to mean tedium and lack of stimulation. You have demonstrated that she operates in two contradictory directions, which is why the reality she seeks does not manifest itself in her life: On the one hand, she wants stable and permanent employment, while on the other hand she loathes and even fears it. What does she create? Both the desire and the non–actualization of her wish, again and again. That is the primary or secondary reason for her failure to attain the desired reality.

Another example: A woman sincerely wants to be in a relationship. However, she associates the term "relationship" with bondage, loss of personal freedom, dread of being hurt and the need to surrender her own identity. What do you think will happen? This woman, too, is walking in parallel roads and thus the creation cannot materialize. The desire is there, but not its implementation.

What she needs to understand is that a relationship is a structure capable of containing freedom and mutual support, while maintaining personal space. A relationship does not necessarily carry negative connotations. She must alter her perception and inner definitions. She needs to integrate the feelings and imagery of a partnership as a wondrous and elevated connection which honours both partners.

At times you humans ask for something from one aspect of your being, but from another aspect, that which you desire contains many negative emotional associations. Why then do you wonder that it fails to materialize in your reality?

ILANA: Thank you. Apropos definition, I am about to conduct three treatments, one after the other and just thinking about it make me feel tired. Could you help me?

MASTER AKIVA: Work is difficult, tiring and grinding. If you regard the series of treatments as work, all the memories of slavery in Egypt flood you (smiling). Consider what you are doing as sacred work. Your inner association will then revolve 180 degrees, which is a truly meaningful turnaround. Indeed, dear, you love being engaged in sacred work which you can accommodate for hours on end without tiring. Moreover, you become filled with the sacred energy and you are empowered, your soul glows and you are happy. Conclusion: you are not going to work hard now. Instead, you are entering a process of doing wonderful sacred work. How do you feel with this definition? Did the apprehension subside?

ILANA: Indeed. Thank you. I now understand the importance of definitions, terms and the narrative we convey to ourselves with words. Sometimes it is sufficient to change a given word which bears a negative payload, for another, a more pleasant word. It is true that sometimes I conduct treatments in that fashion: I demonstrate a person's own experience using different words, interpreting it in an empowering manner.

Now I would like to ask you a question from my father, relating to a woman, his partner, who curses her son, the fruit of her loins, because he is following his own drummer and not listening to hers. He is attracted to members of his own sex. What is your opinion? Is there any way to help them? (I mean the ones being cursed, of course).

MASTER AKIVA: My daughter and student, how great is the suffering endured by humans who attempt to coerce others by force. Of course, coercion is contrary to my credo: "Love thy neighbour as thyself." This love encompasses honouring the path a man has chosen. As I have already said, the soul has many paths, love traverses many roads and fear avails itself of many approaches. That woman is immersed in a deep hole filled with the sticky black tar of fear. Out of a desire to protect, she has launched an offensive. Out of a desire to do what is best for her son, she is doing him much harm. The fear-based approach has many dangers: curses, incantations, sorcery and the attempt to compel another to act contrary to his will and in violation of his freedom of choice. This is the way of the Inquisition.

The way to help the son is to disengage him from the mother's thoughts and desires, which she is trying to force through threats. The disengagement must be effected with the assistance of the Angels of Karma. Protracting the disengagement will transform it into a correction. The soul's light will deliver what is needed in order to heal and will heal what needs healing. The light will be sent to all participants in the creation of the drama.

I would like to point out, that I believe "eye for an eye and tooth for a tooth" to be unacceptable, for it goes counter to the path of light, compassion and love. By following this way, the responding party is dragged down the road of darkness and evil. Jesus said: "But whosoever shall smite thee on thy right cheek, turn to him the other also." Do not resist and thus you will neutralize the evil of the other's energy. It is a well–known tactic of martial arts. Instead of resisting, you flow with the force employed by your opponent.

ILANA: in the midst of our discussion I have had two treatments and I did not tire at all. I am waiting for the third and I am chock–full of energy and I am in balance, despite the fact that I did not rest at mid–day as I usually do.

About compassion, I would like to ask about Jesus...

MASTER AKIVA: "love thy neighbour as thyself," is my response. However, since you need clarification and elucidation, I will bring my explanation down to the plane of human comprehension.

The answer in your awareness is an interpretation and distortion of the truth. Jesus son of Miriam was born a Jew. He was born with a special vision and mission of shaping the consciousness of the masses. Jesus was born with great healing powers that emanated from the high and sublime frequency that contained him. This frequency was instilled in him after his baptism by John the Baptist. The new frequency was actually a process of soul exchange, connecting him with the universal vision of healing by way of compassion and forgiveness. Jesus could see into mankind's psyche and his motives, thus he fathomed that feelings of guilt are usually the cause of disease. Jesus healed through faith and forgiveness. "Your sins have been forgiven," he would say and a heavy burden of worries, anxieties and ill–fate would immediately be lifted. Jesus' mission was very important and his teachings influenced the newly formed faith of Christianity, the daughter–faith of Judaism, with its own interpretations.

It is important to remember that the source of all religion is one. We should focus on that which is in common rather than that which differentiates. Religion is an entry, an approach, an interpretation. As such it is intended to be opened and accessed.

Not every religion suits everyone. The path of hate and separation between man and his fellow is unacceptable, for the deep meaning of the whole Torah is: "Thou shalt love." "Thou shalt love the Lord thy God with all thy heart, with all thy soul, with all thy mind and with all thy strength," and, "Thou shalt love thy neighbour as thyself." Love is acceptance. Love enables. Love is mutual respect. Love is honouring the freedom of the individual, the freedom of nations, to choose what they believe in. Love is enabling every faith to express its unique, interpretive approach, as befits those who carry a particular frequency and follow a specific path. My teaching does not speak of war, but peace. It does not utter hate – it is an expression of love.

Let's return to the example of the woman who curses the fruit of her loins. When I refer the example of Jesus, who taught how not to resist, this does not mean leaving the curse in place, permitting the woman to either shut down life's activity or rob its possessor of free will. My advice is to release the accompanying emotions of anger and hate, the distinctive companions of the Path of Fear. Of course, due to the sanctity of life and freedom of choice, you must do whatever you can to cleanse and deactivate the negative effect. The best way would be to employ transcendence and, even more potently, connect with the light. Commune with the soul's light to the essence of love, to protect your aura: the electromagnetic field that encircles you and guards your balance. Imagine that you are encased by a shield of light, while at the same time you direct light toward the source of attack, as did Balaam, who came to curse the Children of Israel and ended up blessing them.

ILANA: What about doing battle, even preemptively, against those who seek to annihilate you? As I recall, you supported Bar Kochba and the rebellion against the Romans. Does not this contradict the path of peace?

MASTER AKIVA: Dear and beloved, it is not the act that I oppose, it is the attendant emotions. The inner place, whence activity arises, is what really matters. Bar Kochba's rebellion was not motivated by hatred of the Romans, but with the goal of securing freedom and liberty for the Jews. As I see it, it was necessary to act, to restore the hope of salvation to the conquered people, to re-establish faith in God. Of course, the rabble in the rebels camp was driven by hate. Indeed, that was the reason why the rebellion failed.

Bar Kochba was a great emissary. His magnetic personality inspired the multitudes and the whole nation followed the promise he personified. I myself regarded him as king–messiah. Indeed, he was a harbinger of the messiah. The fact that he failed does not disprove that he was from the seed of the Messiah. The same as applies to the Lubavitcher Rebbe, who was considered to be the king–messiah by his followers. His passing from this world has not changed their belief.

ILANA: So Bar Kochba was a messiah? What about Jesus, was he a messiah? And if so, why did salvation fail to arrive? Were there other messiahs? What exactly is a messiah?

MASTER AKIVA: Woe unto the generation if a messiah arrives in their time and they fail to acknowledge him as an avatar. Woe to the generation who is not ripe for his leadership, his light, his innovations. A messiah is an office endowed directly by the high, exalted and supreme God, the Creator of our universe. A messiah is a light entity in whom envoy, redeemer, spiritual leader, prophet and priest are synergestically combined. Such an entity incarnates in a physical body in order to adjust to the world and accommodate its frequencies. Such an entity can change bodies and times and might appear for just a brief interlude. If the world cannot accept its guidance and teaching it is physically extinguished, although the entity survives intact, unless it is the end of its mission.

Each and every one of you has the "Messiah Gene," whose purpose is to alleviate your consciousness and fuse it with the consciousness of one. Israel has had several prophets, more precisely, individuals whose Messiah Gene was activated in order to bring cohesion to the nation and elevate its awareness. Not all of them were recognised as such; some were persecuted and killed.

The purpose of the messiah is to bring salvation. But, if the consciousness of the people cannot fathom the depth and wonder of this truth, it is incapable of accommodating the new frequency. Then the elect, the messiah, cannot fulfil his purpose. That is why solemn and sacred efforts are required to reshape the consciousness of the masses. Learning and accommodating the essence of things – not the surface meaning of the knowledge – the essence being, "Love thy neighbour as thyself."

In the eyes of the people even messianic understanding is perceived as a myths of salvation, thus its roots only reach the surface. In order to receive the messiah, the son of David, in order to accommodate the original light of Torah (written on the first set of the Tablets of the Covenant and broken by Moses as he descended from Mount Sinai and beheld the sin of the Golden Calf), it is necessary to raise the people's consciousness. The original Torah handed to Moses could not have been received by the people, who had committed the sins of lack of faith, intolerance, stubbornness and greed. The original Torah was given from the path of love and light. The second set of tablets inscribed with the Ten Commandments, was adapted to suit the capacity of the masses, to accommodate them. They related to the way of love through laws and prohibitive injunctions from the path of fear, which was then the more comprehensible language.

Jesus brought messages of love and innovation. This is because his perception was ahead of his time and because of his high frequencies, which were identical with his immense capacity for healing. Those who feared innovation developed anger, fear and a great measure of hate towards him which ultimately divided the People of Israel and a great tragedy ensued, lasting for centuries due to the purported karma that adhered to the Jews in the eyes of Christianity.

Each and every one of you contains within him, like a seed of light awaiting germination, the Messiah Gene, that will awaken within you messiah consciousness. This consciousness must be activated and accommodated by the critical mass of the People of Israel. This consciousness will, indeed, become light unto the nations and herald the onset of salvation and the latter days.

All mankind is required to conduct inner self–examination to study their beliefs, improve their choices, be aware that they must choose the path of love and relinquish the path of fear, darkness, ignorance, hate and war. This inner war is waged between man and his inclination to do evil. It is a war between brothers, a war which brought about the destruction of the Temple, a war of annihilation among the nations.

ILANA: As far as I know, Bar Kochba was a political–military leader, not a spiritual one. In contrast, Jesus and the Lubavitcher Rebbe are spiritual leaders par excellence. So how is it that Bar Kochba was a messiah, one who carries the Messiah Gene? Is that the highest truth?

MASTER AKIVA: There is no separation between spirit and matter. Bar Kochba was head and shoulders above all others. He certainly was a spiritual leader, though he was ostensibly not focused in the spiritual plane. In his soul he carried the messiah seed. A messiah can be a military leader, a statesman and yet still carry within him the qualities of an inspiring leader and spiritual teacher. The gene of the avatar was activated in him, ensuring that it was appropriate for him to be the national leader. I observed the gene getting activated, identified the source and consequently regarded him as the messiah–king.

ILANA: based on historical accounts the Bar Kochba rebellion failed, causing great destruction among the People of Israel, countless deaths and exile on a large scale.

MASTER AKIVA: Failure and success are a matter of interpretation. Politically, the rebellion failed. Spiritually, it is considered a great success, for it was a source of inspiration to the whole Jewish nation, Israel. To this day the rebellion remains a symbol of bravery, inner strength and heroism demonstrated against a mighty force. David pitted against Goliath. The clarion call of the few against the many, courage, fervent dedication to national freedom and liberty, are all the fruits of the Bar Kochba rebellion.

Moreover, there is no doubt that ultimately it benefited the Jewish people. The drama of the uprising still affects the fighting spirit, the faith and the fervour of the entire nation.

To this day it is commemorated on *Lag Ba'omer*. It is the victory of spirit over matter, *les grand idea*! Sometimes, the significance of an act does not become apparent for many generations. Another example is the crucifixion of Jesus, which inspired Christianity.

ILANA: With your permission, dear and wonderful Master Akiva and to ascertain that I channell truth, I sought to examine the lives of Bar Kochba, Jesus and the Lubavitcher Rebbe. I wholeheartedly believe in my ability to discern energy, which is as accurate as a computer programme. I surmise that, indeed, all three have very similar energy. I understand that they embodied messianic potential but it was not fulfiled because rather than receiving the approval of the whole nation, they evoked opposition, controversy and strife.

I gather that although a person may be destined to fulfil a role, his mission will not be accomplished if mankind is not sufficiently mature to receive his message. Did I understand correctly?

MASTER AKIVA: you have understood wonderfully well. Preparatory work is required. Fieldwork must include seeding new beliefs, breaking new ground in the national–public arena, re–orientation of the masses toward the concepts of the new age and other tolerant philosophies and alerting the world to the clarion call of "love thy neighbour as thyself" in order to remould world opinion. It should be included in the school curriculum. The motto is: Tolerance, mutual respect, acceptance and enabling.

Time is short and the work is pressing. That is why you are required to work intensely, why you are aroused in the middle of the night to engage in writing. I am pleased to inform you that your efforts are bearing fruit and we highly appreciate your mission. We need you. We need torchbearers of light and liberty. We need the creative talents of statesmen with vision and inspiration, businessmen, healers and channellers. **Everyone who is aware of the light is summoned to the flag of the supreme vision of humanity:**

Unity is divine light and love. The time for union has arrived!

First, take responsibility for yourselves and your interior world and only then apply it to your exterior world.

Ask to be in communion with your soul
Ask to be one with your highest vision
Ask to unite with the Supreme Divine Will
Ask for the consciousness of one, the awakening of messianic consciousness in you
Ask to receive the knowledge of light and love, the original Tablets of the Covenant which Moses received from God on Mount Sinai

Prepare to receive this knowledge. Prepare the ground,

plogh your spirit with the energy of the following sentences: "Love the Lord thy God with all thy soul and with all thy strength," and, "Thou shalt love thy neighbour as thyself."

Here I am Master Akiva, delivering my words as a great beacon of light, as a bonfire rising and expanding in the dark and spreading the glow of light.

Thank you dear, Ilana for linking your personality to the mission, foregoing personal comfort, for releasing your apprehensions of over–exertion and for transforming yourself for the benefit of all. Blessed be, you and all your family, forever and ever.

ILANA: Dear and wonderful Master Akiva, thank you for choosing me as the channell for conveying knowledge. I no longer fear the effort, the unorthodox work hours, as evinced by this channelling, for whose sake I rose at one a.m. and it is now two thirty a.m. I am willing to do sacred work day and night, asleep or awake. I gladly submit to writing your most enlightening words, under your guidance. I send great love to you and all my guides. Be blessed.

Lesson 13

Death, Life after Death, Council of Karma, Soul Rescue

Good morning dear guides; a good and blessed morning to you dear and beloved Master Akiva. I would like to proceed with our discussion. Thank you.

I would like to raise a question. For 31 days I have channelled you. Now, as I edit the book, I have discovered a few lesson numbers with no lessons. Instead of adjusting the numbering, I prefer to add new material. For example, the material with which we started Lesson 13 ended up as Lesson 15. What would you suggest should be the subject of Lesson 13?

MASTER AKIVA: Dear and endlessly beloved. The number 13 represents change. In Tarot cards this number is part of the major arcane, as Death. Death represents transformation, alteration, shift. People are afraid of the shift from the known, from the plane of life (as we know it) to the unknown, the plane of death. Accordingly, our lesson will be devoted to that particular subject. When you are very scared of something, you may refer to it as a deathly horror. This can refer to any aspect of your life: relationships, change, career, health, etc....

Actually, death signifies an altered state of consciousness: An of the chapter of the soul's trials and tribulations on the earthly plane. There is life after death! The soul continues its journey. There are planes of consciousness other than the ones you are aware of. There are further realities of existence, in addition to the physical plane of experience, at the Sphere of Kingdom (*Sphirath Malchuth*), which is where you are now. There are, in fact, an infinite number of consciousness' testing grounds that your soul chooses to experience.

All religions contain this knowledge, but it is withheld from the unenlightened. To maintain the rules of the game being played in the here and now, it is necessary to classify information, compartmentalize knowledge and parcel out data. Think of a computer game. If, before commencing the game, you knew all the solutions and all the moves, there would be no room to experiment or learn. Your experience would be less stirring and tantalizing. You would not develop your inventiveness and your imagination... you would act solely within a technical framework, programmed to carry out missions. Such an existence would contribute nothing towards your evolution. It would give you little satisfaction, enthusiasm or inspiration!

Your soul is eternal. Your soul is replete with enthusiasm, inspiration and the desire to develop and learn. Your soul enriches all of divinity, all of creation! Your soul is the closest thing to God.

From the World of Truth, which pulsates with the most sublime divine truth, the truth of the consciousness of one, the soul draws up an agreement of joint learning! This is the system of "karma." The **Karma Council** is responsible for administering the system. It is a council of higher hierarchies of cosmic justice. These hierarchies are made manifest in angels with specific missions and in light spirits with particular undertakings. Their assignments deal with organizing and regulating the advanced lesson plan of humanity in its entirety.

The system is also responsible for the layer of existence where our life lessons, including individual lessons, are woven. Everyone comes under the jurisdiction and authority of this supreme council. The Sages of Karma include light entities who have incarnated in a physical body, whether in your earthly plane or in astral planes. The cosmic justice entities are in charge of this council, which sits at the Whole Karma Temple.

The Temple contains the entire wisdom of all the spheres (*Sefiroth*) of the Tree of Life. It also contains the measure of judgment, together with the measure of grace, which you call light and darkness. The two are incorporated into the learning experience and employed to teach requisite lessons and the understanding of consequences.

Sometimes judgment prevails, while at other times grace has the upper hand. Sometimes, there is a need for a lesson of difficulties and suffering; on other occasions, there is a need for a lesson of compassion and joy.

The Way of Love and the Way of Fear are the major courses whereby the Karma Council dispenses its lessons to evolving humanity.

For the soul, death is the end of a cycle of karmic lessons in a particular incarnation. The soul is always happy to complete its lessons and proceed to the next stage of its evolution.

For humans, while still in the physical body, not interlinked with the cosmic source of knowledge, it is hard to part with the physical body. It is hard to depart from life as we know it. Knowing that life continues in a different form is not satisfactory or comforting. You mourn those who are parting with the follies of this world. You are very frightened by the idea of losing your physical existence and all your attachments to matter, to relationships and to your physical body, which is your transitory temple.

ILANA: Dear and beloved Master Akiva, might this be the place to speak about trapped souls and soul rescue?

MASTER AKIVA: These matters will presently become clear. And, indeed, you are right, to my mind, to bring up the issue at this juncture.

What is a trapped soul? Can it happen that the soul of one who departed the physical world does not embark on its way to the World of Truth? And, if so, what might be the solution?

Well, the natural course for humans is as follows: Incarnation in the physical plane, transcendence to the soul plane, passage to the astral planes, eternity. As a matter of fact, it all takes place contemporaneously and the transaction is so multifaceted that you cannot possibly imagine or visualize it.

Sometimes a particle of the soul remains stuck in a particular drama, because it has not yet released its hold on its previous life. However, this is learning, experiencing and experimenting.

Since it affects the entire incarnated entity, which is tangled with close family or others by karmic bonds and ties of energy, it is necessary to release the part that is still trapped. This release allows optimal flow in all karmic courses and paths at all levels.

The release is accomplished by Angels of Karma and Messengers of Cosmic Justice. One may summon them to undertake the process, provided one is aware that part of the soul is trapped.

ILANA: how would we know when it is necessary to release a trapped part of the soul?

MASTER AKIVA: Attachment to the departed, beyond the traditional period of mourning, indicates that it was not released; that its energy has not yet relinquished this plane of existence. It may be that the soul itself is clutching at life and those left behind. Or it may be that those remaining alive are the ones clinging to its memory, thus preventing it from embarking on its journey. Unbeknown to them, of course, they are tying it down. When a soul is stuck and unable to continue its journey, it finds itself in a *bard*, a plane between dimensions. The trapped soul is a kind of a ghost, It believes itself to be still numbered among the living, but experiencing ongoing frustration due to its inability to manifest its desires. Such spirit has a negative effect on those physically alive who still mourn it.

Be aware, dearly beloved, that prolonged mourning does not accord with the Divine Will! Protracted bereavement is contrary to life itself and detains its flow! Grief is, of course, natural and necessary, but you must know how to release the sorrow and the pain. You must get up, bolster your faith and go on living! You must cherish the gift of life and its sanctity. Once you become aware that the soul is eternal, that it keeps traversing its course, you will surely grasp the knowledge conveyed to you: It is possible to make contact with the soul of the departed. You can meet with it in dream–state, you can receive messages, feelings and guidance. Sometimes the departed soul of one who was close to you in life becomes your guardian angel or spiritual guide, supporting and assisting you. Learn to expand your vision and insight and understand that there are planes of trans–physical existence beyond what your eyes can see, what your ears can hear and what your five senses can perceive!

Reality has vastly expanses beyond your perception through the physical vehicle of your consciousness!

Expand your awareness! Be in harmony with your spiritual body, through which you connect to the soul's higher, subtler planes, to the comprehension of broader, more comprehensive reality.

Imagine yourself in a house. You can see your immediate surroundings and if you open a window, you will be able to see the yard and the road that passes by the house. But the view is different from the roof and seen from a helicopter your house would assume very different proportions.

ILANA: Thank you, dear and beloved Master Akiva. I request a short break to contemplate and accommodate the new dispensation. Thank you.

(The following day): A woman on my online forum is asking about death. I should note that it occurred right after I thought of seeking people who would do just that. This magnetic attraction is simply amazing. Norma (assumed name) is asking: "I love this life so very much. Ever since I can remember the subject of death has disturbed me, even as a little child. How can it be that one day it will all be over? What went before? When will it be over? I do not want it to be over. And, yes, it even embarrasses me a bit to write all this, for I am aware, beneath the fear, that I believe it will never end, we have existed before and we will exist forever. I fully confess this fear of mine, even if only to let it go. I sense that it blocks me from fully living. Please help me."

Dear and beloved Master Akiva, it appears that we have been waiting for this exact question. Are you willing to proceed with our conversation and answer Norma's inquiry, which is no doubt typical of many others?

MASTER AKIVA: Dear Norma, dear and beloved Ilana, dear and beloved people. Yes, the issue raised is of great significance. Fear of death recurs time and again in your life. The fear is like a whip, motivating the aspect of your lives that has to do with choices and decisions. It is also a stop sign, a signpost saying, "do not enter," preventing you from making certain choices. This fear ties in with the defence mechanism[23] that guides your life.

The knowledge is accessible to anyone who chooses to accept it. Research in the field of hypnosis,[24] leads to

---

23 This was the subject of another chapter. See, Lesson 11, above.
24 See, for instance, Michael Newton's books, *Journey of Souls: Case Studies of Life Between Lives (1994), Destiny of Souls: New Case Studies of Life Between Lives (2000)* both published by Llewellyn; and Brian L. Weiss, M.D., *Many Lives Many Masters*.

the conclusion that the soul survives physical death. Life is eternal, although it assumes many forms. Apart from the physical dimension, the soul has other dimensions of existence. The element that fears death is the ego, the identity you adopt in a given life period, a particular incarnation. All the incarnations together form an entire ocean. Each incarnation joins the one before it and the one behind it, merging with all other incarnations of other individuals.

Words contain knowledge. Words conduct ideas. The lady, who is intellectually oriented, is communicating through her mental body. She knows that the soul survives physical death. She reads books and she has the relevant knowledge.

Deep within she knows it is true; her intuition tells her so and she believes it. But emotionally she lacks the ability to comprehend the process of physically departing from life. Her acute fear twists her consciousness and directs her choices and decisions, thus clouding the warmth and light of her life's splendor.

Mankind is capable of understanding something intellectually while utterly failing to grasp it at the emotional level. Emotional consciousness contains the strongest survival–related fears. It is very fragile and barely affected by maturation. What do I mean by that? It remains, in some sense, in your childhood. Many people react emotionally in a very basic manner, very childishly. Emotions are not processed by the mind. Powerful emotions include anger, rage, jealousy, passion, enthusiasm and love.

Intellectually, you experience your life differently in adulthood. You explain and interpret your emotions to yourself according to your state of consciousness. Are you embedded with a victim pattern, or, conversely, are you conscious reality creators who assume responsibility for whatever transpires in your existence? Are you good natured and forgiving or are you ill tempered, vengeful and a holder of grudges? It all depends on your personality structure, your belief system, whether you give heed to your intellect or operate solely according to your emotions.

Of course, some people operate in complete balance. They may be in tune with their subtler and more refined emotions or they may be more forgiving, taking responsibility even at the emotional level. You probably know people who are overly emotional and impulsive, while others are brainy, cold and controlled. They command their emotions and have the ability to express them rather than holding them in.

In order to help the lady who is scared of death, who intuitively understands the survival of the soul but emotionally suffers greatly from this fear, she must shed light on the dark places in her emotional body, where memories of past lives are stored. These are incarnations in which she experienced the trauma of unexpected death, the shock of losing loved ones, abandonment anxiety and physical, emotional, mental and spiritual suffering. Her acute fear of death indicates that there is a trapped soul fragment, in the manner we have delineated previously. It can happen that a soul is still in a given dimension (a particular incarnation), experiencing trauma and actual fear of death, unable to accept and be at peace with the reality it finds herself in at the moment, at this stage of her existence.

If, using your energy sensing awareness, you examine the situation and ask yourself: Does Norma need soul rescue, what answer do you think you would receive?

ILANA: I have checked and, not surprisingly, learned that you are right. I get a clear, positive message that she is indeed in need of soul rescue. I am continuing to examine the issue, whether all those who suffer from an acute fear of death, excluding those in immediate danger, where the fear is natural and understandable, have a trapped soul particle. I get a clear, certain, positive answer. Yes!

MASTER AKIVA: (With a smile) nice. If so, then your next question would be, how can we help those individuals whose souls are in need of rescue, how do we disentangle them from the bonds of fear?

ILANA: And I would like to add a question: Is the answer true in all cases?

Master Akiva: There is the rule and there is the exception. Processes that align with the rule would, in certain cases, fit the exception. But the common denominator is distributed across the board and similar levels of fear can help us develop appropriate procedures for immediate assistance.

This may be the place to employ past life regression therapy, where the individual's memory trunk is unbolted like a large treasure chest. This chest is the store room of the unconscious. It accumulates and contains the memory of all the previous incarnations of a particular soul. Past life events (parallel lives) can be viewed in the form of a stage play. Naturally, it depends on the extent of the individual's awareness and his accessibility and it can only be done for his greatest benefit. The play or movie, reveals the exact moment in time where his soul became trapped. This procedure provides the opportunity for adjustment, restoration or complete healing. The particle that has been stuck in an endlessly repeating loop transmits emotional content to the current experience until it is released.

Since, as you know, not everyone is ready to undergo this therapeutic procedure, there are additional therapies available for obtaining release. Reversal therapy, healing through breathing, healing through guided imagery and any form of strong autosuggestion with positive healing declarations. Such declarations are life–affirming, disentangling one from the fear. After repeating the affirmations, breathe deeply and contain them in your emotional body. That is the body that needs the breath.

Sometimes there is a short–circuit in the connection between the emotional and intellectual bodies. You have encountered such cases. It then becomes necessary to re-fuse all bodies of consciousness, the physical, ethereal, emotional, intellectual and spiritual, into one cohesive unit. At times you must ensure that a person is connected to his spiritual body. Re–attachment is required. One should do this with intention and declare: "**I choose to reconnect here and now with my spiritual body!**" After every declaration inhale through the nose, hold your breath and then exhale forcefully through the mouth.

Sometimes there is an imbalance in one or more than one body, and, at times, in all. By effecting balance, as described above, you can allay the fear and even release it completely.

A few years ago you received the following declaration: "I am not afraid of my fears! I acknowledge the fear, accept it, smile at it and make a decision not to allow it to influence my choices." This path calls for you to hug the fear. Send it light, contain it through imagery and understanding, until it becomes utterly imaginary, wholly unfounded and literally baseless. Why give it the power to deprive you of free choice? We will come back to this later, when we discuss fears and their transformation.[25]

---

25 See, Lesson 29, **Fears and Their Transformation into Urges.**

Now, let's return to the subject of fear of death. To calm the fear it is necessary to impart knowledge about reincarnation, the survival of the soul and its higher purpose. This would occur on the mental–instructive level. On another level you should connect with the following bodies of consciousness: the physical, emotional, mental and spiritual. You need to open all the centres of energy and chakras, including the superior spiritual chakras, some of which are still unknown to you. That is done in order to allow humans to transcend the plane of doubt to the plane of unconditional faith. Those who possess faith find it easier to accept the higher truth about the eternal nature and continuity of life.

The process of **soul rescue** which you received from the Karma Council, will, with your permission, be discussed now.

* * *

Soul Rescue
Death – End that is a Beginning; a Message from the World of Truth

Light souls incarnate in human bodies. We would like to explain to you, based on the requests received in the Creation Temple and Karma Council, what is soul rescue and why it sometimes becomes necessary. What is a trapped soul and what is your mission in the rescue process.

Let's start at the beginning: You are an eternal soul. Your soul, which is extensive and has a divine source, chooses and is chosen, to experience itself in a physical body. However, it also opts, at times, to experience itself as a pure spirit. The soul delivers itself simultaneously *to each existence it will ever have.* These are "incarnations." Each life is akin to one wave in a great ocean, where each wave is an integral part of the whole ocean. That notwithstanding, each wave has its own unique characteristics and experiential facets. There are high waves and low ones; some are topped by foam. Waves take on various colours: azure, deep blue, green and so on. The soul's purpose is to return, to enrich the divine source, after having undergone and accumulated all the experiences required for its overall growth. All experience is gathered in the knowledge cluster of the soul and amalgamated with the **all-inclusive knowledge reservoir of all souls.**

The soul has a pre–destined path wherein it opts for incarnation in a body (be it physical, ethereal or other). The path incorporates impregnation, birth, life, growth and death. Death is not an end – it is simply the end of the soul's journey in a given physical body and a new beginning on its grand cycle.

All souls that incarnate on Earth (save for very few, the Immortals or gods) are in a kind of a school with preordained stages, which are necessary for the overall experience.

The stage of death is very important, beyond what is understood in your culture. The ancient Egyptian and Tibetan Book of the Living and the Dead provide you some knowledge, most of it lost already, about the course undertaken by the soul.

Since death constitutes passage and continuity, it is necessary to leave behind whatever is not required for the new experience. Things that are considered burdensome, onerous or that weigh down the soul! Think of a person equipped with a great deal of gear (emotional memories – the emotional catalogue) which he loads onto his back. He sets out to follow a mountain track, hiking where the air is pure and clear…. The more he carries on his back, the more difficult the journey. Thus, instead of having a delightful trip, instead of focusing on what he sees, nature's beauty and his present experience, his back aches from the burden, his legs cannot carry him and he lacks the strength to continue. (This, of course, is just a metaphor.)

The question is: **can the soul be tied to earthly life? Can it be prevented from moving on after its passage through the physical experience?** And, indeed, the answer is yes. That is the condition of the trapped soul, a soul in an immediate need of rescue!

It is important to understand that it does not affect the entire soul, for the soul is multi-dimensional. We are concerned with what may be defined as a fragment of the soul. However, since all the fragments together comprise the entire soul, even if just one fragment is affected it impinges on the entire experience. The experience is not always understood. "Each person is an entire world," therefore, "he who would rescue one person, it is as if he has rescued the whole world."

We will go further: Not only is every person a whole world, every soul is a whole world and all souls together are the whole of creation. Every fragment that is trapped and tied down is of supreme importance, because every item in the system affects all the various parts that make up the whole.

How does a soul fragment get tied down and become stuck?

"Emotions," is the correct answer. Deposits of murky feelings such as unrequited passion, rage, extreme worry, great fear, feelings of guilt. Unresolved issues cause the soul to be tied by its spirit to the earthly plane of life, where it no longer belongs!

This causes the soul to find itself in a *bardo*, a limbo, a way station, from which it cannot depart. It is unable to relinquish the earthly experience and proceed with its journey. It cannot internalize its lessons, experiences and insights. It cannot channell its acquired knowledge towards a more enlightened and refined course; its growth is checked! (Growth is the purpose of all souls.)

A trapped soul knows no peace. It is tormented and at times it torments others. It may become a ghost. It is not free of the body, although its physical substance has worn off and thus it has no vehicle through which to express itself. It feels that it belongs to its former life. It desires to be involved in the life of the loved ones left behind.

This form of bondage ties it down and prevents it from reaching the World of Truth. The trapped soul is restless, it has no psychic peace and its suffering is great. Sometimes, it tries to compel its will and ideas on those left behind, even attaching itself to the living as a form of possession. Its presence is the cause of deep distress or unresolved emotions among those left behind. Its presence can inflict health and psychological problems, because the blockage of energy affects the entire family.

This situation is very frustrating. It can damage the entire development process of the soul and the other souls who are members of its soul family. (All souls are related to one another through family ties. You could say that they all have a common source.)

ILANA: Can anything else tie down the soul and interfere with its emancipation and its journey beyond? Do people tie it down? How do you tie down a soul?

You can tie down a soul if you grieve too deeply and continue to mourn beyond the traditional mourning period, at which juncture it is scheduled to continue with its voyage into light, freedom and ongoing learning and development. This is even more true when mourning and grieving goes well beyond the first year following the soul's departure, thus blocking the soul from leaving. Ironically, great love can tie down the beloved soul.

Similarly, anger felt towards the departing soul, even a sense of abandonment, ties it down as well. A feud over wealth and inheritance, a sharp division in the family, quarrels, intrigues and animosity, all of these could tie down a soul who cares for its family. Also, inappropriate burial or, alternatively, no burial, in the case of one whose body was never found. Death resulting from severe trauma can, also, tie down the soul.

In short, intense unresolved feelings on the part of relatives or the deceased, can tie a soul down.

Death is supposed to release a person from the burden of material concerns, from the trials of the flesh, to solve the riddle that is the experience called life.

The process of **past life regression**, in which a person returns to a previous life (actually parallel, since the soul embarks simultaneously on all its experiences) causes the person undergoing the regression to remember his death and the passage of his soul to the World of Truth. The experience is pleasant and liberating. It is experienced jointly by all participants. Following its release from the bonds of the physical body and its experience in the material dimension, the soul is at a state of purification, followed by complete healing and the ability to view the entire scene that is its life. It has the perspective of observing as if from above. It should be emphasised that past life regression may be used for other therapeutic purposes, as well.

Let the departed go! No death is accidental or random, even when caused by a disaster, even when very young children perish. Souls choose when to be born and when to die. There are many ways to depart, to resume the soul's journey past the illusory mist of matter and return to the World of Truth. Once a soul has passed on, it means that it has completed its assigned lesson. If it is done early it moves on early. It has much to do elsewhere. Occasionally souls depart in order to convey an important lesson to their loved ones.

ILANA: How do you release a trapped soul fragment?

Dear people, you may identify a stuck soul by way of the identifiers mentioned above or because a soul has appeared in a dream and caused you discomfort (souls can convey messages in dream state; when you dream of a departed one you really do meet his soul). It is also possible for a medium (whom you find agreeable) to bring information about a trapped soul to your attention. For karmic reasons and for your and its peace of mind it is advisable to release it from its bondage. **Releasing a soul is a spiritual precept of the first order!**

Begin with a comprehensive process of forgiveness, designed for the deliverance of stuck energy and karmic release. If you carry emotional residue in relation to the deceased, you are tying the soul down and burdening yourselves. This residue must be removed. The process of forgiveness can eliminate the negative deposits that are delaying your own soul's development.

Light a candle, invite the deceased soul to be present and say: "**I (your name and your mother's first name) call upon the Angels of Karma and request to heal, release and remove the soul of the deceased (full name of the deceased, including last name and his mother's first name) in all bodies, layers, dimensions and incarnations, here and now and in his/her entire existence. Thank you.**" This must be said with intense intention three times, with the palms placed open on the thighs, facing up.

Then say: "**I (your name and your mother's first name) call upon the Angels of Karma and request to enter a complete process of forgiveness.**

"**I ask your (name of the deceased) forgiveness, if I have hurt you in any way in this life or others. Please forgive me. I forgive you, I forgive myself. Forgive yourself for what has been done and what has not been done (but ought to have been done), in this life and others. I request that the process of forgiveness will operate upon and affect all bodies, all levels and dimensions, in all incarnations, here and now and in his/her entire existence. Thank you."

Then say: "I love you (full name of the deceased) and release you to go on your way. You are free to go. You are free, free, free.

"You came from the great light and unto the light you shall go. May your soul be bound in the bond of [everlasting] life. Amen."

Now take a deep breath. Close your eyes and wait for some form of acknowledgement that your affirmations have been accomplished. You may feel the deceased's presence through some physical sensation, a sense of relief or maybe though your inner vision, your imagination. See the deceased wrapped in light, going upward. You might even see two angels arriving to accompany him. However, even if you did not see or feel anything, know that your action was successful and the deceased has arrived in the World of Truth.

The released soul will be grateful. You will experience a sense of relief. Energy blockages will be eliminated from your life and the lives of your family members. This is a form of **energy domino**. When one soul is healed, the souls closest to it enjoy release and healing as well. Thus the healing spreads far and wide.

As for pictures of the deceased, position them wisely, in one place designated for that purpose. Do not place them in your bedroom. Assign a corner in the living room or study. There is no need to either worship or be in awe of the dead. It is enough to love the deceased person and to accept the fact that his soul survives and exists. One aspect of the soul remains with you, protecting you from on high. You can summon it to come to you in a dream and ask to remember the dream.

Know, dear ones, that when the day comes to end the journey, to transform your energetic phase, the souls you have loved in all your incarnations will be awaiting you.

We wish to remind you that deceased humans who were the object of your wrath, whom you may have even hated, are nevertheless beloved souls. On the soul plane you all love each other dearly. For what lies beneath anger and animosity? Beneath it all there is only one essence – love!

Blessed be in your eternal being, cherish the present of life here and now.

Yours with utmost love,
The Karma and Guidance Council.

Master Akiva: Here I am, Master Akiva. I am thankful for the message and I will endeavour to let it spread and be distributed for the sake of the salvation of countless souls, in every generation. Blessed be in your eternal existence forever and ever more. And thank you dear and beloved Ilana, for your dedication and devotion to the mission of the overall vision of peace and unity.

* * *

Soul Rescue
for Those Who Committed Suicide

Ilana: Three years after channelling that material, I was asked about rescue for those who commit suicide. Here is the supplemental material provided in response.

I address the Karma Council regarding an inquiry by Rose (a Light in the Body instructor). The questions are in regard to rescuing the souls of suicide victims: Is it appropriate to rescue them? Is there an interval that should be maintained before such rescue? Please open our hearts and enlighten us about the high cosmic truth and our mission in creation. Thank you.

I address you from within my soul, in all humility and modesty, with openness and full trust and faith, submission and great gratitude to you for your mission and your purpose in creation and for your being; with utmost love.

THE COUNCIL: Beloved Ilana, our high messenger as creation's mouthpiece, you are now received at the Karma Council, that numbers among its members the Council of Nine. You will receive us as your teachers and we will further your instruction and education in creation, for you are pure in body and soul awareness.

With the force and effect of the laws of creation a supreme and most essential edict had come into effect, which instructs about the sanctity of life: Do not take your life! Do not take the life of your fellow human being or that of your enemy or your adversary. Do not murder! It is expressly stated in the Ten Commandments, which you were instructed to inscribe in your heart. They contain the essence of the holy teachings: the teaching of moral principles for the human race unto its generations from alpha to omega, to the day of salvation and beyond. From eternity to eternity, forever and ever.

The act of taking life is a distortion of this moral principle. There is no clemency or pardon for murder and manslaughter. It is a desecration of the most high. It is the taking without permission of the life of a soul: a life that was created and animated by the Holy and Blessed One, the exalted and glorious Elohim *in whose own image* you were created. Alas, you have either forgotten this or you have taken it to the regions of the ego, which has developed and expanded, till it overflowed its banks with hubris and disregard of the laws of creation. The sin of the Tower of Babel is the sin of the shut heart, the result of man's arrogance whose ego regarded itself as a living god.

ILANA: It is men who sin but not souls. I am saying this. It seems to me that it is me. Souls are pure. They are entitled to redemption, clemency, grace and salvation. Isn't it so, dear and esteemed guides?

THE COUNCIL: The soul has its own system of trial and error, paths of choice and paths of formation, which include lessons in the times and dimensions in which it is immersed and even in parallel existences.

ILANA: Is it at all permissible, then, in order to rescue souls?

THE COUNCIL: Nicely said and thank you for asking, dear and beloved priestess of ours.

Soul rescue is carried out by souls whose mission is instruction and accompaniment of souls from one class to another, from one level to the next, from stage to stage. Rose is one such guide. You are such a guide.

The conditions for qualification for this path are complete purity of heart, high spiritual evolution in the avenues of grace, compassion and mercy. You may ask, in your heart, whether you should rescue a soul and when would be the best time to do so and the Angels of Karma will assist you in your mission. You are emissaries, intenders and callers of angels, endeavouring to direct their hearts toward lost, suffering and confused souls in the hereafter.

Not all souls are in this state after passing on. The vast majority are awakened by the light and are delighted to come home. This homecoming, called transition or death, is the process of shedding the physical body.

ILANA: Please forgive me, but I fail to understand: Is it permissible to rescue the souls of those who have perpetrated the sin of taking their own lives?

THE COUNCIL: It is permissible, but only 40 days after their death. This is because the soul needs to learn the appropriate lesson and draw fitting conclusions.

ILANA: I get the feeling that the transmission of material is not flowing smoothly. What is the reason?

The reason (the guides from the Karma Council are smiling) is that we are in conference… and you are an unconscious but active participant with your supra senses. The ruling has been made and is being transmitted down to you at this time. Please wait and soon you will be able to receive it in one conceptual continuum.

When rescuing those who have committed suicide, emphasis should be placed on forgiveness, which is the absolution of sins and transgressions and the liberation of the suffering soul from the impediment caused by pangs of conscience. Emphasis should be placed on the supreme sanctity of life. During that particular soul's next encounter with life it will remember and it will be forever committed to safeguarding the sanctity of life. For these souls we provide the following affirmation:

"In the name of the energy of grace and compassion, in the name of unity, in the name of the ascension of all, I request release, full karmic healing and full and comprehensive rescue for the soul of _____ (full name: first, last and mother's name); I request that the soul be brought into the covenant of full forgiveness. I ask that this soul be required to declare that it chooses the sanctity of life and that it shall honour life in every form in which it finds expression. I ask the soul to accept the energy of healing and clemency unto all its parts and to deliver them to all its fragments, so they can unite in one whole.

"I ask to encode the karmic lesson in the psychic structure and inner circuits of the soul.

"I ask that the soul shall unite with its soul cluster and that the injuries which have caused the tear within itself, between itself and its fellows and between itself and the sanctity of life, shall be healed."

To all the ascended emissaries, thank you for the holy process.

ILANA: Thank you so much. Is there an appropriate procedure for the relatives of one who has committed suicide? Is there something they should know?

THE COUNCIL: The relatives of one who takes his own life endure great emotional torment. They flagellate themselves with their feelings of guilt: Why didn't we listen, why didn't we see (it coming), why didn't we act differently, better? Why weren't we there for him?

Suffering is valuable. It teaches. The suffering should cause the relatives to ask themselves: Are we self–aware? Are we aware of other people? They should learn to transform the suffering into a learning experience whereby they will respect the sanctity of life and become fully attentive to the needs of their own inner being and that of others.

They need to relinquish the pain and attachment to self–flagellation after 40 days or at the end of a year of mourning. They need to let go, to release and thus be healed.

Blessed be His name forever and ever, says the Seraphim choir.

ILANA: Thank you. Did we receive the complete procedure or is there anything else we should know about suicide?

THE COUNCIL: Dear and beloved, thank you for such an excellent question. Suicide is a soul lesson about the power of despondency and hopelessness. People need to learn about hope. It is always possible to seek help. Never fall into the arms of despair, never lose the hope that is embedded in the innermost heart of your creative awareness.

ILANA: Thank you very much. I would like to say that suicide victims do give up hope, but sometimes that is their solution for preventing emotional or physical pain. Do not they have the right to commit suicide if they suffer from a terminal disease, for instance? Is no allowance made for such cases?

No, beloved. Suicide is suicide. Every suicide is brought about by acute pain, inner torment, separation, loneliness or a sense of deep despair. If hope exists, if even a single ray pierces the darkness that distorts vision and reality, suicide will not be the last resort.

The act of suicide is an act of self–elimination. It is taking your destiny into your own hands, with complete lack of faith in the attributes of heaven and the means that could be of assistance to you. It means you have no faith in life. No faith in the miracles that life has to offer. You have no hope. Loss of hope and utter despair, dear and beloved Ilana, are the most severe ills of society and of the individual. And from here stems your mission, beloved, as an exalted messenger, as a ray of light in creation, generously spreading hope to your readers and students, to all who were created. It is a mission of tremendous importance. Hope saves lives.

Be aware. Spread the knowledge generously. The good rays of hope that accompany you will continue to refine knowledge through you.

Be greatly blessed for your inquiry, dear and beloved Rose. It is crucial to all of creation.

Blessed be dear and beloved Ilana, an envoy from high in your world. You are blessed for being a pure and untainted instrument, increasing in greatness. Your brilliance is expanding through the dimensions. Be blessed.

Be blessed all of you beloved people, who are evolving at the alpha and omega of creation. Be blessed.

Holy, holy, holy is the Lord of Hosts and we are his angels. The Seraphim choir is blowing the golden horns and playing the rays of the sun of creation.

Praise the name of God, blessed be He forever and ever. Praise, praise, praise! Amen.

Lesson 14

What Are Dreams; Soul Dreams

ILANA: Good morning dear guides. Good morning to Master Akiva. I call on Master Akiva and ask to proceed with our discussion. Thank you.

MASTER AKIVA: Good morning my talented and beloved student. I thank you and appreciate the fact that you set an alarm clock to make you rise early for the sacred work of creation: Together, writing the Book of Light whose purpose is to open a portal to admit the flow of knowledge from the light, to expand mass consciousness on planet Earth. There is no doubt that any apprehension of undue effort, spiritual or physical, which, as you can see, are inseparably bound together, has been lifted.

I am glad to inform you that we are keeping to our schedule and proceeding with the mission. Ask, my daughter and you will be answered.

ILANA: Thanks. I set the alarm clock for four a.m. and woke immediately. My eyes are certainly tired and desire sleep, but my spirit is firm and determined to continue and work.

I woke from a dream in which I had a key to the old Lotus

Centre. In the dream the apartment (where the centre was located) was different from the one I rented for my spiritual centre, Lotus, but nonetheless there were similarities. It was an old apartment at the centre of Mount Carmel. I found the key and checked to see if it fits the keyhole. I entered. The apartment was lit. There was a gigantic aquarium full of live fish. There was a lot of furniture. I recalled that the furniture was mine and wondered why it was still there. In my dream I figured that I have not paid rent for three years and I had no presence there. I tried to recall how I found the apartment; I remembered a real estate agency in the area. I recalled that, in the dream, the owner was an old lady who taught the Bible. She was considered difficult to deal with, but I was on good terms with her. Her name was Zipporah. I thought she may have died and no one is aware of what's happening with the apartment. I thought of keeping the apartment and not telling anyone.

But then I thought that it would be more appropriate to check and see if there were relatives who would inherit the apartment. I then thought that I may have to pay property taxes for the last three years, as well as the power bill, since it was not cut off. I thought I would probably get around it and not have to pay anything. Then I recalled that the landlady is the mother of an acquaintance, so I called to tell her about the apartment. As it turned out, the landlady had not died, but was living in an old folks' home. The owner of the real estate agency did not want to deal with her and therefore he took no interest in what was happening to the apartment. Meanwhile, I thought I could offer the apartment to another acquaintance who actually has had difficulty finding a place to live. However, I thought it would be too small for her needs and she could find a furnished apartment for free. I conveyed all this information to the landlady's daughter.

Then, the alarm clock went off. This is the second time this week I dreamed I had a key to the Lotus Centre (my erstwhile spiritual centre), that it is still furnished and my numerous possessions have remained there. I think it is highly symbolic. I will be glad to receive an interpretation, to shed light on its meaning. Also, I'd be happy to obtain additional information about dreams and what they are exactly. Thank you.

MASTER AKIVA: My dear and beloved student. The purpose of a dream is information. Dreams carry coded messages from the subconscious, from higher worlds, from the kingdom of truth, from the dead, from guiding entities and from memories mixed with the soul's interpretation. They also contain emotional experiences relating to facts, some of which will serve in later times and other dimensions. Lessons are learned from emotional experiences at the level of dreams and not in the physical dimension. However, there is no dream that does not have a hidden meaning. Remember that!

An excellent way to deal with dreams is to remember and interpret them, according to your path and ideas, in the way you understand the truth and according to your own experience.

It is very easy to interpret your dreams. Keys to your temples of knowledge and accumulations of (spiritual) assets are available at many levels. You are spiritually very rich, but you are unaware that you have both the contents and the keys. Your Lotus Centres are active and bear fruit. As for the landlady who taught the Bible, she is linked to Zipporah, wife of the Biblical Moses. Your presence is where the nation's giants, rabbis, saints and countless kabbalists and spiritual leaders may be present. Even when you think you are no longer at a given location, your spirit is upon it. The large, lit aquarium, filled with fish, is a sign, dear and beloved, of great abundance and blessings. It shows that your influence remains in place long after you depart from a given location or from the company of a person and you leave much light and life in your wake.

ILANA: Thank you for the informative and fascinating explanation. I would like to add John's inquiry; he wants to know why it is so difficult for us to interpret dreams. Why do we receive things we are unable to understand?

MASTER AKIVA: "Difficult" and "easy" are subjective concepts. Some people find it easy to swim among the mysteries and depths of dreams, to penetrate the heart of the matter. For others, it is trying. Dreams are experienced, just like reality. Nobody "gives" you an experience, prefaced with the words, "Here is an emotionally powerful experience, whose purpose is to awaken your consciousness. Do you agree, today, between two and three in the afternoon to undergo such experience?" (Laughter.)

You experience events not because your body–personality (ego) chose them, but because it is an assembly of experiences your soul opts to experience for its own purposes. Think of the soul as a supreme aspect, an aware element, the divine within. In contrast you can think of yourself as a toddler, who as yet cannot process explanations and interpretations of the abstract meaning of things.

Ilana: An excellent and entertaining explanation, to my mind. I will clarify and refine my question: What is the right way to relate to dreams? Is it just an experience that you either remember or forget when you wake up? And if you remember a "bad" dream – by which I mean a dream that leaves an intensely oppressive sensation such as fear, what should you do with the data that affects you? Is there a way to heal, to comprehend, to be restored? What do you suggest we do with the data that rise from dreams?

Master Akiva: First, you would be able to get a handle on the complexity of your entire personality, the sum of your parts. Second, you can obtain information about your rich inner world and receive facts about your reservoirs of data. Lastly, you can accommodate messages and use them for your benefit in everyday life.

As to a "bad dream," it can produce pearls to act upon. For instance, Pharaoh's dream: "… Seven other kine that came up after them out of the river, ill favoured and leanfleshed; and stood by the other kine upon the brink of the river. And the ill favoured and leanfleshed kine did eat up the seven well favoured and fat kine." (Genesis 41:3–4): This dream left Pharaoh oppressed and fearful, causing him to consult Egypt's wise men. After Joseph interpreted the dream, Pharaoh used his knowledge to his advantage, preparing for the bad times ahead. His proactive action saved Egypt from hunger.

There is no information that cannot be used. The question is, what for? Harsh dreams, such as dreams of persecution, evince the existence of fear residue, an urge to escape some sort of confrontation on the earthly plane. Ask yourself: where is the truth and where is the fear? Try to think of ways to face up to and overcome the fear and transform it into an impetus for positive action.

You can use the energy of a "good," dream as a source of nourishment and inspiration. Creative individuals are influenced by the dream–state dimension, expanding its effect beyond the screens of physical reality.

If you wake with an oppressive feeling and the sense that you have experienced a nightmare, respect the feeling. Relate to yourself gently and ask for healing of the memory of the experience, including the emotional body.

ILANA: Of whom do we ask? And, is there a way to heal the disturbing experience?

MASTER AKIVA: You could ask the Dream Angels to assist with the healing. Ask to be released of the emotional flooding. Imagine sending light to yourself. Visualize a white fall (akin to a waterfall) of light that reaches from the sky and washes over the length and width of your body, including your aura and the emotional body (a part of your being that is not physical but delicately ethereal). Use your breath to settle down and balance yourself up. Envision the remnants of the dream departing from your body and dissipating.

Well, it wasn't just a dream, it was a real experience. The experience came to awaken you and bring the belief system you are clinging to into your awareness. I would advise you to seriously consider the residue left by your dreams.

Now, with your permission, we will shift to another type of "dream." Since it cannot be defined precisely, people use the term "dream" in three contexts:

a. Dream – a nocturnal experience, a kind of a psychedelic projection of bits and pieces, at times irrationally tied together. An experience, either pleasant or unpleasant. In your perception, dreams are distinct from reality.

b. Dream – a primordial idea which may be disconnected

from reality and even be defined as a fantasy. You sometimes say about someone that he is a dreamer. You say, "I have a dream that one day..." and, "it's not real, it's just a dream."

c. Dream – the heart's yearning. You relate to it as an emotional or romantic generator. "I have a dream that one day..." you sigh.

d. Also, "I have a dream," in the sense of a vision, a goal to be desired and attained, even though it might seem hard to attain at present. You sing "Imagine All the People" (by John Lennon).

There are individual dreams; there are dreams of a vision for a nation, a country, a continent, even a global vision for all of humanity and the whole planet.

Know that a dream is a supreme vision of great value. It transports from planes of high consciousness, seeping into the awareness of leaders and influencing their opinions. At times it takes hold of a single individual, at other times it penetrates the perception of a group of visionaries. These are not necessarily politicians, generals, public figures, celebrities or familiar and influential individuals. They could be children, obscure poets and any soul receptive to visions.

If an individual who lacks any influence receives a vision, he in effect becomes a conduit, carrying the vision's frequency. This is a kind of relay station that broadcasts in all frequencies, simultaneously. The message is received at the telepathic tier of vision operatives. These operatives belong to a group of people who have the ability to influence others. Great value attaches to the person who is both a conduit for direct reception of the vision and capable of shaping reality. Prophets and visionaries are such people. They receive a direct transmission, believe themselves to be conduits and act accordingly. They do this as ambassadors of creation. Though the substance of the message is often rejected by the majority or by the ruling powers, its acceptance is not the primary purpose of the transmission. Even when people are angry or fearful when they hear the message, even if they do not believe it or agree with it, as soon as they are exposed to it, it affects them, whether consciously or unconsciously.

Clearly, if every message is equally influential, you may filter the information that gets through to you. You can choose the information feed according to your preferences and decide why and to what extent it will influence you. For example, do you know how much you are affected by newspaper headlines? Even the front page, which you barely glance at, contains words, which are energy and ideas that project themselves onto your consciousness.

ILANA: Dear and beloved Master Akiva. News headlines are designed to boost ratings and increase sales percentages. That's why they are always overly dramatic. More often than not, newspapers carry reports that sow fear. How is one to protect himself from such energy? Is it, in fact, necessary?

MASTER AKIVA: Your question is good and aimed at high consciousness. It asks for defence against the control and manipulation of your frequency. Know that once you have been exposed to exciting or frightening information, it is received by your emotional body and penetrates directly into your subconscious, which stores and recalls everything perfectly.

You can counteract the volatile effect by meditating on Holy Scripture and on reinforcing ideas. For example, tell yourself, "Love thy neighbour as yourself," "The nation of Israel lives!" and so on. Work on positive affirmations that combine imagination and emotion and tell yourselves: "The world I live in is wonderful, just the way God created it," "The world is a stage – and we are all actors." Remind yourself that there is no coincidence, everything is a multi-participant drama.

Clarify and focus your awareness. Regard news reports the same way that you regard messages that point out your own inner beliefs: beliefs in peace, security and economic stability or, alternatively, fears regarding social and economic issues.

When you feel anger at your leaders for disappointing you,

take personal responsibility and understand that through your beliefs, as individuals and through public opinion, you enabled them to assume office. You appointed them! Accordingly, look to your own motives and beliefs. You may decide to take action and pass new laws regarding the appointment of public officials.

You could do individual checks by means of palm reading, numerology, graphology and psychology and enact them by law. This could prevent unpleasant surprises and the appointment of unqualified persons to high office.

Remember, "A man sees the eyes, while God sees the heart." The façade can be deceiving. Therefore, since you may not be possessed of intuition and the ability to see that which is hidden, employ the pseudo–scientific tools referred to above. Try to penetrate the depths of the personality. Place the emphasis on loyalty and dedication to vision and achievement, not just self–aggrandizement.

There is no need for anger, fear, helplessness or hopelessness. Face the truth, accept it and then ask yourself what you can do to change it. What is your liability for the situation? How do you intend to act on the issue and, in general, from now on?

This resembles my instruction regarding your self–image. You must accept who you are. If there are elements of yourself you do not like or are displeased with, note them with equanimity. If you are able to change them, do so. If they cannot be changed, accept them. But, do not be angry with yourself, do not disdain yourself, do not belittle yourself. There is a reason why you appear as you do and for everything that transpires in your existence.

Know how to accept and accommodate the truth without suppressing or ignoring it, without covering up and without apology. Do not compound your negative feelings, instead, immerse them in compassion and love.

Do not rush to attach negative labels to yourself or the world. Beware of this tendency, because it reinforces an undesired reality. Expressions such as, "The whole world is against us," are very dangerous. Please, go back and examine your stock of idioms. Just because someone has coined a lovely phrase does not mean it reflects the truth or should be adopted.

Expressions are statements of ideas and beliefs. Learn to examine them. Does the expression, knowledge or belief stem from the "path of fear" or from the "path of love." Choose your beliefs carefully and do not let interested public leaders influence your emotions and opinions. Do not let them influence your sure inner knowing, that creates and shapes the reality you are experiencing for yourself.

ILANA: An hour has passed, the birds are singing and it's

getting light. With your permission, we will take a short break to accommodate what has been said. Thank you.

MASTER AKIVA: Well, of course it all depends on you capacity to accommodate. We are going to proceed with the subject of dreams which, as it turns out, is very important and very... real.

It is very important for the individual to get in touch with the level of the soul and its dreams.

The soul's dream is the vision board of the corporeal personality. Some people dreamed as children, in purity and innocence, that when they grow up they will "do something." They must remember those dreams because they were the soul's wishes. Of course, some dreams should not be interpreted according to their surface layer since they contain messages. For example, a child may want to drive a garbage truck when he grows up. That is the surface of the dream. The inner message would be that this child is impressed by the fact that a large vehicle lifts and empties trash cans. He would develop an interest in cleanliness. It could, for instance, be ecological awareness for the benefit of the environment. At any event, instead of laughing at such dreams, try to relate to them as messages that bring an inner concept in the language of children.

Some children dream of being a physician, for example, but become afraid of attaining their dream when they reach adulthood. The goal seems difficult, impossible even and they give it up. **Please do not give up on your soul dreams! Ask to reconnect with them.**

However, know that if the child wants to be a physician, it means that he has the desire to help others and heal them. There are numerous ways to accomplish this and learning medicine is not the only path to his ultimate goal. It is possible that his lesson is to go through his sense of fear and not give up. Even if it is difficult, he should study medicine.

Commitment and dedication to the goal are the means to realize soul dreams and to ensure success in every field of endeavour. **Sometimes people are not in touch with themselves and their soul. They lack a clear soul vision and they have no purpose to guide them.** *These people are not happy!* They define themselves as lacking inner drive and ambition. I am not saying that ambition is either a positive or negative quality, but deep within them there is only ennui and emptiness. Their lives have no meaning. They are robot–like. They tire at work or, alternatively, from their inability to find employment. Actually, the disconnection from themselves and from their source of enthusiasm causes them to live exclusively in matter. Their soul spark is weakened and does not light up their path. They lack the inner fuel that would fill them with activity containing vision and meaning.

The way to help these people, provided they seek help,

is to reconnect them with their soul dream, which is their supreme vision. It would restore their sense of being alive and give meaning to their experiences, even the painful and challenging ones. It can be done by pouring waterfall–like flows of energy unto their aural bodies and by affirmations. These affirmations are in effect new codes, reprogramming their "software." They settle in both the consciousness and the sub–consciousness, creating an energetic flow of activity. It is like magic.

Affirm:
"I opt to connect with my soul and be under its full guidance and in its light, here and now in my entire being!
"I choose to tune into the dream of my soul.
"I combine vision and self-actualization in my life.
"I always manifest my soul dreams in full, here and now."

The dream is knowledge from the supreme goal of the soul for its fulfillment; the dream always carries an optimistic message for your supreme benefit. Usually, it will be related to other individuals. It will be meaningful and provide mutual stimulation.

Soul dreams are not – and I repeat and emphasize my words with all possible weight – they are not material (in orientation)! They have no relation to material accomplishment!

Dreams may include material achievements. There is no contradiction whatsoever between dreams and matter, but matter is not the essence but rather its insipid attendant. A soul dream of a human being cannot be, "I'll get rich and become a millionaire." A soul dream can be: "I will be a person of great influence; I will help others to earn their living." Such a dream may have added value if the dreamer becomes wealthy.

Do not fear getting in touch with your dreams. It will promote your understanding of your soul's supreme goal, of comprehending your lessons, which accumulate in a circle, for many purposes. It will cause you to live exuberantly, from a place of significance and inner spiritual growth.

You manner of treatment, Ilana, could indeed include **connecting with the soul dream** and an infusion of energy from the dream to the candle of the soul, which is the source of inner soul light and the embers of life. It is located at the core of the emotional body. It is an opening through which one can be filled with the force of life and the capacity to contain it.

ILANA: Thank you for your words, dear Master Akiva. In order for me to accommodate, I ask you to sum up our discussion today.

MASTER AKIVA: Dreaming is part of reality. The dream connects you to expanded reality. Dreams expand your overall understanding. A dream is an opening to the supreme vision of your soul and a key to perspective on all your lessons upon earth. Dreaming gives your life a sense of hope and inspiration. It is a tool for action. **honour your dreams and follow their footsteps in your soul's path.**

I thank you dear, Ilana, for your dedication and commitment. You have devoted two hours before dawn to our learning and for that your reward will be great. We love you and appreciate your way. Your dreams are being fulfiled on a grand scale. Have strength and courage. In my name and the name of the Karma Council and the Torah sages, in the name of the high and exalted Metatron, in accord with the will of the elevated and exalted – our Creator. You are creation's envoy, thus, honour your office and dedicate yourself to it.

Thank you and see you in our next session.

A Dream Deciphered

ILANA: Dear Master Akiva, I'd like to share with you and hear your opinion about a dream I had before I woke up, that has left me with an unpleasant sensation. In my dream I am driving my car to a steep mountaintop, the road is narrow. I climb and suddenly I see a road sign: "No Entry!" I have already passed the sign and want to turn around. However, there is no way to do so. The road is very narrow.

Nonetheless, I go back, I think I did turn around somehow. However, the place is so steep, that I become apprehensive, feeling an impending wreck and sensing danger. I ask for help from up high. "Help me," I request, then I imagine an accident, then no–accident. Nothing really happens and I wake up feeling fear and oppressiveness. I'll thank you for telling me the meaning of the dream, which seems to me to be an important message, even crucial for my life.

MASTER AKIVA: Dear and very beloved Ilana. First, settle down, for we protect you and you are safe, protected, guarded in God's world. Your value, importance and presence in the world are more crucial than ever now. Second, you are really standing before a very steep rise. The path is narrow – few have ever enter it and emerged intact. This is the "*pardes*[26] path" to higher worlds. Not just anyone can enter. Actually, you could have proceeded. You could have disembarked and continued on foot. And I recommend that you do so now, when you meditate and ask to see what takes place up there. You were so close, you could have actually entered. Only the road sign caused you to turn around and go back.

---

26 *Pardes*, literally the word means "a citrus orchard." It is also an acronym (formed from four words, *Pshat, Remez, Drash, Sod*) that refers to certain approaches in Biblical (and especially pronounced in Cabbala) exegesis. Each type of *pardes* interpretation examines the extended meaning of a text. As a general rule, the extended meaning never contradicts the base meaning, i.e. the *pshat* (or plain, contextual meaning of the text). *Remez* is the allegorical meaning. *derash* includes the metaphorical meaning. And *sod* represents the hidden, even occult, meaning.

Your faith is still undamaged and at a moment of danger and fear for your existence, you addressed High Ones. They helped you to avoid rolling downhill and losing your life. The awareness of the request for help accompanied you in your dream and it goes to show that your faith is getting stronger and is paving an upward path for you, to glory. By glory, I mean the halls of glory of creation, the supreme worlds, as they are referred to in the Cabbala, which are hidden from the unenlightened.

The root of your soul directs you toward devotion to the goal and an intrepid upward climb. As the divine tree that you are, your roots are grounded deep in the earth, in the ancient root system of the nation's forefathers, its leaders and elders. Your treetop rises and climbs to new apexes. You give fruits to the masses, like the generous tree in the well–known parable. Do not fear to give away your fruits, for fruits that are not given, fall to the ground uselessly and rot.

This is a time of immense growth for you. It is a time of accretion of pure and sublime frequencies that only few in your generation could reach and accommodate. Beware not to lose your way due to misinterpreting the road signs. Know however that you are accorded protection and your path is unique. You have the potential to ascend to soaring summits, to the bright, veiled light of the profound, esoteric truth emanating from the Cabbala. Know to pay attention, to halt when necessary, to turn around when needed, to be careful and responsible, but, I reiterate: *Fear not*! There is no need to allow the element of fear into your creative repertoire for the latter is powered by the consciousness of light.

In the case of your dream, in the optimal situation you would have parked the vehicle and proceeded on foot.

ILANA: Dear Master Akiva, there was no place there to park. If I were to have parked I would have blocked the traffic coming down. Otherwise, you interpretation is wonderful and an eye–opener.

MASTER AKIVA: Well Ilana, my dear and very beloved tree of God, do not limit your conceptualization to the confinement of matter. Do not lend your thinking to the concrete form practised by those who have not ascended to subtle worlds of intelligence and wisdom. Think creatively and spiritually even when you find yourself in a material vehicle. Next time, try to convert the car into a flying chariot or an aircraft of some sort, try to work without physical limitations, You can do it, you have a talent for it.

This is a message dream of great importance. I am grateful that you have shared it with me; actually, I asked to share it with you (smile). We work as a well–trained and coordinated crew and you always were one of my favourite students. Continue with your dedicated work. May goodness and mercy follow you all the days of your life and may you dwell in the house of the Lord forever. (Accord, Psalms 23:6.)

I am Master Akiva, who emphasize to you Ilana and to all of you, to pay attention to your dreams and to take them with all seriousness. Thank you.

ILANA: Thank you, in my eyes it was an exciting and wonderful message. Should I include it in the book or file it as a personal communication.

MASTER AKIVA: There is no such thing as a personal communication and all your experience has accumulated for the benefit of all. Believe! Release the perceived need to keep things, get in touch with giving and the need to share and to give freely and lovingly. There will be souls among your distinguished and dear readers who would find good and beneficial use for you and your experiences, including the ones in dream state. I am Master Akiva in the service of all, conveying the message, Love thy neighbour as thyself.

* * *

ILANA: (another dream) Good morning dear and beloved guides, good morning good and blessed Master Akiva. I woke up today at three thirty a.m. Moreover, I did not sleep well and tossed and turned on my bed all night. It seems to me that this would be a good opportunity for a channelling.

I woke up from a dream that has left me feeling guilty.

In my dream I had two babies, but it appeared that I had forgotten about them. One, to whom I eventually returned, was a little girl. She had fair hair and she was chubby and very cute. We were somewhere outside when I suddenly remembered that I have another one, smaller, whom I had forgotten for hours at home. I explained to the little girl that we have to go back, but she resisted. However, finally I convinced her that it was necessary. At home, we still did not approach the baby. I remembered that his name was Michael, Michael Lewis's namesake, I think. I thought to myself that if he was not fed for a long time it would not be really bad, fat cells will not develop in his body and when he will have grown he will be skinny and well-shaped. In the meantime, I put the little girl to sleep in her stroller. I lay down in the double bed and I tied the safety belt around the girl in the stroller. I noticed that her legs were exposed and I covered them with two wool blankets. She fell asleep. I noticed that her mouth was making sucking motions and I placed a pacifier in her mouth. She spat it out. I thought it was for the best, so that she would not need braces when she is older, at a prohibitive cost. (Very practical thought on my part, I should note.) I still did not attend to little Michael, to check on him.

I woke up with a very unpleasant feeling of guilt about my neglect of my babies. I would like to be provided with an interpretation. Is it possible that the smaller baby is a book I thought about publishing earlier with the Council of Karma and several other guides? The book Alchemy of the Soul which was pushed aside because of the book we are working on right now or is it something else I am neglecting?

By the way, I felt a great deal of love toward the talking little girl I had. I will be very happy to be given an interpretation of this dream.

MASTER AKIVA: Dear and beloved Ilana. There are many souls under your supervision, whom you nurture as if they were your own tender children. As if they were your own flesh and blood, with utter dedication, total love and all the wonderful motherly skills you have been endowed with. What is motherhood? It is synonymous with accommodation, total acceptance, breastfeeding/unconditional giving, dedication and unconditional love. That is perfect motherhood. That is its purpose. To be a mother is a calling of the soul who came to develop and nurture skills of extraordinary giving, providing and dedication.

You speak with shock about the babies' neglect. However, that is not so. You have forgotten to whom you entrusted their care. The message is: Know how to let go. When the day arrives and the baby chicks need to learn to spread their wings and fly, release the worries that something went wrong. You have figured out in the dream that every apparent mistake has a positive aspect. The baby will not develop excessive fat cells, which would cause him anguish in adolescence. He therefore can wait. The baby girl turned down the pacifier, thus, her teeth will remain straight. Note the common threat that passed through your thoughts, was long term planning. You thought about the braces, the appearance of the baby boy when he grows up. You must understand that there are no mistakes and everything is for the best. You need not take everything as your own personal responsibility. Let go and let the universe take care of all people, in all matters. Be in a state of love, as you are and do your best. You did not neglect the souls entrusted to your care. Indeed, you forgot, but someone else arrived to assume responsibility for them.

As to your assumption, that it was symbolic of books, that is actually one layer of interpretation. Dreams have manifold meanings. As you know, the book you are not attending to at present and, supposedly, neglecting is the baby Michael. No harm will come to it. It still needs to take shape. Its energy will solidify and take shape in the future. It will also be well known. And the baby girl is, indeed, our joint book. You do not need to worry at all (the pacifier was superfluous), it is taking care of itself, it understands its value, it will distribute itself, it will become well-known and will be a beautiful book of great value on the bookshelves of the universe.

ILANA: Thank you.

Lesson 15

Soul Mates and Inner Completeness
Personality Fragments and Their Effect
Purifying the Vessel

ILANA: Good evening to all my guides. Good and blessed evening Master Akiva. I call upon you to proceed with our discussion.

MASTER AKIVA: I am ready, for the time is at hand, the time is ripe. I am glad that you set aside quality time and accommodate all the material said here. What would you like to ask?

ILANA: I'd like to tell you that I have read one of the channelled messages, the one about war and peace and understanding truth, to the participants of my tarot course. In a magical way, every one of your words ties with their previous discussion, which was pessimistic. They were sure war was imminent. They were moved and excited by the message. I think we concluded and understood the dissertation.

I would like to pass to you a question that came up and is of an interest to me, as well. It is about soul mates. Everyone is looking for his soul mate. Nevertheless, I do not think we understand the meaning of the concept. In addition, I was asked if a person has just one or several soul mates. And, do homosexuals and lesbians have a soul mate that matches their sexual preference?

Also, what is a complementary flame? Is it like a soul mate? What is holy union? Is there such a thing as an energetic complement? If so, is it a person in a physical body and how does it affect us? Or, is there no such thing? I will be grateful for your response.

MASTER AKIVA: Dear and beloved, exalted and wise – I am referring to all those who are asking. People desire to be whole, to feel a sense of security and belonging. People look for themselves in others; seeking validation of who they are, of all of their substance: emotional, physical, intellectual, energetic. They seek one person to contain and hold them, to reinforce and encourage, who'd be there for them in times of need.

You should know that whatever you pursue outside yourself, you will find within. It can be found by opening the heart's core and by being in communion with your soul, which would allow you to feel the wholeness to which you yearn to return. That is so because, initially, you were in communion with your soul and, through it, with the Creator of the world.

The source of your soul is a cluster of souls formed from one soul root. All the souls that were formed with you are sister souls, which you term soul mates. They may be incarnated as either gender and it is not relevant to either sexuality or a particular relationship. You recall the great closeness, camaraderie and brotherhood you felt for your twin souls and now you yearn for a similar bond.

Thus, a twin soul is a soul that was formed simultaneously with yours and has identical characteristics to your own. A twin soul could be of either gender. A twin soul can be your friend, girlfriend, parent or child. It will not necessarily fill a sexual role in your life or even be in any relationship with you.

A complementary flame is something else altogether. It is an energetic complement, intended to make you whole and intensify the experience you undergo in a relationship. The complementary flame is an essential part of you. However, you will not find it in another person in your outer world. A complementary flame can exist between you and an angel, an extraterritorial alien or any other light entity. When you encounter your complementary flame, a holy union takes place. There is a function in you that corresponds to the complementary flame and you must first activate it, although it sometimes works automatically, depending on your genetic makeup.

ILANA: It is evening now. The tarot study group is over. I

thought I would channell, but I see that right now I lack the capacity to accommodate it. I kindly ask that we continue later, maybe tomorrow.

MASTER AKIVA: Gladly. You need balance and rest. We will see you later, dear and beloved disciple. The subject is indeed very important. We will deal with it later. You are invited to set up an early wakeup and then receive the broadcast. I am Master Akiva, in the name of all the senior guides.

ILANA: Good and blessed morning to you, dear and wonderful Master Akiva. I slept a little and now the birds are singing and the sky is filling with light. I love this hour very much. I will be glad to proceed with our discussion. I want to tell you, that I feel a little discomfort that I read your channelling to others, but I feel I did the right thing, because I saw the effect of your words, with their innate wisdom and logic. What do you think?

MASTER AKIVA: Dear and beloved Ilana, rest assured about reading the material. I was with you at the time. I wanted you to observe the effect of our communications. A facial response is much more effective than a response by e-mail, delivered in a few words. You are not acting from an ego level, if that's what is worrying you. You are a clean channell; really clean. You must let go of meekness and the tendency to hold on to information. The knowledge that comes through you is crucially important and, accordingly, it will be published in a book. It is an important book of light, whose influence you can hardly fathom and it is better that way. Do not concern yourself with the consequences, as you currently understand them and how the book will be published and distributed. Immerse yourself entirely in the activity. You occupy yourself with it devotedly and with dedication. I have heard your request to transform your personality and become a soul in a body. Well dear, that has already been the case for quite some time now. Certainly there are certain human aspects still in need of healing, but they are very few. A fragment of you is afraid of misleading. That is ego. It is an inner voice that tells you to keep a low profile, not to stand out, not to draw attention. Well dear, that aspect needs to be healed and released. I ask you to call forth that fragment of yourself, exude your soul light on it and reunite it with the rest of you. You have no reason to worry. It is important that you believe that about yourself, so you will not be apprehensive about being with others, even in crowds. Even if you say nothing, your presence will raise their consciousness and energize their inner flame, their soul candle.

It is not you, but a fragment of your ego that speaks to you, as evinced by the reactions when you shared the material with other. Feel the truth of my statement.

ILANA: Thank you. I accept what you are saying as nothing but the truth. I call forth that part of me that desires to remain apart, mute and unnoticed. I remember that as a child in school I behaved that way. I was very shy. I didn't want to draw attention. Now it's more of a defence mechanism. I ask that portion to elucidate what is hidden within me, which affects my life and the reality I create.

What is your name? Present yourself!

The fragment: Lonesome I sit... In fact my lonesomeness is better than keeping company with sly foxes who bite the hand that feeds them. I stay away from dens of gossip and slander. I live according to the injunction, "Blessed is he who did not sit in the seat of the scornful.[27]" I have been hurt by people who disappointed and betrayed me, turning their backs on me at a time of crisis and trouble. I carry beliefs influenced by the priest Elazar the Essene and you are his reincarnation.

ILANA: Well, holy, dear and beloved fragment in me. I embrace you and seek to comfort you and heal your isolation. Remember, "Love thy neighbour as thyself," remember forgiveness and know that I am undergoing a great transformation and the soul is guiding me and my path now. The soul, the Great Light, God, are telling all my fragments to reunite and undertake the mission of spreading light. I ask you, please, to join us, gather your courage, replenish your faith in mankind, whose source and essence are good and you are one of their number. Join me

---
27 Accord, Psalms 1:1.

and accept the healing of the soul's light. I, as the I Am, am channelling to you light of purity, truth and love.

We will always act from truth, but it will be the highest and most exalted truth from the highest levels; a truth of purity, holiness and great compassion. We will act out of the wisdom of the High Priestess of the Tarot, who teaches what to say, when and how much to reveal. We will function from a firm and clean connection with the I Am and God's will. There will be no errors. We will receive whatever comes with love and understanding. That is the way of truth. Would you accept all this?

Elazar the Priest: I accept your words with love and submission, great teacher. I join your camp. Please understand, I was very arrogant, I erred in my interaction with others, for I was hurt by their betrayal. I was left alone in a cave to pay for my sin of hubris. Guilt and fears were my companions. I renounce them and return to join the leadership, which is my natural place, due to my role as go–between and communicator between high worlds and the *Sphirath Malchuth*. I am proud to be... humble and in touch with compassion. I thank you my daughter. A great thank you is conveyed to you from all parts of the soul I have gathered around me, who have caused you to stay home out of acceptance of fate, out of an outlook that "My home is my castle," or in this case, "my temple." It is time for you to go out to the world. I, with all my strength, will remain with you and convey through you my knowledge. A great thank you to wonderful Master Akiva, who brought me out of my dark cave.

MASTER AKIVA: Welcome, comer to the light and to the ranks of leadership. Your presence is needed.

Dear and beloved Ilana, everyone has many parts to his personality, formed over countless incarnations and through the soul's experience in the plane of corporeal life. Traumas, fears, lusts and accomplishments that were singed into memory adopt independent identities and affect the individual's personality. These are personality fragments. I find it proper to emphasize that you do not suffer from a split personality and to legitimize and acclaim the process you have put into effect.

Some fragments drive you and other fragments impel you in different areas. Some are positive. Others hide in the shadows, due to their fears and your lack of acceptance. Maybe your career will be guided by an ambition fragment, built for success, ensuring that you climb the ladder of success and become wealthy and prosperous. In that case your status will rise in your own eyes and others'. Conversely other parts, maybe just a single one, will affect you negatively in the area of relationships, for instance. This damaged fragment will carry patterns of fight or flight and it will try to "protect" you from being part of a couple. This is just one example of the numerous possibilities in your life.

Apply yourself to putting your house in order, calling on all fragments and letting them have their say and then accepting without judgment, with compassion, understanding that they function based on the experiences they have accumulated, which they are seeking to protect and avoid from harm.[28]

Acceptance, accommodation, sending them light and providing them with knowledge of your main purpose, is the best course of action. (This course of action was received from Orin, channelled through Sanaya Roman.)

Understand that you are composed of personality fragments. This will help you not identify too much with any drama or negative emotion that might arise and generate difficulties for you.

Instead of saying, "I am angry," "I am hurt," "I suffer," "I am sad," say, "there is anger in me," there is vulnerability in me," "there is sadness in me,", "there is suffering in me." You are not all these feelings; you are whole and transcendent. These emotions are frequently evidence of an inner battle, linking with the truth of the ego and not with the high truth flowing from the level of the soul.

When you are linked to a high, soul level truth and conduct yourselves accordingly, you realize that you have chosen and created the event. You can then take responsibility for

---

28 See, Lesson 11, above, dealing with defence mechanism.

all that has transpired in your life. You understand that if you feel hurt and anguish, some part of you chose to feel that way because it is in need of healing and compassion. Instead of identifying with your unaware fragments, your "shadow parts," choose to identify with your enlightened, aware parts, which are on the path of compassion and high truth.

When you say I think, which "I" do you mean? Which is the real you? Are all your personality fragments damaged and isolated or is there a higher self, a superior "I," a spark of the Great God?

You are God–created. You are an instrument and a temple. You feel all kinds of emotions and think all manner of thoughts, based on your comprehension of truth at any given moment. How you perceive reality translates into the type and intensity, of your experience.

When you are aware of love and soul–truth, you accept everything with love. This experience is pleasant and you, accordingly, accommodate high frequency, cleansed thoughts and feelings that are gentle and pleasant.

However, if you choose the path of fear for any reason, including lack of awareness of your freedom to choose, it is harder to accommodate your experience. The thoughts and emotions that reach you have a low, compressed, barbed and edgy frequency. They stem directly from your energy system, from the part that prompts you to fight or flight (first Chakra, base, root).

Remember that it is in your power to choose the quality of the experience. What do I mean? Situations will be presented to you on the game board of your life. You will have to contend with challenges and missions. They will offer targets, they will shape your personalities. Their goal is to peel away your lack of awareness and provide you with the soul lessons you need to learn.

You can undergo these trials with hardship and anguish. Or leap over them, to a state indicative that you have understood the lesson and need to learn it no more. You can react either with love or with fear, with the low truth of the body or the high truth of the soul.

You need to understand that you are not the victim of a destiny that lays snares and pitfalls in your way. Remember that you have created and continue to create what is happening to you, out of a **well of creation** containing the beliefs you are clinging to, consciously or unconsciously. These beliefs correspond to your thought processes, the *quality* of your feelings and desires. Fears and imagination–generated scripts also affect your life and create diverse situations.

It is time to clean up this well, with its accumulation of deposits and pollution.

First, the relevant beliefs must be identified. However, not everyone has the ability to see inwardly, clearly and perceptibly. It is easier to point an accusatory finger at others and thus avoid responsibility, to blame parents, society or corrupt leadership. It is easier to play the innocent victim to whom things simply happen.

Well dear, let's roll the stone off the mouth of the well and examine the clear truth below the grimy water: **You are never a victim! Even when you are abused by another person or nation, remember that God has taken us out of the house of slavery and we are free and liberated. Every external subjugation is indicative of inner suppression. Difficult experiences point to the correlative beliefs that attracted them.**

Do not resist the experience. Accept it, then look inwardly with equanimity. Observe the negative belief that attracted the situation to you. Place that belief under the wings of your higher self. Choose to heal it by this intention.

Intention and imagination, together they form the most powerful healing force there is! With the power of intention and imagination you can heal your life on the individual, micro level, as well as the collective, macro level, until the whole world is healed.

It (the well of creation) is a receptacle. You can empty out any contents that are unsuitable, soiled and foul. You can wash it out and pour in whatever you like. When it is clean, its contents will be clear and sweet..

Now we will dispense to you the "vessel meditation," to cleanse your inner space. Breathe deeply. This provides nutrition to your body systems and refreshes their substance. Exhale slowly through your mouth. With every breath, imagine a blue wave of water washing you outside and inside. Now your body assumes the shape of a pitcher or jug.

Notice its shape. See its outer contours in your mind's eye: its outline, texture, colour, size. Is it ornamented? Is it smooth? What is it made of, ceramic, clay, metal, glass, porcelain, wood or some other material? Does it have a neck? Does it have handles? Is it tall? Is it short? Is it wide? Narrow?

Now look inside. How does the inner surface look? Ask to receive an image. Do not think logically about the inner surface. Let your subconscious send you the true condition of your inner state.

What does the vessel contain? Is it empty? Is there liquid in it? if so, what colour is it? Is the liquid thin, thick, maybe greasy? If it is not liquid but solid, what does it hold?

Does the inner surface seem clean? Dirty? If dirty, how does it look exactly? Is it rusted? Is it glazed? Is it covered in scum? Or is it something else? Is it cracked? (Do not let your ego participate in the process, because it will want to show you a beautiful, perfect vessel. Ask that the image will reflect the high truth of your soul.)

Now, if you have found something spoiled, cracked or disharmonious, ask to have it repaired and purified. If you are not sure of the result, if you have the shadow of a doubt as to whether your ego has presented you with the perfect ewer continue nonetheless.

Your vessel is brought to the workshop of the clay–maker, its creator. The table is crystal clear and glowing. Your vessel is placed on it. Light, like the refracted light of brilliant precious stones, is projected on it; it is bathed in a waterfall of clear water suffused with a pink glow, the energy of love and compassion. Imagine that you are inside your vessel and that you are the vessel. Receive the cleansing.

If there are cracks and breaks, if the walls are too thin, if there is any disfiguration, feel how the clay–maker's large, sensitive hands mold you anew, repairing and healing all that is in need of repair and correction.

Declare with utter intent:
"I affirm the complete healing of my vessel now!
"I affirm now that all unnecessary exterior layers shall be removed from my vessel.
"I affirm that the process will take place gradually,

harmoniously, in perfect balance, for my highest good and according to my personal rate of evolution!

"I affirm the expansion of my capacity to contain and accommodate love and the Creator's light!

"I am an instrument of Divine Will, a vessel containing the highest and purest truth!"

Now close your eyes and imagine, feel and acknowledge the process. Have faith and trust the feelings that arise and flood you. Accept and honour these feelings. Ask the angels to help you go through the process harmoniously. It will not begin without your full approval and only when your intention is pure and clean. It will take place at the exact right hour for your evolution, but it will speed up the peeling away of unnecessary layers and hasten your enlightenment. Take all the time you need, rest a little, drink clear water and bless it: "**God has made for me a pure heart and a new spirit is set in me.**" Drink with great intention.

Be at peace. Be in wholeness. Tune into great healing and spiritual growth. I am Master Akiva, delivering my holy teaching and my words for the unity of the Nation of Israel and in order to speed up salvation. Thank you Ilana for the devotion. Let there be a will that Messiah shall come soon and end the suffering of the people of Israel and all nations of the world. Amen and amen!

ILANA: Thank you for the exciting process. Interestingly, I sought information about soul mates and similar matters, yet the discussion turned in this direction. The moral I have learned: We have the ability to ask in one direction, but the answer we might need is in a different place altogether.

MASTER AKIVA: Well dear, I see that you have comprehended the essence of things. When you search for something externally, be it an energy complement, a complementary flame or a soul mate, know to first find it within. What is inside is a reflection of what you find on the outside, accordingly, the process of inner cleansing of the vessel, which is you, was brought forth.

Thanks and all my love and we will go on with our discussion later. Messages will continue to be conveyed through others, who will present you with questions all day. Be tuned in and know how to combine it with my knowledge and what was said here. Hear the question beyond the question; delve into the essence of the question. Have a fruitful and successful day and abundance of love.

ILANA: thank you so much. I hear the Israeli national anthem playing in my head ("As long as in the heart; within, a Jewish soul still yearns. Onward, towards the ends of the east, Our hope is not yet lost, The hope of two thousand years, to be a free people in our land, the land of Zion and Jerusalem.")

MASTER AKIVA: I am asking that you pay attention to the inner meaning of the song, not just the surface layer. The words "a free people" not only means a people that is not enslaved to an external power or an empire, it means one that is liberated in its beliefs, thinking, feeling and acting as a free people. Thank you.

Lesson 16

The Spiritual Senses and Enlargement of Vocabulary
The Frequency of Holiness

Good evening dear Master Akiva. I would like to continue with our discussion, on any subject, direction and path you might choose. Thank you.

MASTER AKIVA: Dear and beloved Ilana. "How sweet is the intoxicating taste of success." "Bitter as wormwood is the taste of failure." This is how you characterize concepts, by way of flavours. Indeed, you animate ideas with all your senses. For instance, "How pleasant is the fragrance of love" or, "how repulsive is the odor of betrayal."

You use images of light, shapes and sounds to express inner impressions and even abstract concepts: "His wisdom enlightens like a candle," "Loud silence," "Food pyramid," and more.

In fact, the terminology by which you explain and define a given experience is taken from concepts generated by your five senses. It is difficult to meaningfully describe the colours of sunset and sunrise to a blind person or a symphony of enchanting sounds to a deaf person. Likewise, the mute cannot express his feelings in words.

However, the deaf and the blind can tune in to the gist of the expression and figure out its meaning according to the extent of their inner senses. You can explain colour to the blind through the use of sound, texture and tactile contact. You can teach a deaf person to enjoy music through reverberation and vibrations, all of which can be felt by the body.

Why am I using these analogies? In order to form an aperture in your understanding of the holy and ascended teaching of the light.

You can only recognise tastes you are familiar with from your own experience. You can only understand music in the scale you are acquainted with. Your understanding equals your comprehension of reality. Through your understanding you accommodate information. Information can only be processed through the tools you actually possess: the vocabulary you have accumulated, your insights, your spiritual awareness and your ability to contain.

Let's use you, Ilana, as an example: A very talented, clever and intelligent student. Nevertheless, you are unable to process mathematical or physical formulae, because that is not your language or your conceptualizations. A person can only channell knowledge he is in tune with and which he comprehends. Of course, it is also the preferable state of affairs, otherwise chaos would ensue. The one who is charged with conveying knowledge must assume responsibility and participate in the internalization, comprehension and accommodation of the information being channelled. For this reason you will not be provided with material you are conceptually unfamiliar with.

You will certainly be presented with material that is new to you, but which you are able to assimilate. Every person is a channell of specific frequency, able to receive particular sources of information. As a rule, no channell is suited to everybody.

Accordingly, great importance attaches to every person who chooses to dedicate his life and submit to becoming a channell that connects between the higher worlds, the sublime kingdoms and the earth plane. It could be a channell with practical and possibly verbal capacity or even one capable of permeating the unconscious and energy bodies of people in its vicinity.

ILANA: Dear and exalted Master Akiva, I understand that today you communicated with me through all the people I have met. Your conversation here reminds me of what someone told me today. He often receives a great deal of knowledge on high frequencies but, according to him, it is difficult for him to translate it to words and transmit to others. I suggested that he learn to write it or to transmit it telepathically. He said that even writing is difficult for him. This ties in with your previous statements. Nevertheless, I wonder why you chose to raise the issue, what is its significance?

MASTER AKIVA: There is great value to language, vocabulary and concepts. There is significance to examples, the use of allegories and metaphors. There is a particular way to discuss things with a farmer, for instance. Such discussion will utilize the terminology of seasons, sowing, harvest time, when to let the fields lay fallow and more. The conversation with a technician will be handled differently. It will involve machinery, maintenance, workshops, cleaning facilities and the like. One manner of speech suits children and a different one suits adults. There are many paths of communication and it is important to find the precise language that suits other individuals.

You may remember that as a child it was difficult for you to communicate. You had a rich level of expression, but could not use it since it would have alienated others and would have made you feel uncomfortable. So you brought it down a notch, to speak in a more folksy fashion.

ILANA: Indeed. I felt strange and different, and that I did not belong to the society around me. I always looked for meaning and did not understand why people settle for material gratification. Life appeared trite. I certainly was an outsider.

MASTER AKIVA: Dear Ilana, your source is the high spheres and you have always possessed very high frequencies which differ from those of the people around you. Even when you did not speak, people around you felt that something else, different, emanated from you. Sometimes they felt threatened by it. People feel each other's energies, even if they are not aware of it. They are attracted to those with similar frequencies to their own. They are repulsed by those whose frequencies are different from or at odds with, theirs. Those with higher frequencies avoid those with low frequencies. Those with a low frequency detest the holders of high frequencies, whom they perceive as haughty and intimidating.

Humans, like animals, can smell different energies, as well as similar ones. There is a psychic olfactory sense that operates in your relations with others. People say, "I smell something suspicious," or, "I smell a strange character," or they "smell good and pleasant energy." Conversely, when they get an unpleasant energetic sensation, they get a very unpleasant feeling in their noses.

Likewise, physical sight has a psychic equivalent known as clairvoyance. Physical hearing has, as its complement, that inner voice you hear – not through physical ears. It could be the sound of a heavenly voice, a prophecy emerging from within and even an actual voice materializing out of your brain. We have already discussed the olfactory sense. As to the sense of taste, you taste not only physical food, but also the spiritual variety. You say that things were said in good taste or, "the taste of Torah is sweet," and the like. The sense of touch, too, has a parallel psychic sense. You feel energies and their texture, some are smooth while others are rough.

To summarize, every physical sense has a psychic counterpart. There is a spiritual head, there are spiritual hands and legs and the same holds true for every bodily system. Why is that? Because, essentially, you are spiritual beings manifested in various planes of existence, one of which is the physical, your flesh–and–blood body.

To be more precise, I define you as spirit in the flesh. This is a superior definition of a human being, one which will enable you to emphasize your spiritual and inner essence. You are a soul encased in a physical body, a spirit materialised in the flesh. Get in touch with your spiritual aspect and accept that there is no contradiction between that aspect and your earthly, physical expression.

When an idea is dressed in words, a window is opened to insights into human nature and the meaning and purpose of life. All you have to do is enrich your inner vocabulary, in order to interpret your life experience from different angles.

For example, when you become familiar with the term "lesson," as an analogy to the process of life, it is much easier to deal with life. You seek meaning. What is the lesson, when will it end, does it attract other lessons to my experience? Once you become familiar with the term "karma," it is easier to translate your life experience.

Enriching your spiritual lexicon will link you with a spiritual perception of your physical experience. It will bring you in touch with your true essence.

ILANA: Dear Master Akiva, I am very tired, let's continue in the morning.

MASTER AKIVA: Excellent, it is all proceeding according to the higher purpose. Tonight, you will have a very meaningful dream relating to our conversation and I ask you to remember it. In the morning we will analyse and interpret it. You are welcome to arise during your sleep and visit with me, for a conversation. Much love and appreciation. I am Master Akiva, the emissary of love and light.

ILANA: Good morning dear and righteous Master Akiva. The time is 6:06 a.m. I am barely awake. It took a while for me to fall asleep and I slept very little. However, my fierce will and determination to proceed with our study have caused me to get up nonetheless. My eyes are still tired. I do not remember the latter part of the dream. In it, I looked at the sky and I was awed by the gigantic paintings of the angels, near which were written all kinds of things. In the dream I knew or at least I think so now, that they were painted by an airplane. They were huge and white, like clouds. I do not remember the rest of the night's activities, which as usual were intensive. Could you, nevertheless, analyse and interpret the memory of this dream? Thank you.

MASTER AKIVA: Good morning dear, Ilana, envoy of the angels spirit. Well, even if you are strongly committed to a particular goal, you must still reach balance among all your bodies. The physical body needs sleep to rest and replenish its reservoir of energy. That's why you had to sleep, though you did not want to. As to your dream, on the surface its meaning appears obvious.

This is what is happening: You are looking at the sky. You see angels and their energy, which is embodied in the words you see. You see messages. They appear gigantic, for they are composed of spiritual elements. They are white, because they are pure and free of any human interests. You know how the painting was created, because you penetrate the higher worlds and seek to understand the secrets of creation. Why did you receive them in the form of painting rather than an actual manifestation? That has to do with barriers and interpretation, allowing the brain to assimilate and accommodate, as opposed to actual manifestation.

Let me tell you something you might not know: you did in fact meet angels and received messages from them. You are constantly in touch with the angelic realm, for your purpose in creation includes observing both worlds, the higher and the lower, the heavenly and the earthly, the spiritual and the material. Your function is that of a go–between. On the one hand you bring messages from the angels, God's envoys who are ceaselessly at his service. On the other hand, you convey human requests, prayers and yearnings. Sometimes you even defend them and request the abrogation of soul agreements, karmic releases and transformations, linking with the way of truth and light, the way of love.

In your case, your purpose is crystal clear and you are fulfiling it efficiently and with great dedication. Everyone has a task and a purpose, both on earth and in heaven. Sometimes, the relation between the two is not obvious. You might ask how do people with very ordinary jobs fulfil their spiritual purpose? What is so transcendent about mundane, uninspiring occupations? The answer is that beneath the surface everything is spiritual and possesses deep meaning.

You have a memory surfacing now, dear, Ilana, that you saw it fit, yesterday, to go to the flower shop and purchase a large bouquet of white flowers, to raise the frequency, spread a pleasant fragrance and bring joy to your heart and soul. You like to frequent this store because the salesman is a great soul, spreading light and love. You see how happy he is to sell flowers that spread joy and happiness, peace and healing, harmony and beauty. The spark in his eyes, his willingness to generously add ornamental$1grasses free of charge, the discounts he gives, all these create good feelings among his clients and uplift their spirits. He performs his job with love; from the heart. He thus fulfils his purpose in life wholly and completely. His spiritual purpose is to spread healing energy by raising the frequencies in his environment. His purpose is related to connecting between the plant kingdom with all its healing qualities and generosity and the human realm. His purpose is wholly spiritual. On the material plane, he sells flowers.

Now, do you remember your favourite gas station attendant? Why do you especially like to have him gas your car, when there are so many other convenient stations and even at that particular station there are so many other attendants? It is not for his good looks. You recognise his great and enlightened soul. He does his work with love and dedication. You feel that he truly enjoys checking oil and water, slipping a good word here and there. This person is carrying out his goal. His spiritual goal is to provide energy and recharge human batteries! On the material–physical plane he does it through filling tanks with gas, thus fueling your ability to traverse distances.

Every corporeal job has a spiritual cause and radiance. When a person performs his assignment, however mundane it may be, with love, dedication and enthusiasm, he fulfils his goal and he is in tune with his spiritual task.

ILANA: And what happens when an individual fulfils his task, which, you say, has a spiritual meaning and yet he is not satisfied, he is even angry, bitter and unmotivated. Does he fulfil his purpose?

MASTER AKIVA: Dear and beloved Ilana, indeed, everything has a deep and hidden spiritual purpose. When a person is at odds with his manifest existence, his job, his duty or his profession, when he is not satisfied with his way of life, then he actually does not accept the yoke of heaven. He is not in touch with the spiritual significance, even if it is in the hidden layer of his being. He does not accomplish his purpose. There is no task so demeaning that it does not contain a lesson at the spiritual layer, at the soul level.

You know what? If you add next to every occupation the word, "spiritual," its meaning will suddenly become clear and change fundamentally. For example: "Spiritual – CPA, spiritual – shoemaker, spiritual – baker, spiritual – teacher, spiritual – captain, spiritual – statesman, spiritual – plant owner and so on.

ILANA: Amazing. I am truly impressed, so simple, yet so deep. Adding "spiritual" next to any occupation, adds meaning that promotes our understanding of existence. Let's say we change the word "school," that children love to hate, to "spiritual school," then all the teachers, who would be now considered "spiritual teachers," would approach their task and the children for whom they are responsible, differently. I sense that the essence of sanctity and value would enhance our daily lives as a result.

MASTER AKIVA (pleased): Indeed dear, you have well understood and internalised what was said.

In order to attain spiritual transcendence and spiritual union with the original way of teaching, the original teaching of "love thy neighbour,[29]" you must commune with the holy frequency. This frequency contains a deep sense of gratitude, love of God and immense respect. It contains purity of intention, thought and action. Imagine, the Holy Temple (in ancient Jerusalem) or the Tablets of the Ten Commandments: Your sense of sanctity is imprinted in your most ancient memories. Every individual can ask to tune into the experience of entering the Temple and even beholding the Ten Commandments.

We will now engage in such a guided memory exercise. Its purpose is to get you in tune with the sanctity of life, the fusion of spirit and matter, the inner unity between supreme vision and the high purpose of souls and its implementation at the material plane, human beings who are spirit in the flesh.

An energy exercise devoted to the communion of spirit with matter. The exercise will be conducted by the Ministering Angels of the Lord.

Dear and beloved, blessed and wondrous, divine sparks in the physical body, each and every one is a great world of wonder, a pure and special world. We address you collectively and individually. We know you. We greatly

---

29 See, Exodus 32:15–19.

esteem and respect you. We see the brilliant purpose and meaning of your life.

We cherish and sanctify the holiness of life, the holiness of those who sustain life's frequency in their physical body and integrate the infinity of the spirit with the material dimension. We have come especially for you. We dedicate to you our time, we sanctify your time. There is neither time nor space and therefore there is no barrier between us. The divine curtain is removed, the screens rise and our energy reaches you directly.

Breathe deeply... Make room in your body, the sanctified temple of your physical and your spiritual heart, the centre of your soul, which operates the divine spark of life. Keep breathing through the nose, which breathes angelic energy of the holy white frequency. Convey the breath to every cell and system of your physical body. To all your centres of energy, those you are or are not familiar with. The breath contains God's light, the sanctity of life. It permeates you... contain it... exhale gently through the mouth, your centre of expression and communication.

Do that several times, until you feel serenity and a pleasant sensation. You might feel dizziness. Now stabilize your breath: inhale and exhale in a way that is natural for you. Bring into your awareness the following idea: "**With every breath I bring into myself the holiness of life.**" Say this three times, inhaling and exhaling each time.

Wait a bit at the end of the affirmations.

Now say to yourself: "**I contain the holiness of life.**" Repeat this three times. At the end of each affirmation take a deep breath of the holy white light that enters you.

It is calm within you. Holiness is pervading your heart, your eyes. Holiness, purity and compassion permeates every cell of your body. It is raising the frequency of all your bodies: the physical, the emotional, the intellectual, the spiritual. It enters your entire being. The holiness enters your brain, your subconscious reservoirs, the storeroom of memory and experience, your projector of creation. Holiness suffuses your thoughts and your feelings. Holiness is radiated through the palms of your hands and the soles of your feet. It is expressed through your actions. You are an entity that contains greater holiness, more and more and more.

Acknowledge your self–value. honour yourself. Relate to the holiness of spirit within your body, the holiness of life. Revere the holiness that is expressed in all of creation. Know and remember that all of creation contains this holiness, including animals, plants, rocks and crystals. You have the ability to imbue your daily life with holiness, imparting deeper value and meaning to your experience of life, whatever it may be.

Blessed be in your eternal being.

"Holy, holy, holy, is the Lord of Hosts and we are his angels," sings the choir of the Seraphim and the Ministering Angels of the Lord blow the horns of Heaven which penetrate the illusory projections that separate spirit and matter.

MASTER AKIVA: Holiness confers an added quality to your life. Material and self–indulgent goals slowly dissolve. New, more enlightened objectives replace them. Every minute becomes imbued with meaning.

Opening up to the spirituality within is the reason for your existence. To inhale holiness is, in essence, to be in a perpetual union between spirit and flesh, material and divine, the lower self of the body and the higher self of the soul. It expands consciousness, raises awareness and gives you to understand that you were created by God. It is to recognise who you are and to retain holiness in your thoughts, feelings and actions. It causes you to honour, accept and cherish yourself and the embodiment of the spirit in you, the soul in your body. Thus you will honour and cherish all others, your fellow–travellers. Then the following will be fulfiled:

"And thou salt love the Lord thy God with all thin heart, with all thy soul and with all thy might" and "thou shalt meditate thereon day and night."[30] "Thou salt love thy neighbour as thyself."[31]

---

30 See, Deuteronomy 6:5 and Joshua 1:8, respectively.
31 See, Leviticus 19:18.

Acceptance of every human being will cause the consciousness of peace to infuse the material plane of planet Earth. Awareness of holiness will become part of the world of free choice.

Consider today as a festive day, the day of giving the Torah at Mount Sinai. You are invited to participate. Wear white or any other festive clothing that has a high frequency and gives you a good and pleasant feeling. Light a candle in your home. Buy flowers for your house or clean and decorate it. Know, when you clean it physically you also clean it spiritually and energetically. Ask to raise the frequency of your home. Ask to raise the frequency of your body. Consider it your last day on Earth, a day in which you celebrate your life experience. honour the air you are breathing. honour the body that contains your soul and supports it during your life journey. Listen to music that lifts your spirit and makes you happy, excites you or makes you feel calm.

Know that you are in a frequency of holiness and that you commune with angels of the Most High. This knowledge will alter the way you conduct yourself in your relations with others.

At the end of the day be grateful for the gift of holy life, for the holy frequency, for today's present and its new insights. Insights about yourselves, your purpose on earth, your ties with other people and the effect you have on each other.

Ask to dream holiness at night.

Repeat this experience as often as you like. Remember there is no need to separate between that which is holy and the mundane, instead, allow the holy to permeate the unholy.

Of course, I am not suggesting a role reversal between the profound and the profane. I am saying that **it is time for holiness to enter your life and your perception.**

Here I Am, Master Akiva, the bearer of the truth teaching of, "Love thy neighbour as thyself" speaking to you and suffusing these words with my spirit, my inspiration, my love and my frequencies.

Blessed be in your eternal being and thank you Ilana, dear and holy messenger, most beloved, who apply your body and your life to the knowledge of light and holiness.

Lesson 17

Communication
Mutual Influence
The Language of the Spirit

ILANA: Dear and beloved guides, good morning; a wonderful morning to you dear Master Akiva. I am asking to proceed with our discussion.

MASTER AKIVA: Good morning to you, dear and beloved Ilana. Please stop worrying as to whether you got up too late and about not arriving on time for our study. Despite your great motivation, you have to consider your physical body's needs. Besides, to wake up before six a.m., on a holiday, would be considered too early by most of the population (smile).

Fears, conscience pangs and guilt feelings are sure to bring you down. Therefore, you must be very forgiving and compassionate, healing with light and love. Fear leads you into a trap, the path of fear, as you may recall. Only through forgiveness and compassion can you return to the "path of love."

I would like to dedicate our conversation to the matter of

mutual effect between personal and national creation.

Dear human beings, you are involved in the process of creation, which is joined with all elements upon the planet known as Earth. You are one of many parts, an organ or maybe even just a single cell in the organic system of a large and highly complex body.

Due to the isolation programme embedded in you, you fail to understand the entire picture: How you are part of Earth. How Earth is part of you and you are part of her. You do not see the relationship between life and the air you breathe and the plant kingdom, which provides oxygen. You fail to notice what is so obvious to us here in the heavens, that all is one, that all is connected with all else. The common denominator is:

Life!

You separate the various kingdoms: Human (which you consider the main and most important), fauna, flora and inanimate. Thus, you separate yourselves even in your thinking and learning from planet Earth. If you were wise enough to change your division, even by one word, your ability to observe and be aware of your environment would profit greatly.

What do I mean? All of it is life: **All that is upon, below and above, in earth's atmosphere is either alive or is**

life. Mankind is but one family in the amalgam that is life. Animals are no different than human, except in their degree of awareness and willingness to receive the Creator's light. There are simpler and more complex forms, but it all comes under a single, common definition: **Life.**

As I have explained and repeatedly emphasised, it is important to be precise in your terminology. If, for example, you understood that plants are an intelligent life form, you would relate differently to cutting down and destroying forests. The fact that you do not speak the language of animals, which is heard on the higher and subtler planes, does not prove that they are mute and lack intelligence. That is your interpretation, based on the experience of your five senses, which is narrow and judgmental.

A universal language exists beyond definitions of good and evil. This is the language of life. It is transmitted through the energy sensing conduits, through telepathy, in subconscious pathways of which you are not aware. This language does not have words. It cannot be written down. Its form of communication is direct with the source of all life. The way to understand and get in tune with it, as King Solomon learned, is by opening a new channell of awareness. This channell includes the expansion of insight into what life is. It encompasses knowing that God is the creator of the world and has permeated creation with His spirit; that there is much more that is common to all creation than that which differentiates it. This knowing includes the realization that "man looketh on the outward appearance, but the Lord looketh on the heart.[32]" God explained it to the prophet Samuel when he commanded him to go to Jesse's abode in Bethlehem and crown one of his sons king. He did not disclose to the prophet the name of the elected son or gave him his description. That was why Samuel initially erred in his selection.

The inner senses penetrate the illusion screens of outward appearance, which mask the essence of truth and the spirit of things. This inner dimension is operated from the divine spark which is within it. Sometimes the spark is reflected in people's eyes. At times, however, the spark is buried under many layers, of body–personality (ego).

It is a wondrous language. It is holy and blessed. The language is a bridge, a channell of communication. It is easy for those who speak it to communicate with one another. Here, too, there are differences in the quality of the language and the energy level, but its speakers can convey their clear wishes and even express their hidden thoughts and feelings.

In order to communicate with members of another nation you have to learn a new language. You can learn any language by devoting to it desire and passion. That is one kind of communication, **verbal communication**. Since you have

---

32   1 Samuel 16:7

gotten so used to it, you have, for the most part, forgotten that there are alternative channells of communication, some obscure and not comprehensible (to you).

Another important channell is **emotional communication**. This communication is beyond the verbal form and usually parallel to it. It is not necessarily similar. You may convey one message verbally, while emotionally you are transmitting an altogether different, even contrary, message. You have a need to please, to excuse, to deceive, to hold on to your inner truth.

There is a less known form of communication, **body language**. Through involuntary motions you broadcast the truth reflected in your inner conception. Listeners are certainly affected by these, apparently covert, communications channells. You can sense when a person is broadcasting trustworthiness and you trust his words. Alternatively, you may feel inner discomfort and know that he is lying.

Some people are skilled in the use of the language and have the ability to manipulate their environment. Mostly, you would notice the use of this subtle language when politicians are making speeches and are trying to convince you.

Since you are composed of several bodies, each body has its own unique language.

The physical body uses body language, in the form of movements and motions.

The emotional body uses the language of feelings, conveyed through energy.

The mental body uses language expressed verbally, in written form or by the spoken word.

These are the languages you know and speak, some better than others.

Since you have additional bodies, it stands to reason that you should become familiar with their languages. We will point out here your **energetic body**. Its method of communication is purely energetic. It is neither verbal nor emotional, though it has an effect on the emotions. Humans have a frequency, which is energy. This energy is in constant communication with its environment. People feel energies that differ from their own. They feel energies of anger, sadness, despair, as well as joy and love. People are intuitively attracted to pleasant energy and reject its unpleasant counterpart.

The spiritual body is the closest aspect of your spiritual essence. It contains the most integrated pools of knowledge and assemblies of communication with the Creator of the universe. It, too, has an important language. This language unites all of life's kingdoms. This is **the language of spirit**.

It is neither verbal nor emotional. It is not a language of motion nor is it an energetic form of communication. It is above all the others (in frequency). Its spirit suffuses all other languages. It is the language that links and unites all of creation. It is a universal language spoken by all who possess intelligent awareness. It does not distinguish between plant life, inanimate objects, fauna or countries.

ILANA: I breathe to accommodate the knowledge, so that it does not just verbally pass me by. This breathing is an excellent way to receive information beyond its word level. It is a way to connect the verbal with the emotional and the energetic. I wish to know how to speak the language of the spirit. Could it be taught as a second foreign language in schools? (Smiling, but mixed with amused seriousness.)

MASTER AKIVA: (Smiling, pleased.) And why shouldn't it be? In fact, it is the first language used to communicate while the fetus is still in its mother's womb. The language of life is the most extensively used communication channel. You can accommodate it and even speak it as fluently as if it were your mother tongue. Actually, you may call it your father's tongue, if we relate to God through His male aspect, as the Creator of the world. There are individuals whose spiritual language channell operates involuntarily and is open continuously. These people are exceedingly sensitive, gentle and very loving.

When you understand, experience and feel the unity that is

present in all of creation, you understand and know that you are within the unity, present in the spirit residing in your body. Then, there is no place for the separation that creates the path of fear. The path of love becomes your natural course. The universe is a safe and protected environment, abundant with goodness and filled with love for you. You naturally fulfil your role in creation, to tend the Garden of Eden that God had created before He created Adam and Eve.

ILANA: It is both wonderful and amazing in my eyes how everything really connects with "Love thy neighbour as thyself." Simply amazing. All of life is love. But forgive me for I have interrupted. I do however want to hone in my inquiry: What is the way to know the language of the universe, the language of spirit? I want to be able to use it on the level of father's tongue. (A smile.)

MASTER AKIVA: Dear Ilana, you already speak it fluently. You should improve and polish your speech, your knowledge of common idioms in the language and focus on listening. Naturally, understanding and knowledge of the language can only be acquired when you are aware, when your willpower is activated and implemented, in order to reach it, teach and enhance it.

When you have set, as a goal, the learning of a language, when you dedicate yourself to the goal and devote of your time to it in order to achieve proficiency, your goal will be attained. It depends on your faith in yourself and an innate talent for language acquisition. However, consider this, if there were a mysterious language containing knowledge and data regarding the codes and riddles of creation, wouldn't you passionately desire to know it? It is true in this case as well. It depends on how much you truly want to know it.

However, let's say that there is in fact such a language, but you are unaware of its existence; the unknown is hidden from you, concealed. You would not be able to accommodate it, simply out of a will to do so. When you lack knowledge of the existence of a given thing, it is not in your power to obtain it. Such is the language of the spirit.

That is exactly why I tell you to be precise with your definitions. Study! Expand your vocabulary! Acquire education, in every area and as much as possible. Learn, learn, learn! Do not ever stop learning. Learning is not just a means to gain new facts. It is a way of expanding, it is the experience of life itself, which includes the lessons needed for your evolution.

The first step toward learning the universal language of spirit, the common language of the Creator and all of His creation, is simple: Be aware of the existence of the language. Then, express a reality–forming intention:

"I affirm that I will know the language of spirit!

"I affirm that I will understand the language of spirit."

The next declaration, for which you will open your inner channnell, is: "I am in touch with the intelligence of the consciousness of life and the language of spirit."

Breathe deeply after each affirmation. Repeat it three times. After every one, breathe in, deeply, the energy of the affirmation, inhaling it, halting a bit as you assimilate the energy, then exhale, through the mouth, gently but firmly, thus you activate the energy in all bodies simultaneously.

As I have made clear, it is not enough just to ask for something. You must connect all bodies to the experience. Through the spiritual body, you add faith. Through the emotional body, you experience it. Through the mental body the willpower of intention will be added. Through the physical body, which participates by breathing, action and manifestation will be included. Now, the process begins to assume a corporeal reality. All you have to do is express an intention and events begin to unfold around you.

In order to learn the language of spirit, you have to develop awareness of your inner dimension, the entire emotional and thought content. You must open the channnell to receive your external environment. You must develop energetic sensing ability, open the heart's core and learn to feel compassion and love. You have to learn how to be attentive, to listen to the truth emanating from all your bodies, your highest and most genuine truth. Such attentiveness should expand to encompass all that surrounds you, other people and their real needs and true desires, which may even be hidden from their own perception.

This attentiveness should include the intelligent animals, the intelligent plants, the stones and rocks, the crystals. The song of grass will be heard in your hearts in its entirety and it will please you like a heavenly angels' harp. Listen to the earth and sky, to the land, to the seasons. Listen to the smallest pebbles, the beetles and the tiniest arthropods. Listen to your bodies; listen to mother earth's body, whence you were formed from the elements: fire, air, water and earth. Cherish the unity of creation; understand the unity of the universe. Thus, you will accommodate the meaning of **Love thy neighbour as thyself.**

Everything is your neighbour, materialised in myriad forms. Creation is you; you are part of it, inseparable. Animals, plants, rocks and people. **Others** should become **brothers**! "Other" is a word that denotes separateness. Brother is a word that denotes unity.

"And the whole earth was of one language and of one speech." (Genesis 11:1.)

By "the whole earth" I mean that the language of the spirit shall unite all of creation and all the life kingdoms will be in harmony, peace and unity with one another. That is the deep meaning of the verse in Genesis 11:1. Eleven is the number that unites heaven and earth. One is the number of unity – all is one.

I would like to end this chapter with a verse that you might understand at another level and with a deeper meaning: "Hear, O Israel, the Lord our God is one Lord." (Deuteronomy 6:4.)

I am Master Akiva, who brings the message of unity to the whole of Israel and the nations of the world, to all of creation; installer of the way of the bright light of the truth that is love.

ILANA: Thank you. I am thrilled and feel a fire burning in me. Interesting that yesterday I corresponded with a woman who had written me a very agitated e-mail, where she told me that her husband, who has brain cancer, has lost his power of speech and is not able to express himself in writing, either. I advised her to develop a telepathic ability. Then, I was filled with compassion and much understanding and advised her to accept. Not to resist, not to be afraid; to settle down and to settle him down. To understand that there are no coincidences and what is needed the most for him now, for recovery and strength, is tranquility. I explained to her how in a conversation, especially, idle conversation, we very often become empty and tired energetically, mentally and emotionally as well. The body has its own intelligence, directing its healing and collecting energy and we may need a time for gathering ourselves inwardly, disengaging, tuning into our inner realm. I have advised her to accept and to say, with full intention: "Thy will be done." She is doing her best (which is a wondrous and even spiritual ability) for him. There is a time for everything. A time to act and a time to rest, a time to speak and a time to be quiet, a time to communicate outwardly and a time to tune in inwardly.

It is astonishing how things happen. Yesterday, I met a man (whom I have mentioned in our fascinating conversation yesterday) at the supermarket, ostensibly, by sheer coincidence. Of course there is no such thing as coincidence. I told him about the message that came yesterday and he told me how naturally he functions exactly in that fashion in the world. The world is astonishing and everything is connected with everything else. Thank you, wonderful Master Akiva, the wisest of all people and most beloved, for the privilege of communicating with you.

MASTER AKIVA: Thank you, beloved Ilana, God's envoy, a channell for the angels, a mouthpiece of the truth of "Love thy neighbour as thyself." Now you comprehend your importance in creation. Now you can look back at your life, from the perspective of a soul who knows its purpose and see all the pieces coming together in a single perfect tapestry. There is no error, there is no coincidence, all is exactly as it should be. Be blessed, you and your household forever and ever. Blessed be your day, it is a festival day for you, for the whole nation of Israel, for all of creation, which is greatly anticipating the reunion of intelligent consciousness.

Look around you. All of you who are aware of the message, look around you, look directly at your inner being, expand and enhance the direct communication that exists with the world of spirit. Live the language of spirit and teach it to your children.

May there be a will and the messiah will come soon, a messiah who is the intelligent awareness common to all creation. Amen and amen.

"Holy, holy, holy, the Lord and His host and we are his angels," blow the host of seraphim in the heavenly trumpets that are designed to awaken the consciousness of unity of all who have been created.

ILANA: After reading the material, which still makes me feel a burning fire in me, I suddenly saw in the word "life" – a living sea. I saw the word God as a divine sea; I saw all of creation as a great sea of life and God's presence in it. It awakens in me a real wonderment and great gratitude. I also feel the effect of the lesson seeping in and getting absorbed in all of my consciousness, expanding and deepening it greatly. Thank you and much love.

MASTER AKIVA: Indeed, that is the effect of the knowledge as it is absorbed and seeping upon all planes and which is altering what has been before. Ask for its expansion and full assimilation and accommodation. Thank you. Here I am, Master Akiva who is proceeding with his study.

Lesson 18

The Sanctity of Words, "Crime and Punishment," Identity

ILANA: Good morning dear and beloved guides; a wonderful morning to you dear and beloved Master Akiva. I am asking to proceed with our discussion. Thank you.

MASTER AKIVA: Good morning to you, dear and beloved Ilana. It is high time for our daily labor, the sacred work. "Time is short and work aplenty." Therefore, you gladly accepted an early wake up you set yourself.

ILANA: I have set up the alarm clock for 05:30 a.m. I have found it to be a convenient hour for our daily study. I was in the middle of a dream which I do not remember, when the alarm clock went off. I woke up immediately, feeling very happy and said: "Beautiful." It was an especially fast wakeup and I got up quickly, filled with enthusiasm and gratitude. I prepared to contain the holiness by intention and readiness, on the one hand and the breathing that fills one up, on the other. I prepared herbal tea (sage and verbena) and I am very excited to start our lesson. What shall we discuss today?

MASTER AKIVA: this is the 18th consecutive day of our joint

sacred work. Its purpose is to raise public consciousness, expand cosmic–human awareness and plant light idea seeds of world peace, through, "**Love thy neighbour as thyself.**" **As you and our beloved and honoured readers can see, these five words contain the comprehension of human nature and the essence of life.**

As a matter of fact, it can even be found in a single word. For example, think of one such word that is meaningful for you: **God.** You cannot read this word without being flooded with feelings and associations: faith, understanding creation, truth, divine decrees and more. If you take this word into your daily meditation, say it repeatedly and ponder it, a host of ideas and concepts will arise and influence you.

I repeat: words and ideas are very important. If you could observe their energy, sense their fragrance, their flavour, their light and their colours, you would be more selective when choosing your words.

I would like to relate to news headlines. Lacking deep comprehension of the innate significance of words, while having a clear knowledge of their aim, which is to captivate mass attention, they sow the ideas of fear, pain and war, the harshest karma of the planet in your nation and your world. Headlines "scream" to get attention and to shake up your emotions.

In scripture, by contrast, words are chosen with focused

intent, with judicious insight into the power of words in creation, they aim to connect you with the divine spark that forms your essence.

People do not block words said in anger. They resort to curses, threats and verbal abuse. They even use similar expressions about themselves. You are your own worst enemy. That is why it has been said, "Life and death are in the power of the tongue." (Proverbs, 18:21.)

Words have magical power, With their energy, the whole universe was created. Think of sorcerers in books and movies. How do they make magic happen? By uttering magical incantations. Think of yourselves as sorcerers. You are usually unaware when you make negative affirmations about yourself, you might cast a curse upon yourself within the context of a particular statement. You do the same thing when you curse others.

I want you to be aware of the extent of your influence. Also and this is of crucial importance, when you utter a particular word or idea, you assimilate it into the vessel that you are, which is linked with all of creation. Thus, when you speak in the language of love and compassion, you accommodate its energy and essence, thus absorbing it into your aural body, activating in you identical energy of compassion and love, purity and godliness. The same goes for thoughts, which are the silent expression of words and ideas. Words and thoughts have the same effect on you.

When you use words as a weapon, it indicates that you are holding great fear energy. It fills up the clear channell with soot that obscures your vision and fogs up your sense of judgment. This soot burdens breathing and creates emotional and physical illnesses. By clear channell we mean all your energy centres, when they are untainted so that energy flows through them unobstructed. Soot symbolizes the negative thinking of fear energy. It is generated when you use words to hurt, to insult, to speak ill of somebody, to gossip or to criticize someone, including yourself. Your operation and control centres, known as chakras, are blocked as a result and they cease to operate. It is like pouring sugar into your fuel tank, introducing a substance that is incompatible with a machine that needs a clean, pure component to continue running. Well, you, too, are a well-oiled machine that is activated by natural life energy, your intrinsic fuel, whose components are thoughts wrapped in emotions.

We have already discussed the idea of mutual influence. Each one of you is an energy carrier. And each one of you is an energy receiver, according to your inherent capacity.

ILANA: Dear Master Akiva, I understand and accept the idea in general, but the following question arises: If day in and day out I am a person who has harmonious thoughts and emotions, filled with love and light, why would I contain the negative elements of others? I am referring to the evil eye, curses, spells and so on. I understand how those who constantly carry fears and anger would attract such energy (like attracts like – a cosmic law), but what about those who are dissimilar?

MASTER AKIVA: Dear and beloved, my talented student, the answer lies within your question. No one is clean of negative thoughts, guilt or fear. They float up from past memories and experiences and they might be stirred up as a result of identifying with individuals who carry such feelings and talk about them. It could be the result of accidentally reading a headline on the front page of a newspaper. The fear energy immediately adheres to you.

The negative energy you have absorbed will stay with you for a while. The cleaner you are within, the less your balance will be affected by external negative energies emanating from those around you or those far away.

ILANA: I wanted to ask you what I can do in defence, but now I understand that the solution is simply to purify myself within, again and again; to get rid of fears and apprehensions, let go of anger, to forgive both my fellow human beings and myself and ask forgiveness, be it from another person, or, at a different level, another nation. I understand that only pure love of truth, unconditional love freely given, can serve as an effective defence. Is there any other way to avoid susceptibility to disasters incurred by negative energies? What happens when people intentionally curse, not to mention those who place a spell on others?

Are they punished in any way or are they free to do so due to freedom of choice?

MASTER AKIVA: Good and well. We have arrived at the important subject of reward and punishment and the question of the righteous man who suffers while the evil man enjoys blessings.

Out of the dual concept of this corporeal dimension, the Sphere of Kingdom (*sephirath malchuth*), you can observe both sides of the coin. You see day and night, complementary opposites that form a whole. You see black and white as opposites, found in the symbol of yin and yang, interwoven and forming a balance between the male and female aspects. You also see good and evil as opposites. Notice that these terms are subject to numerous interpretations, most of them subjective. They characterize a particular frame of mind, reflecting widely accepted opinions in a given time, in a given culture or region. Different people have different, even contrary opinions. Each side believes it is right and just, that it is the good side, while its opponent is, no doubt, evil. Every enemy is automatically endowed with negative characteristics.

The dynamics that motivate your thinking lie in the tension between your urge to act justly and your inclination to bestow rewards. You might be surprised to know that it is also true for the way you relate to yourself. When people feel unworthy because they have erred they punish themselves.

Guilt feelings light up a fire deep inside. A person may, consequently, develop physical and psychological ailments and incur ill–luck in all aspects of life. This is an outcome of the ancient notion of reward and punishment. Punishment is expected, especially when one has trespassed a given norm of conduct. Reward and punishment are effective tools of *human* management.

Already in kindergarten it is used freely. "Were you a good kid? Have a piece of candy." "Were you a bad boy? Go stand in the corner. You may not participate in the class activity!" Sounds familiar? It is how employers relate to their employees, commanders their soldiers, partners in a relationship to one another, parents to their children. As a result, you ascribe these human qualities even to God, the exalted and sublime.

Good and evil are subject to individual interpretation. For example: A small child passionately wants some candy. He turns to his mother, who is busy preparing lunch for the family. She refuses, saying "Soon we'll eat lunch." The mother denies his request, his wish because for she sees the long term consequences and she is concerned with the greater benefit of her child. In her eyes, it is bad to eat sweets before a healthy and nutritious meal. She does not want her child to lose his appetite just before the meal. She also considers the candy not too healthy.

No doubt you would agree with her, right?

Now, what is the truth in the child's eyes? Does he understand her correctly? He thinks it would be excellent to eat candy right now. Who needs lunch, anyhow? And it is too bad that his mom is refusing to give in.

The notions of good and evil are perceived in distinctly different ways here. I do not want you to judge the child as having no understanding or that you should identify with the mother. This is just an illustration of reality perception in relation to "evil versus good."

Look at the regional map of the Middle East and observe the existential issue you Israelis have with the Palestinians, with the lands of Ishmael, the Arab nations. In your eyes, you are the good guys. But the other side regard themselves as the good guys and you are the evil ones, who robbed them of their land. Who is right? Everybody is right. Every side interprets the truth according to its perception and according to its interests.

People tend to think that it is God who punishes and rewards them. Actually, it is you who harshly judge and, accordingly, punish yourselves. You also are the ones who feel deserving due to your good deeds, charity and success and you reward yourselves, accordingly. God allows this. God accommodates all of creation and does not get involved in trifles.

We, your guides, see your overall objectives from a high

perspective. We see the probabilities and potential possibilities of your conduct. We can warn and prevent unnecessary disasters. We can also encourage you to take certain actions, in order to fulfil your potential. Usually, we do not get involved with decisions and personal choices. We do, however, get involved when the destinies of nations hang in the balance.

We do not necessarily see war as a manifestation of evil. At times it is necessary, in order to revolutionize the existing order, to uproot rotten foundations from the system, from the perceptions and beliefs of a nation. Sometimes, only the sword brings you to choose peace and co-existence. Accordingly, if a battlefield is necessary in order to draw you near the Creator, to enhance your insights about overall peace in your region, so be it. We will not judge the war as bad but regard it a necessary evil that promotes goodness and peace.

There is more than one way to reach a goal and here your freedom of choice comes into play. You can arrive at a comprehensive peace that would allow abundance and prosperity for both nations, Hebrew and Arab – the descendants of Abraham – in various ways. These can be easy and pleasant or, difficult and painful.

There are those who learn easily, while others require much suffering and hardship in order to develop insight. A skilled artist can sculpt stone quickly, but the flow of water takes eons to make an impression on embedded rock.

You perceive death as a bad thing, whereas in our regions it is a natural process of transformation for the soul, which emerges from the bonds of the flesh in a manner akin to the cocoon of a butterfly. It returns to the World of Truth.

Since death is not bad, is it therefore not good, either. It is simply an integral aspect of life. There is no need to fear it. True, the sanctity of life commands you to hold on to it till your last breath (which is the reason why it is worth your while to learn the way of peace and make war unnecessary). If you would respect yourselves and your fellow humans equally you would understand that justice is global, not just locally yours. You would tend to forgive, forego, allow, enable, and communicate. You would embark on the easy road to peace, which is inherent in the verse, "Love thy neighbour as thyself." Indeed, your enemy is your neighbour; likewise, your lover is your neighbour.

ILANA: my ability to absorb… I do not think there is anything new here for me and I am hungry for new knowledge. However, I think that for many recipients there is at least added clarity here. Dear and beloved Master Akiva, could you add new aspects of reward and punishment, peace and war?

MASTER AKIVA: People hold many incredibly contradictory ideas. People want peace, but hold on to ideas such as, "there is no choice but war." People desire to be rich but are attached to beliefs of want, hardship and debt accumulation. You must examine yourself and remove the ideas, beliefs, emotions and thoughts, which are in opposition to your wishes. You must understand, **the inner content shapes the outer effect.**

This tie in with what I explained previously, about a creation that is woven in two different and opposing courses. Together, they disable your desires and reinforce what exists, including dominant elements of undesirable fear.

I say again, you must choose your channellls of information, be they newspapers, books, television, internet or people. Meticulously choose your thoughts. Scrupulously sift out all the negative emotional deposits, which clog up the filters in your well–oiled body machine. Deposits that cause energy blockages exist in your physical, emotional, mental, even spiritual bodies.

The most appropriate request would be the use of prayer, which is a cluster of words carefully chosen, as if they were medicinal herbs. Such prayer should be done with focused intent. You are invited to breathe deeply and say: "Cast me not away from Thy presence and take not Thy Holy Spirit from me." (Psalms 51:11.) Repeat the process three times. Imagine a waterfall of copious white light that washes over you. The light enters your body and cleanses it of all the negative energy deposits and obstructions that have accumulated in you, whether in this life or previous and parallel incarnations.

Let the white light, with its bright crystal frequency, purify your inner realm. The light will strip away the layers covering the inner diamond at the core of your being. This is the creation diamond that contains the divine spark and your true identity, which you have forgotten. Express gratitude for the process. Repeat this exercise as often as needed. It will cleanse you and purify your inner content. It will heal your thoughts, beliefs and feelings.

I Am Master Akiva, the herald of the message of unity for the people of Israel and the nations of the world and of "love thy neighbour as thyself."

ILANA: Thank you dear and beloved Master Akiva. I am overcome with fatigue and I must end the communication. Did the entire message come through? Is there something we did not discuss yet in this particular lesson?

MASTER AKIVA: Our lesson for today is complete. Dear Ilana, learn how to measure things not by quantity, instead, measure content by its quality. There is no need to enlarge or shorten a given lesson, for time is of no consequence. If we were able to transmit an idea, we are satisfied. Now we ask you and our dear readers to absorb the material and accommodate it. Consciousness will then do its thing, the seeds will be planted and, at the right moment they will germinate and put down roots, until they grow into trees for the glory of creation, till they are akin to the Tree of Life itself.

Thank you for your attention; now it is time for you to assimilate the material.

Here I Am, Master Akiva, who passes my words to you from the sanctity of the words that were carefully chosen and which contain creation's holy energy. Thanks and all my love. Thank you dear and beloved Ilana, who has dedicated the morning of this Saturday for our joint holy work for the good of unity, for the well-being of the nation of Israel and all of creation, in accord with the will of the exalted and lofty God.

ILANA: thank you dear and wonderful Master Akiva. I am smiling because I remember how we started the conversation, with your idea that a word is a whole world and the five words, "Love thy neighbour as thyself," can be an entire universe.

MASTER AKIVA: And so it is. Our lesson for today is complete, but its effect will last forever and ever.

* * *

ILANA: (I slept a few hours and returned around noon.) Dear and wonderful Master Akiva, I have just received a call from a friend's father, asking me to send him protective energies. Before that I dreamed dreams. At the end of each one I had a karmic and spiritual explanation. It was as if I was being provided with an experience, followed by its moral and the applicable perspective, from up high.

I remember that in one dream I had a little girl or maybe she was someone else's and I was somehow involved with the story. Suddenly, she disappeared. I thought I should have watched her more vigilantly, not taking my eyes off her. A search was conducted in the Indian subcontinent. It involved a voyage on a ship. Because it was a voyage, I looked for a suitable hat to wear. At the store I went to where there were hats in many strange shapes. I found a large–brim hat made of straw and cloth that covered as much of my face as possible. The saleslady did not want me to buy it, because it was worn by the low caste in India. I agreed not to wear it.

On the ship, I sat next to a young, handsome man who was a physician. Then he sat close to another woman who I knew, who was my friend or actually the friend of the little girl's mother. I now remember that I was, in parallel, two different characters. (Maybe this is an interpretation many hours later, after my brain had time to filter the dream). Anyhow, I perceived the man and then the woman as a manifestation of infidelity. I felt there was some sort of a romantic connection between the man and myself.

Then I saw the events a few years later, as an observer. I saw a ship carrying a physician, whom I now knew had kidnapped the baby girl. He was leading a group of young ones, one of whom was the little girl, who by now has grown into an adolescent. I saw her from the back. She was thin and shapely, her hair blond, straight and flowing. I knew she was believed to be the doctor's daughter. I knew this was the karma of all the characters involved and that is how it should be. Later I was provided with an explanation of the drama: This story came to teach me a perspective beyond the duality of good and evil. The fact that I wanted to wear a large hat was symbolic of judgment and of a role being enacted. The advice I received, to be without a hat, placed me in my truthfulness and kept me honest, with no place to hide, in a neutral place without judgment.

I will be glad to hear your interpretation. Before that, I would like to say that I just had a phone call from a woman who seems to be in distress. She told me that her nine year old son has speech difficulties. Usually I do not answer the phone on Saturday, unless I know it is from family members or a close friend, but since my father had sent me an SMS, I picked up the phone, thinking it was him. At first I wanted to ask her to call the following day, but I thought about your words that it is not work I do, but the holy task of saving souls. So even though I needed to rest and recharge my batteries and Saturday is a holy day, I agreed to see her.

Needless to say, it is not for material recompense or even spiritual reward, but because I felt compassion coupled with the ability to accommodate her.

What do you think? I will be glad to have your answer and to continue our conversation. Thank you.

MASTER AKIVA: Dear and beloved Ilana. The shivers that just went through your shoulders and the sensation of heat in your heart, relate to the excitement with which I receive your words. The heart's intention is what counts. You have transcended your personality, your beliefs and your personal needs, to commune with God. There are many ways to reach the mountaintop. Yours is the way of enlightenment.

The Sabbath is sanctified for inner work. However, in our last conversation it was said that one ought to sanctify all days, day and night, waking hours and sleep. Indeed, you are engaged in holy work. It relates to salvation and healing of souls, to altering and reshaping the cosmic collective consciousness. It is the path of the great compassion of "Love thy neighbour as thyself."

The case in question was sent to you as a test and a lesson. You did well! Your inner motive was purely to assist the woman and her son. Flexibility is the secret to listening, to intuition, to the guidance of the soul. It is interesting that the woman told you that her problem is lack of resolve.

She did not come to reflect you to yourself, not at all. To the contrary, this came to show you how attentive you are to your intuition and emotions. The brain is an excellent instrument for situational analysis and interpretation, for logic and intelligence, however, the mind is capable of erecting barriers that are too rigid.

As to the dream, it came to show you that beyond the pain of betrayal, the loss of the baby girl, the guilt, fears and all the impulses created by the drama, there is an overall plan. It relates to the Karma Council and the supreme goal of the participating souls. Each has its own truth, that leads it to action or, alternatively, to inaction, which is also a form of action, passive in nature. In the short term, one can see all the evil caused by the kidnapping. The long term perspective, many years hence, reveals the cause of the event and the influence of each of the participating characters.

The hat, indeed, is the role. Not wearing one, despite the considerable variety offered, is the choice not to undertake a limited role, but to leave the head exposed in order to receive truth.

Supreme perspective is tied to avoiding judgment. It relates to understanding and accommodating the high cosmic truth, which has a supreme goal. There is no coincidence, there are no errors, there is no evil. It is all from God. As a rule, most people find it difficult to digest this truth. They identify with a name, a family, a gender, a tribe.

They identify with a place of residence. They identify with their favourite football or basketball team. They identify with their country and nationality, which is the foremost identification of the population on earth.

However, there is also a superior identity, composed of higher elements: Identifying with humanism, identifying with the soul, with God, with all of creation upon earth. When people identify with this group they transcend judgment, war, separateness. They opt for and identify with giving–taking–giving, which is love and compassion. They opt to identify with peace and unity.

Identifying is the source of karma: Identifying with a role, with a specific emotion, with a script written for joint learning process and produced as a multi– participant, splendid and magnificent production.

Accordingly, non–identification, non–attachment, not holding on, are openings for the great release. This release is a portal to inner transformation of the old belief systems that no longer serve the choices of humanity to proceed and climb the ladder of light, to advance along a path of spiritual evolution from earthly human to a higher identity, that of soul and spirit.

ILANA: Dear and wonderful Master Akiva, did we somehow start Lesson 19? And I thought that the communications today was too short (smiling).

Master Akiva: Everything interlinks with everything else. There is no separation. Lesson 19 will be conducted tomorrow. It will be the 19th continuous day of our meetings, arising from deep commitment and great devotion to our joint holy work. This lesson has evolved and expanded according to your capacity to accommodate, dear. Actually, every one of these lessons is an idea that can be infinitely expanded and differentiated into many layers. Each can be made into a separate book. Remember that at the start of our conversation I said, "Love thy neighbour as thyself" expands, branches out and leads us to writing this book of light.

As to working on the Sabbath, physicians and emergency crews, for example, are always on the watch, because saving lives supersedes the command to observe the Sabbath.

Ilana: Dear Master Akiva, I do not think that saving lives is at issue here. There is no immediate danger to lives. Maybe I am a bit torn inside: I am not religious, I am not observant, except for keeping the commandments "thou shall love the Lord thy God with all thy heart, with all thy soul, with all thy mind and with all thy strength," and, "love thy neighbour as thyself." I try to light candles on Sabbath's eve and I fast on Yom Kippur (the Day of Atonement). I am secular, yet I believe fervently. Maybe because of the communication with you, with the Righteous Ones, with the Angels, I am debating the matter. The question is: Can I work on the Sabbath? Is my work considered holy work?

MASTER AKIVA: Dear Ilana, are you expecting a license from me? Put all fears and apprehensions aside, get in touch with the higher, pure truth your soul is showing you. Did you not feel, through your clean channell, a readiness to receive the suffering woman today, on the Sabbath? It is you who gives yourself a license. It is you who can treat another individual today, after you have been recharged during your morning sleep, following our joint endeavour of channelling.

Know dear, you are fulfiling one of the most important commandments and apparently you have no need to follow others. It is not out of disregard; instead, it is due to intelligence and the soul–mending work accomplished in previous incarnations.

ILANA: I really have trouble with the idea. I am afraid to desecrate the Sabbath.

MASTER AKIVA: The Sabbath was intended for you! Besides, I do not see any desecration in what you are doing. It is a giving and expansion of your ability to accommodate. Remember, concepts can be deceiving. When you relate to something as work and desecration of the Sabbath you feel heavy guilt. What you do is holy work and that is the unblemished truth. You have the mission of being an intermediary with the high worlds. However, if you are now experiencing a sense of great oppression, first deal with your inner cleansing and cancel the meeting. It is a test for you!

ILANA: My stomach is doing flips and my insides are on fire. Something inside is not letting me see the woman on the Sabbath. I do not know if it is ego or fear. Is it my intuition; is it my close ties to your guidance, to your presence? I simply do not know the right answer. I assume that if it were right to receive the woman, as I thought earlier, I would not feel what I am feeling right now. It is apparently a very important test for me. This is the way I see it: Is it right that I see the woman? Yes! Do I want to receive her? No! Can I accommodate this? No! I am calling to cancel!

I did it. I apologized and explained that I am willing to see her, but I am unable to do so; an overwhelming force controls me. What do you say about my choice? By the way, I just postponed her until tomorrow, so it is not critical that I see her today.

MASTER AKIVA: I respect your choice. At any rate, it is simply a trial. The divine will and your soul, which is so much in tune with it, has needs, urges and effects that you are not yet familiar with. There is no transgression of any kind at issue here. It is about accommodation and an inner need for sanctification, for respect of that, which is holy, honouring tradition and divine will. Whatever happened, you learned much about yourself and your inner realm.

ILANA: I have settled down and started deep breathing again. There is a smile and a sense of relief inside me. What a strange trial. It was a lesson about inner attentiveness to truth, a lesson about compassion, accommodation, intuition and self–recognition. Who am I? What are my beliefs? What guides me? Do I know who I really am beneath the autobiography I have authored with so much talent and identified with for the last fifty years? I feel a sense of quiet, love, sanctity, purity and joy. It is a sign that I correctly and deeply understood the lesson I set for myself today, which is tied to observing the Sabbath and the sanctity of my inner truth.

MASTER AKIVA: Such sensations are the best indication as to whether or not we have completed a lesson. Thoughts can be deceiving and lead one astray. Feelings are faithful to the inner truth.

Dear Ilana, what you have understood is the extent of your inner commitment to accommodate holy writ. The violation was not of the Sabbath but of your sense of inner commitment. What was in danger was your sense that you are privileged to hold that, which is holy.

Accordingly, self–fidelity is important and I refer our readers, who are participating as viewers in your lesson experience, to the same conclusion.

What are you, dear Ilana? You are God's tree (Ilan is Hebrew for "tree"). Your roots connect you to the earth and the sky. Your trunk holds the spirit; your treetop reaches up to higher worlds, not seen by physical eyes. Your golden fruits are most precious and whoever tastes them tastes the flavour of fruits of the Garden of Eden. Your personality no longer controls your decisions. It participates, based on freedom of choice and mutual respect, but the soul assumes responsibility for execution.

One should ask himself "Who am I?" "Where do I come from?" "Where am I going?" You may be surprised to learn that when material goals alter, beliefs are replaced and may even change radically and your inner identity unravels and is woven anew.

Identity is one note, one sound, of a divine and wondrous symphony, one you became aware of at a given moment in the present. Notice the other notes, the range that shifts to other sounds, to the music of the soul.

As you change, your identity shifts and you cease identifying with the body's personality, its wishes, urges, fears and beliefs. New goals appear. New beliefs are woven into the tapestry of your consciousness. You replace isolation with unity. You transform from a body's personality that lust to get and take for itself, to a soul–in–body that accepts in order to give, to influence. A soul that implements, with all its being, the understanding of the essence of the entire Bible: **"Love the Lord thy God with all thy heart, with all thy soul, with all thy mind and with all thy strength,"** and **"love thy neighbour as thyself."**

That sums up lesson 18.

I Am Master Akiva, the harbinger of the message of truth of the bright, veiled light, whose time of revelation to the people of Israel and all the nations of the world has come. I bless you, those who receive and take in the message into your essence of being. I bless and bestow upon you, dear and beloved Ilana, my close guidance. And, a blessing of peace upon the nation of Israel. Be strong and we shall be empowered. Amen!

ILANA: I understand that I tuned into the truth at both its levels. The first was of the personality. A personality that defines itself as secular and flexible in its thinking, found it appropriate to see the woman on Saturday. It was not for the money, I need to emphasize, but out of giving and compassion. Therefore, my gut feeling, which said, "yes," was that of the personality. But the higher truth, that of the soul, said otherwise. The gut feeling of inner discomfort after I did what I did, told me it was wrong to see the woman on the Sabbath, for the matter could easily have been postponed. I think it was an excellent and important lesson. When one seeks the truth, it is important to be precise. Is it the truth of the personality? Is it the sole truth? Or is it the truth of the soul?

A person should act according to his choice, be it the way of the personality or the way of the soul. I chose the way of the soul and its full guidance. Even my personality does not know the motives, because I am not in tune with religious edicts. After all, the personality is subordinate to the soul. It is well and good that I could function on both levels out of choice. I thank you dear Master Akiva for guiding me to act in accord with my heart's command. Thank you. I shall remember this lesson and incorporate it into my treatments. I can examine the truth of the personality, the truth of the soul and the path a man takes. I really love such lessons.

I suddenly recalled that the woman told me she has a triplet. For me, it is symbolic of the three truths I can see. The first is that I do not accept patients on the Sabbath. The second is that if I so choose, I can accept patients on the Sabbath. The third is that I choose not to do so, even if I do not exactly know why I have made this choice. That is the high truth of my soul. How lovely…

MASTER AKIVA: That is how one should handle life situations: see all aspects, examine the truth at all its layers, learn how to go deep below the surface and proceed to the coded message hidden within. Blessed be in your eternal being. Your capacity to accommodate is growing and as a result you are able to extend the lesson. You are unable to fathom the extent of your strength and depth of your roots. Sanctity is the truth that guides you at present, dear and beloved Ilana, who is with Angels and saints. The spirit of the Lord is upon you. And I, Master Akiva, am with you.

ILANA: I am thrilled by the splendour and the holy ambience about me and within me. What a great privilege. I am happy and filled with a sense of goodness. Thank you, wonderful Master Akiva, great messenger of God.

Lesson 19

How to Become a Channel of Knowledge

ILANA: Good and wonderful morning, dear and magnificent guides. Good and wonderful morning to you, dear Master Akiva. I ask that we proceed with our discussion. Thank you.

I should point out that I woke up at two a.m. and again at three, out of a desire and impatience to channell. I love this feeling. I would love to channell until the day I die, whenever that may be.

MASTER AKIVA: Good morning, dear and beloved Ilana. You walk in the way of Spirit, linked with all of your psyche and soul to the divine will. It is an urge from the high worlds, planted in you, after you agreed with all your might to the commitment. It includes utter devotion, perseverance, eagerness, dedication. Your personality has renounced its desires. It has relinquished its attachment to fears, lack of self–esteem and lack of understanding of the nature of your mission on higher planes. The personality has yielded to the light of the soul that has seeped through your outer layers, peeling them off and stamping you with the Seal of the Great Light.

I see that you marvel somewhat at the vast change that has occurred in you. This is not a temporary, transient change, but an anchoring of the overall tendency to be a clear channell on a daily basis, to embrace the great light.

Your mission is to contain frequencies of bright light, to fasten them to your being and to transmit them: to be a super receiver–transmitter, broadcasting the high worlds' transmissions and the divine will. You were told, long ago, by Archangel Metatron: "Write every day," but you did not take it seriously. Do you know why? Because you belittled your self–worth; you thought it enough that there were other channellers, much better known, who write and publish books. What new material could you add? Not to mention, the difficulties entailed in distributing your books. In other words, your ego–personality was, to some extent, your stumbling block. However, you did write. Apart from our conversations, you have enough material for several books. But you did not persevere and therefore did not see the dynamic pattern of how things were evolving.

In order to succeed you must persevere. If persistence is absent, it indicates inner resistance that blocks the flow. This resistance may be due to fears and apprehensions, which affect the conscious will.

ILANA: Dear Master Akiva, every day I am afraid I'll have nothing to write. However, I tell myself, **"I am linked with the knowledge. The knowledge flows through and in me.**

I am a clear channell for knowledge." I breathe deeply until my breathing becomes easy, until there is no longer a clutched feeling in my chest. This indicates that fear has been replaced with faith. This statement is appropriate for other situations, as well, such as preparing for a test. Yesterday I read a Cabala–oriented book by Rabbi Michael Lijtman. It seemed familiar, as if things that I was aware of at a certain level were now clothed in words. I wonder if I would be considered a Cabala scholar[33] even though I did not study Cabala under the guidance of a rabbi or is the ego playing tricks on me? I would love your opinion as we proceed with our discussion. Thank you.

Rabi Akiva: Your soul root is of a very great *mekubal*. Since you embraced him, his knowledge became embedded in you and it is seeking to burst out through your great light. You are unaware of the great deposits of knowledge that are latent within you. The knowledge embedded in you yearns to awaken. You remember what you knew a long time ago. Highly talented individuals actually received instruction and training in another time, in another dimension.

As was said by King Solomon, "There is nothing new under the sun." The deep meaning of the verse is, "In the beginning God created heaven and earth." All the ideas, all the concepts, everything, was part of the ancient creation. Human beings, over the generations, have picked up the

---

33 In Hebrew, *mekubal* (plural, *mekubalim*), a term for someone who dedicates his life to studying Cabala.

knowledge they previously received through their spirit, that which their consciousness could accommodate. They have processed it and interpreted it in a language appropriate to their understanding.

Everything exists, has been in existence, will be in existence. Imagine a vast, bottomless lake of cosmic knowledge. An endless lake, containing knowledge in every possible area you could possibly fathom, even those whose existence your consciousness has not yet grasped. When a person is aware of the lake and needs its water and let's imagine the water to be clear, clean and delicious, he can fill a pail with water. Some may bring a tiny cup, others a large pitcher, some will carry many bucketfuls for the benefit of humanity. Be that as it may, the lake will remain full and all the water taken will not even be noticed.

You can dig canals to carry the water to your fields. The water will irrigate your crops, which provide you with your daily bread. Think now of those irrigation canals: In order for the water to flow without hindrance, they must be regularly maintained. Clean them up, dig them deeper and wider. Potentially, each one of you is such a channel. The channell is not always clean, deep and wide enough to accommodate, nor does it always extend all the way to the source. But you can be such a knowledge channell.

ILANA: I opt to be such a channell of knowledge. How do I do it?

MASTER AKIVA: Thank you for your question. There is only one way to be a clear channell: connect to the source of your soul; reach your soul light; express intention and desire. You must be devoted and dedicated in order to maintain the channell.

The power of prayer, the power of intention, acceptance of responsibility for the contents of the channell, beliefs, thoughts and emotions, all these bring great inner purity, which can contain the knowledge of the bright light, of the infinite lake. The earth is a channell for reaching heaven, which is infinite. As is written in Genesis, "In the beginning God created heaven and earth." Concurrently he created them and the two are interlinked. One is the reflection of the other. As was said, "As above so below." Therefore, when a man isolates himself from the higher world of spiritual knowledge, which is the source of his soul, he finds himself in a dry creek bed, is awareness cut-off from his origins. But when he connects his awareness to the heavens, when he links his channell to the infinite, the earth transforms from a narrow channell to a treasure. The infinite lake discharges its endowments abundantly. He discovers a hoard of riches in spirit.

ILANA: Is Cabala the only way to reach the source? Is there but a single path? Or, are there other ways?

MASTER AKIVA: The way is one, but it has many interpretations. One should tune into the channell to which his soul leads him. Not every way suits everyone. Sometimes you should return to a given path later, when it is in harmony with you. The source of all paths is one. All roads lead to Rome.

I accept the way of Cabala, which contains the purest high wisdom. I have been leading you along this path and have enabled you to taste it. Not every person who crosses the threshold of Cabbala comprehends it in the same way. Everyone fills himself according to his thirst and his ability to contain.

ILANA: I am requesting a break, so that I can accommodate the knowledge and also catch up on some sleep. A fatigue has descended on me, is there a way to be rid of it?

MASTER AKIVA: Whether asleep or awake, you carry on with our studies. Go, sleep, dream and remember the dream. We then will interpret it and it will tie in with our continued conversation. I release you for a break. Blessed be in your eternal being. Here I Am, Master Akiva, conveyor of the bright light by way of "Love thy neighbour as thyself."

Ilana (A few hours later): I am back with the dream. In my dream, I am driving a vehicle on a mountaintop. It appears to be the road to Safed. The vehicle starts to drag. I find, next to the gear shaft, to the left and a bit higher, a new device that looks a little like another gear shaft. It has a broad handle and two positions - one, up, with a red light, the other down, with a green light. I pull the handle but it does not help with the drag. I shift it back to its original position. I fail to understand the purpose of this new device. Nevertheless, I climb toward the top, where there is an inn and a garage. I ask the owner to repair my vehicle. I add that maybe it is not out of order and I just pulled the transformation handle (he told me that it is a transformation handle) and maybe it just needs to be restored to its place. At any event, I ask him to check the vehicle. In the meantime, I enter the inn and talk with the owner and her daughter. The owner tells me that her sense of smell is highly sensitive: She can actually smell breakdowns in vehicles! I am impressed. I tell her that my sense of smell is good, but maybe not that good.

Meanwhile the garage owner is examining other cars. The one he is checking is severely damaged, but I can see that it is not mine. I insist that my vehicle is fine, that it only underwent a transformation and I am ready to pay for the inspection. I announce that I am Arthur Amit's daughter, in order to be well-treated, for it seems to me that the man would recognise the name. He wants my father to pay or else my sister, whom he knows and whose name (in the dream) is Anat (actually this is a good friend who is a rich VIP). However, I insist that it is my vehicle and I should be the one to pay. The cost is more than NIS 300. I hand over four very large red notes. I know I should get change and the woman says I should be getting 22 NIS.

The dream seems to me definitely spiritual, with a message of spiritual ascension. Safed is a spiritual centre of *mekubalim*, where the holy Rabbi Isaac Luria taught the Zohar. The ascent is of course a spiritual ascent. The vehicle represents all my bodies (vehicles of consciousness). They had a bit of a difficulty climbing, but with the aid of the transformation handle they made it. Wow. Now I see that I came to repair my vehicle, my current incarnation, but, as it turned out there was no need for it. I identified myself based on my ancestral reference, signifying status. But I insisted on recognition of my own self, for in the dream it was I who acknowledged my own worth very highly. The payment was with four notes. The number four depicts matter, framework. It is the Emperor card in tarot, indicating spiritual and material power. I gave more than required; therefore, I was entitled to a return (change). Twenty two is the number of masters' masters in numerology, those who have the good of the planet before them and who are known for their high ideals.

This is how I interpret the dream and I feel happy about it.

In half an hour the woman who asked to meet yesterday will arrive. I think the meeting will raise ideas for further discussion with Master Akiva. Therefore, I will not channell any further now but wait until the end of the meeting, at which time I will not be pressed for time. Thank you.

[Later.] It was an excellent meeting. The woman was blocked energetically for five years and suffered all kinds of side effects from the blockages in all her chakras' systems. I have reconnected her with the light, with the soul, with life and with forgiveness, which was hard for her. I also treated her son. I think, about my dream, that maybe the stop to give the vehicle a check-up indicates that I should rest and rebalance. Therefore, I will proceed with the channelling later. I feel really tired.

MASTER AKIVA: Dear and very beloved Ilana, the dream is a gateway for understanding the reality you are experiencing at a higher level. In everyday life people do not usually appreciate their accomplishments. You do not tell yourselves: How beautifully I am progressing spiritually; I have accomplished much of the repair work I have undertaken for this life, etc.

Your dream contained a message about your spiritual state. It is very easy to interpret: Spiritual ascent is like climbing the mountain. Unlike your previous dream, where you encountered a stop sign, in this dream you kept going. When you had trouble with the car, you created a new instrument board, designed for transformation. And, indeed, you underwent a great transformation, which allowed you to proceed with your spiritual ascension. This time you reached the summit and even got to know some people there. The mechanic, the garage owner, her daughter, they are spiritual guides in earthly form. Your spiritual guide, who referred to her sense of smell, indicated a possible developmental direction for you. You have made use of your spiritual sense of smell, your intuition, to reach remote events.

You exhibited a great deal of courage and self–awareness in the way you interacted with the machine. It is a superb message–dream, reflecting your current awareness through an action–drama experience, known as a dream. **Every dream shows you your inner substance, including parts you are not familiar with.**

On a deeper level, you are told that you need not be afraid of transformation, of using new inner tools, which will be disclosed to you in time. Trust yourself, your intuition, your ingenuity and creativity. Otherwise, you have interpreted the dream very well.

Messages come to you in dreams as well as in your waking state. Messages can reach you through the Internet, by way of e–mail, forums, sites, TV programs, movies and books. They can also turn up through people who might say a word, a sentence or form an idea that ties in with a question you may have. They make you aware that there is a tie between your inner and outer worlds. Someone hears you and transmits messages; all you need to do is be attentive and open. This, ties in with the start of our discussion, that you should prepare yourself to be a channell leading from the ocean of infinite knowledge. Willpower, awareness, intention and practical implementation will enable you to become a channell.

Channeling is, in fact, enabling. Enabling which is a two–way communication with a source that is usually not physical. When you are in a state of channelling,[34] the channell opens up, becomes cleansed and receives transmission from the source you have connected with. You connect with a source that matches your frequency and your soul's will and intention.

In ancient times channellers were known as prophets, disciples or spiritual teachers. The founders of religions were, of course, channellers. Artists and creative individuals are natural channellers, through a channell that fits their particular talent.

ILANA: Dear and wonderful Master Akiva, I have received inquiries from people asking what is channelling. Some are even afraid of it. They associate it with séances, ghosts and all sorts of scary things. They also ask if it is possible to become addicted to channelling. What would you say to them?

MASTER AKIVA: Dear ones, you should not be afraid of yourselves! Do not be afraid of the truth. But at the same time, you should know how to distinguish between different kinds of channelling and different kinds of channellers. Some are clean and pure and transmit a true message. Some are less clean and according to the frequency of their personality, they convey half truths and even lies.

---

34 Additional material regarding the nature of channelling may be found in Chapter 35, infra.

Bringing a person to communicate with his soul opens a portal to the high truth, which will then be revealed to him. This truth leads to an understanding of the verse: "Love thy neighbour as thyself."

Through channelling you strengthen your energetic and telepathic connections with all of creation. You discover that separation is just an illusion to which you have become addicted.

Channeling is not an addiction. Is looking with your physical eyes addictive? Is listening addictive? Channeling is a natural ability that needs to be developed. It relates to the sixth sense that enables humans to gather truth, even from that which is concealed.

Is it possible to communicate with spirits, with the dearly departed? Of course! That is because their energy and their souls exist and can be sensed, interacted with and dreamed about. A séance is a form of channelling, though it is not safe or recommended.

In order to channell, you need to learn about energy, how to erect energy defences, how to be balanced and more. It is a path of awareness that must be properly developed and understood.

Here ends our discourse for today. I Am Master Akiva, bearer of the message of unity for the Nation of Israel and all nations of the world, and, "Love thy neighbour as thyself." Thanks and love.

Lesson 20

Creating Reality
The Intelligent Consumer & a Recipe for Happiness
Parables for Consciously Creating Reality

ILANA: Good morning dear and beloved guides. Good morning dear and brilliant Master Akiva. I would like to proceed with our discussion.

MASTER AKIVA: Good and blessed morning dear and so very beloved Ilana, I would like to congratulate you on your perseverance. Please remove all feelings of guilt, because they reduce your ability to accommodate (the messages). Now I will discuss accommodation and its role in creating reality. The subject of **creating reality** has become popular in your generation and I like that very much, for it is time that people learn to take responsibility for their lives.

The raw materials for creating reality are found in your creation conduit. This conduit affects the physical self, including your health and your surroundings. Since it is now known that everything is energy, it stands to reason that beliefs, thoughts and emotions are clusters of energy.

Knowledge of energy provides an understanding of the energy system, your chakras and aural bodies. When your energy bodies operate as they should, the life energy (chi) enters and fills them up, bringing balance to all the elements in your body, the cells, the organs and the entire organism. When the energy system is functioning well, life energy pours into your physical body, your emotional body, your mental body and your spiritual body. You feel well. You are in complete balance. You feel and express abundance, love, faith, empowerment and vitality.

However, when the natural energy flow is disrupted, you become blocked. It manifests itself in various ways. You may feel an unpleasant inner sensation, which will sooner or later spread to your entire physical body. Next, the sensation would spread to the mental plane, to the thoughts, the inner knowing, forming reality out of these inner substances. "That which I was afraid of is come unto me." (Job, 3:25.)

Disruption of the energy balance is caused by flawed and spoiled substances that are antagonistic to the sanctity of life. They are tied to the path of fear and not to the path of love: Apprehension, worry, fright, anxiety, are all forms of fear. Feelings of guilt are an inner fear caused by a failure to act in what you consider a correct fashion. Self–criticism, another form of fear, tells you that you are not okay, you have acted inappropriately and your behaviour warrants punishment, which you then anticipate. Self–pity, despair, anger, hate and desire to avenge, are by–products of the great fear that enslaves.

If you look at it this way, you will be able to classify every negative emotion as a **product of fear**. Imagine yourself as a shopper strolling among the aisles of a supermarket. You can choose what to buy and what to purchase not. Imagine that you choose only the products made of love and self-acceptance.

Every thought, every emotion and every belief can be thought of (by analogy) as a supermarket item. Check its ingredients. Learn to be an intelligent consumer.

Ilana: Thank you dear and wonderful Master Akiva. I am still amused by your picturesque idea, taken from our everyday life and so familiar. Simply great!

Master Akiva: Thank you. Ideas are abstract in nature. They come from both the higher and the lower worlds. They are in a different dimension to yours. Humans, depending on their patience, skill, basic beliefs and frequency, fish ideas out. They then decide what to then do with their catch, whether to throw it back or keep it. You can keep an idea to yourself or share it.

Allegories are very convenient for conveying ideas. We'll call this particular allegory: **Fish - Something Material.**

Ideas are products that can be interpreted. They are like a seed conceived by awareness that puts out roots, according to the capacity of the consciousness to accept

it. **An idea can be a type of a speed of light**, transmitted from the path of love, facilitating freedom, no–time, infinity, eternity. Conversely, **it could be a type of darkness seed,** sent from the path of fear, including the essence of fight or flight, accompanied by negative feelings.

The intelligent consumer who wants to maintain a healthy life–style plans his diet accordingly and watches what he eats. He focuses on food that is beneficial (a healthy mind in a healthy body) and he maintains his figure. He learns all about the importance of food types, vitamins, supplements. He knows what his optimal intake of calories is. He may sign up with a fitness club. But here's the question: Even if he knows all this, will he live by these rules?

The measure of implementation is more important than the measure of theoretical knowledge. This is true in every walk of life.

Now, let's proceed with the **diet allegory.** Let's say that you know the **recipe for happiness,** that it is **easy** to prepare and following it would make you feel wonderful. Would you use it? Apparently you would. We'll call it hunger and thirst for happiness. But some people would settle instead for their usual portion of suffering, because they would not want to make any effort.

The ingredients for the **recipe for happiness** are easily

obtained. They are not expensive. It requires a few basic materials.

It is easy to make the recipe and it will bring you all that you yearn for: It will slake your hunger and quench your thirst. It will cause you to be in that ideal state you desire. Daily usage insures results and even miracles.

Now, are you going to use this recipe? What do you think? It seems to me that a few of you will not use it. Others will be glad to share the recipe with their friends and neighbours. This is because the side effects of a daily use cause true love and immense happiness to blossom in their hearts. This love is the way in which you see yourself. It is also how you accept others, your family, colleagues, friends, buddies, acquaintances and in fact the whole world.

Well, dearly beloved, the secret recipe, the recipe for happiness, is being handed to you right now. Actually, it is provided in various forms. We will use baked goods as a metaphor.

Your happiness recipe contains but one basic ingredient: love. Freely given, unconditional love, pure love, giving–receiving–giving, love thy neighbour as thyself! It is a natural resource found in the heart of each and every one of you, if you'd just look, if you'd just allow it to emerge.

ILANA: Amazing! I am accommodating your words. Soon

my son Yoav will come from his army post for a short while and I will make him breakfast, before I drive him back to his post for another two weeks' duty. I assume that there is a link. Therefore, with your permission, wonderful Master Akiva, who never ceases to amaze me, we'll take a break until our next encounter, later today. Hold it! The penny just dropped. This is really funny. I am discussing recipes, fish, ingredients and here my son surprises me, arriving at short notice and I am about to prepare a meal for him (LOL) So as to implement the message, both literally and in its deeper sense. This is simply grand!

MASTER AKIVA: Indeed, laughter is healthy. I join in your joy and I am looking forward to our continued interaction. Thank you dear for channelling the material in such a flowing and delightful way.

ILANA: I am back (on the following day), dear and wonderful Master Akiva, would you please summarize the idea?

MASTER AKIVA: Good morning dear and wonderful Ilana. Well, these were allegories about consciously and unconsciously accommodating awareness. I ask that you carefully sift through your beliefs. Be meticulous with your thoughts and scrupulously select corresponding emotions. This will bring you closer to the high truth, which you will sense within you. Place less faith in sensational messages, which spread fear–based beliefs. Take responsibility for your inner reality. Ascertain how to develop your inner–

truth–meter, independent of outside opinions. Think for yourself and choose your beliefs.

Trust your impressions and know how to identify their source: is it in the frequency of love or the frequency of fear. Everyone needs to be in tune with his heart, with the guidance of his soul. May you choose goodness, for the benefit of all, the People of Israel and the nations of the world and may the visions of the prophets, Jeremiah and Micah, about the latter days, be fulfiled.

Choose light and be light unto the nations of the world.

Here ends our lesson, I Am Master Akiva, for the unity of Israel and the nations of Earth, bearing the banner of "love thy neighbour as thyself," of the superior and the most exalted consciousness.

And thank you Ilana, for enabling the lesson and for returning to allow us to complete it.

Lesson 21

The High Truth of the Soul

ILANA: Good morning dear and wonderful guides, good morning dear and wonderful Master Akiva. I would like to proceed with our discussion. Thank you.

MASTER AKIVA: Good morning to you dear and beloved Ilana. You are well–disciplined and properly dedicated to our work, the holy mission. What would you like to discuss today?

ILANA: Thank you. Well, I thought we could discuss a subject raised by one of my patients. She told me that anger has stirred up in her lately and she has no idea why. She told me that she does not know what her truth is and what her desire is.

In a phone conversation a day earlier, another patient talked about interpretations by a person she had separated from, how he would interpret an action of hers. I told her that his interpretation is irrelevant, that his intention and desire are of no consequence. What matters is that she should know her own truth and stick to it.

I see a connection. Some people get carried away by the

desire of another, perhaps because they have a need to please.

What can you tell us about truth? Wait a minute. Something amazing! I suddenly heard the verse, "Thou shall love the Lord thy God with all thy soul and with all thy strength," as clearly as if it were broadcast on my neighbours' radio. I have never heard it in the morning.

MASTER AKIVA: Dear and beloved Ilana. The subject of truth recurs in our discussion, because it is the essence of our message. The truth is perceived differently by every religion and by every thinking person. It is subject to diametrically opposite interpretations when two people are having a dispute. The truth may be ambiguous or it may be obvious.

Ask yourselves: **What is truth?** As I have already explained, you cannot understand and digest the highest truth. You can however comprehend the truth according to your own belief system.

Anger is a by-product of the failure to maintain your inner boundaries. Sometimes it is due to an inability to perceive the high truth. **Every time you are angry it fogs up your vision and you fail to see the high truth that contains the situation you are in at that moment.** Anger blinds the eyes. Anger diverts you from the high, clear soul-truth. Anger is characteristic of the individual who suffers from the **victim pattern** and sees himself as a victim of circumstances. Actually, he is a victim of negative inner emotions that block the inner flow of the life energy. The most distinct of these negative, blocking emotions is anger. It evokes inner chaos, flooding the emotions and harnessing the intellect.

Some people can rein in their anger. Others are ruled by it. Anger shakes up your emotions, some of which you were not even aware of until anger waved them before your eyes. **It is like a red flag to a bull.** The bull is you. The red flag is anger. The bull's reaction of getting mad, charging and launching into battle, is how you appear when angry.

Some express their anger outwardly, while others hold it in, because they seek to control it, are ashamed of it or are simply afraid to employ it at the moment of truth. They will direct their anger elsewhere, maybe at someone perceived as weaker than they.

The **victim's pattern** is characterized by helplessness, ineffectiveness, suppression and internalization. Victims lock away their anger and direct it against themselves. They are mad at themselves for their failure to react, in real time. They accuse themselves of cowardice and hesitancy. They criticize themselves harshly, thus further damaging their self–image.

However, if they feel a sense of overload and are unable to bear their anger, it bursts out with no check or control.

They may hurt whoever is nearest. Maybe they are pained by their failure to maintain boundaries, which of course is linked to the **lesson of truth**.

Do you know what your truth is? Are you willing to stand in front of others and tell them what that truth might be? What is your true desire? Are you afraid of potential confrontation, of getting hurt? Maybe you do not believe that you have the capacity to convince others? Maybe your self-image is damaged and that is why you are afraid? Some people are afraid to speak the truth, as they perceive it, preferring to hide it, even from themselves. They would excuse a lie by saying they do not want to hurt others. Accordingly, they would see themselves as good, as do-gooders.

For sake of the deeper truth, why do they want to avoid hurting others? And why should their truth is perceived as injurious? It is because they fear being hurt by a confrontation with another's willpower. They are afraid of the truth and its consequences. There is no good or bad, there is only truth. When you realize that you are afraid of the truth, you are empowered to correct yourself. This leads to the stage of assuming responsibility for creating your reality.

You must remember that your belief system, parts of which are unknown to you and linger from other incarnations, is what attracts events and situations to you. These are growth situations, which enable you to empty out what you have accumulated and take a good look at them. When anger rises in you, be truthful and courageous and ask yourself why you are angry. What is it in me or in the other, that has caused it to surface? **Always know your high truth and strive to express it.** As you become clear about your boundaries, your desires and your purpose, you will be able to explain things to the other party. Ambiguity of intentions creates a state of untruth in relationships and raises veiled anger among both sides. One might become angry at hearing a certain truth expressed, because one interprets it according to one's inner images and subjective understanding. On the other hand, one may sense a different truth hidden beneath the words. Lack of clarity creates ambiguity and uncertainty. These, in turn, awaken hidden fears.

ILANA: Some people do not know their truth, certainly not the high truth of their soul. They are not in tune with themselves and they come to me, asking for assistance. How does that happen and how can I open their eyes?

MASTER AKIVA: people are fed by rumours, by the opinions of others, by education and norms. They do not find their own truth: What they actually believe. They do not trust their gut level feelings, their intuition. They do not believe in themselves. They look for confirmation outside themselves. Their inner connections are loosened up and they become distanced from their soul–truth. These people vest others with the power to twist them. They become enslaved by willpower stronger than their own. They follow and worship the strong and influential. They invalidate their own opinion, replacing it with the dominant public opinion. They try to be like everybody else - although they do not know what everybody think and feel. They simply want to belong, to belong to the majority opinion. They actually want to live in unity instead of separation, though their path, of course, is erroneous.

The message I wish to convey to these people, who are far more numerous than you imagine, is: **You belong when you feel you belong! The way to belong, first of all, is to truly belong to yourself, to be attentive to your heart, which is interlinked with your soul.**

Connection with the soul and the higher self strengthens you and guides you to trust your inner sensations. When the connection weakens, it weakens you. The way to belong, to feel secure in your existence, is to strengthen your tie to your soul, to your higher self. These would give you constant accessibility, on a daily basis, to your high truth.

The high truth of the soul, of course, is associated with taking responsibility for everything that happens, that you have summoned into manifestation. You have done so to observe and study the configurations of your inner creativity. Its importance for your ability to consciously create your reality is very profound. When your inner configurations are based on fears, whose source is shrouded in fog, it may affect the conscious desire; even divert it from the path of its self-actualization.

For example, you want more money in order to feel secure and live in material comfort. You learn the laws of reality creation. You watch movies, purchase disks and books and sign up for study courses. You feel that you have acquired the knowledge and you then attempt to implement it in your own reality. For some unfathomable reason, you are unable to become rich. Is the method wrong? That's not it. The reason is that negative beliefs accumulate within you, some of them contradictory, which neutralize the desired object. We have already discussed the creation of two contradictory paths that cancel each other out. Furthermore, the path of fear is the more powerful one. It blocks the desired manifestation.

Why is it more powerful? Because its purpose is defence! Fear based beliefs attempt to protect you from harm. A defensive block can arise from an experience that forms a belief in your subconscious that would endanger you.

Why, for instance, would you be afraid of accumulating money?

Maybe you harbour beliefs from previous or parallel incarnations or beliefs you have acquired in your parents' home or from your society. "He who accumulates assets accumulates anxiety." (*Mishna, Nezikin, Avot* 2:7.) Maybe there are traumas imbedded in you, caused by loss of property, which have greatly hurt you: beliefs that formed a defensive screen, preventing the manifestation of the desired reality.

How do you know whether you have negative beliefs based on fear? You will become aware of them, when you consciously attempt to create a scenario, which fails to materialize over a long period of time.

I suggest that we return now to the subject of anger and the high truth. **The high truth of all souls is but one and contains the message of unity:**

You are an eternal soul that reincarnates in order to mend itself. You accomplish that by way of external relationships, which reflect to you your inner beliefs. Is their source the path of love or is it the path of fear? All human beings co-operate with you. This is anchored in soul agreements you have entered into with them while you were still in the World of Truth, before occupying your body and before returning to the World of (biological) **Life.**

Accordingly, when someone provokes you to anger, know that he is actually helping you observe yourself within, enabling you to become aware of a negative belief that has surfaced in you. Ask yourself: What is truth? What is the deeper truth? What does this truth show you about yourself? What does the truth you have perceived allow you to correct within you? Therefore, after the truth has been rendered, thanks to an external agent, you can forgive him. As a matter of fact, you should understand that you have chosen to be hurt, for you failed to see the truth about yourself – it was more important for you to be more right than the other guy. After you are kind enough to forgive yourself, you can transcend to the next level of insight. Forgiveness engenders gratitude.

Had that external agent not presented to you your inner pattern of creation, it would have to repeat and reconfigure events and situations for you, over and over again. That is a good reason to feel gratitude toward the person who angers you. Likewise, thank a nation who angers you.

ILANA: Dear and wonderful Master Akiva. **What is the way to establish forgiveness between people who have quarreled and of course on a higher plane, hostility between nations?**

MASTER AKIVA: Thank you dear for an excellent question. Well, because communication occurs through many channels apart from speech, you can transmit understanding toward the other party, who, although he may not understand how and why, will feel his anger evaporate. He will sense the release of resentment and act accordingly. He may even contact you and you will be surprised to hear that he seeks forgiveness and reconciliation. Even though he may not make physical contact with you, you will still sense that his anger has faded. Consequently, you are no longer bound by any ties. They may subsequently become tighter or looser, according to particular soul agreement and personal choices. This is a process of karma release.

Know that when you are holding on to a powerful emotion toward another person, religion or a state, you become tied by energy which forms karma. Karma is an energetic association leading to joint lessons.

ILANA: Dear Master Akiva, if people have negative karma between them, will they converge and interact in this life, until it is released?

MASTER AKIVA: Negative karma forms the core of a tie. It might find expression through ties with others. Let's look at the example of a couple who has divorced and its erstwhile members are left with negative emotional residue. They will develop negative patterns of relationships, trust and betrayal. They will harbour resentment, anger even fear. Perhaps they will attract new partners who help them deal with the negative inner contents. It is similar to the role a soul takes upon itself. If it is unable to fulfil it, it will pass it over to another. The task will manifest as long as it is necessary.

As to the person you have separated from or divorced, you will meet again at another temporal juncture, maybe in the next life, in order to complete and heal the negative karma between you. This can cause thorny and knotty patterns among family members, for example. Humans arrive with negative karmic baggage that must be released and corrected. That is why you sometimes have a smooth and pleasant relationship with one parent or child, while with another parent or child it is much more arduous.

The way to release karma is always through the path of love, which includes forgiveness, compassion and gratitude. Unconditional love releases karma, no matter how negative. The path of "love thy neighbour as thyself" is a conduit of karma release, as well as personal, general and collective means of transcendence. That is the only way. There is no other.

ILANA: Dear and wonderful Master Akiva, I understand the path when it concerns two individuals. But how does it relate to nations? Specifically, **how do we establish peace between the Hebrew people in the Land of Israel and the Arab people in the Arab lands?** When our lives are threatened we must prepare for war. Is there a way to attain peace without war?

MASTER AKIVA: Dear child, your question is great and most important. The entire Host of Heaven has been dedicated to the mission and vision of world peace. It is not an easy course and I cannot just drop a magic formula here to hasten the process. The path has to be prepared. Our book, with many others, is paving the way. They plant transcendent ideas of peace, brotherhood and unity in the awareness of the masses. Readers who agree with the message plant within themselves the seeds and, in turn, help to disseminate them.

ILANA: Dear Master Akiva, I feel a sense of oppression as I read these words. I understand that there is no magic solution and yet I believe in miracles. In my treatments, I see wonders every day.

MASTER AKIVA: Dear and beloved Ilana, let go of worry and put your faith in God. Go back to the course of faith and understand, first of all, that internal processes are indispensable. There is a need for a sea change in the individual as well as the collective consciousness, in the area of connection between people and their source, with the high truth, the soul's path light. Time is of no consequence. Through the high dimensions, the boundaries of time and space are removed. Visions of peace and brotherhood, wealth and prosperity, light and love, are now being projected onto the screens of consciousness. People must first acknowledge that there is another option, that the universe is a place of plenty and enablement; that what is best for them, is what is best for their fellows, that the highest good is common to all the children of Adam and Eve.

Many visionaries have dedicated themselves to the task. "Time is short and work aplenty." (*Mishna, Nezikin, Avot*, 2:15.) It is for this reason that you are waking at dawn to write, a mission to which you are dedicated for the 21st straight day. You will recall that this endeavour began after you received the "pigeon message."

ILANA: Indeed, a pigeon flew into my house. She hid behind a planter and would not leave. I sent her healing energy. She made her way to the balcony and a day later died there. I felt that, in addition to a personal message, there was a message to the People of Israel. I asked that the pigeon would atone for the People of Israel and I meant it from the depths of my heart. The time is 07:07, a lovely hour.

MASTER AKIVA: This is a crucial time for the People of Israel and, indeed, the nations of the world. It is necessary to tune into the supreme, comprehensive vision, for the good of the whole planet. The state of global warming symbolizes your global need to unite and consider the existing resources, to think of solutions for the emerging situation. Visionaries are needed, prophets, messengers, clear thinkers capable of making decisions, activists and doers. **Vision must precede implementation!**

Everyone who feels enthusiasm and vision must harness himself to the mission. We commenced our conversation with the issue of high truth. I have endeavoured to outline the method of connecting to the high truth.

I call upon the Angels of Service to guide this process. Thank you.

The Process of Tuning into the High Truth is brought here by the Angels of Service, who blow the trumpets, in order to awaken hearts.

Breathe deeply, several times, till you feel serene within yourself. Become connected to the high truth frequency. Do that by employing the power of intention and declaration. Say the following and after every sentence breathe deeply and internalize the frequency in all your energetic bodies. Say each sentence three times with total intent:

"I connect with the light, with the high truth.
"I connect with the supreme vision of my soul.
"I open up to contain the high truth.
"I am fully in tune with the high truth and connect with the vision of action."

Energy of the high truth will now enter through your crown. Know, that the connection has occurred, things will start to surface to the conscious awareness and the transformation process has begun.

Blessed be in your eternal being, we are the Angels of Service, envoys of the Blessed Holy One.

I, the Lubavitcher Rebbe, have joined the process and bless the People of Israel with the coming of salvation and of Messiah in these times. Amen and amen.

MASTER AKIVA: Thank you. Request internalization and accommodation of what has just been said. For that purpose, we will end our 21st lesson. Thank you dear, Ilana, for your willing participation in the process, for enabling it through your channell and for holding the high truth frequency that is anchored in your being. I am grateful to all who have participated in the process, who are paving the path to the nation's unity and to salvation. I Am Master Akiva, the bearer of the message of unity, of "love thy neighbour as thyself." Be at peace.

ILANA: Thank you for the exciting process.

Lesson 22

**Personal Responsibility for Inner Content
Negative Energies and Means of Protection
Preparation for the Consciousness of One**

ILANA: Good morning dear and wonderful guides. Good and brilliant morning to you dear Master Akiva. I am asking that we proceed with our discussion, this 22nd consecutive day.

Yesterday, at the conclusion, I felt as if I had physically strained myself. My breathing was rapid, as if I had been jogging and it took a long time for me to settle down and regain my balance. I thought maybe my frequency was too high. Could you instruct me about that? Is it related to frequency and is it about frequencies in general?

MASTER AKIVA: Good and blessed morning, dear and beloved Ilana. Well, I am happy to inform you that your mission has been accomplished! You have harnessed yourself to a great effort in order to channell certain material and transfer it in the best and cleanest manner. Do you remember your fear of undue effort? Do you remember that you chose to release and transform it? Now you are reaping the fruits of the transformation and you have realized that it was well worth it. **Perseverance, decisiveness and greater effort, these are the secrets of success.** We have indeed discussed the subject, but I want to emphasize it for our wonderful readers and for you. Apply it in all aspects of life. Many artists, including yourself, tend to wait for inspiration, for the muse to impart its grace upon them. There is a better way. It relates to perseverance, dedication, investing effort, training and practice on a regular basis, in accord with your willpower.

A well trained and skilled individual will attract his muse by himself without waiting for it to arrive. When you decide to write, write on a daily basis. If you choose to paint, do it on a daily basis. It is true that sometimes you will attain a sublime creation, but not at other times. It is true that every day fruits of differing quality will be plucked from your creativity garden, some unripe, others bursting with flavour and others that you must discard because they have decayed. Do not be angry with yourself; do not criticize yourself, enable creation without impeding it. At the end of the creation process, if you love the product, distribute it, publish it, produce it and promote it. If, however, you do not like it, put it respectfully aside. Maybe later on you will find it appealing after all. Maybe it is an overture to another creation that will arrive later. Regard yourself with respect and honour what is created through you.

As to your interpretation regarding your bio–physical reaction and the emotional storm you felt following our last channelling, it is acceptable. It is, however, only one layer. The ability to digest and internalize the rising materials is one side of the equation. The other side is the major effort you have invested, that enables all the information to surface and flow freely by way of the written word. Yes dear, you have made great efforts, though in real time you did not feel it. Do you know why? It is natural to all athletes, artists and creative people. I am talking of total submission to a particular enterprise. When you undertake it with passion, ardour and even pleasure, time disappears. Your physical body and its biological needs are pushed aside and you dive totally into the process. You are detached from all reality of time and space and engaged with the creative source within you. It is a pleasant and intoxicating state of being.

Well dear, you entered this state last night, enabling important material to come through you. Since you are an active, critical and full participant in the transmission of the message, your discretion, vocabulary, insights, writing style and your entire spirit all participate in the writing process. Consequently you felt the effects of your efforts. Was it so terrible? Is there something wrong with devoting an effort to secure desired results? What you have observed is that by breathing, awareness, energetic linkage and most of all, by utilizing your remarkable power of intention, you quickly recovered and attained balance.

Do not be concerned with effort and fatigue, because you have the ability to restore the energy reserves in your body simply and naturally. Sleep is a natural and vital way in order to replenish your reserves; the same applies to meditation, cessation of external activity and rest. But, ask yourself whether you are overexerting yourself by choice or whether an outside agency demands the effort. The first case is different than the second in that, when it is your free will choice you gladly make the effort and your positive spirit recovers quickly. However, when you act unwillingly and even out of compulsion, negative residue like anger and self–pity will remain in your body.

Naturally, it depends on your inner reference. If it is positive, no negative residue will remain in your body to disrupt your physical balance. But if your attitude is that of a victim and you feel displeasure, bitterness, anger, self–pity and so on, your balance will be disrupted, prompting energy blocks in all your energy systems, as well as your physical body.

Why were you blocked? Is it because someone "worked you to death"? Is it because someone exploited you? Or is it because someone made you angry and upset your natural balance? The answer is, no and no and no. The blockage was brought about because of your own inner attitude.

This can also provide information about how you relate to negative energy from other individuals – curses, sorcery, the evil eye and energy parasites. **Your inner approach**

is the key. With your inner approach, you supply the external approach that penetrates and seeps inward. If inwardly you are loving and supportive, you will be filled with pleasant energies. They provide you with balance, a sensation of relaxation and a feeling of satisfaction. However, if you are inwardly filled with criticism, anger or self–pity, you will create an opening for negative energies to take up residence within you and disturb your balance.

I want to emphasize that it is you who enables access for the negative energies, just as you enable access to positive energies. No–one is at fault. Such thinking is characteristic of the victim syndrome, of one who fails to take responsibility for himself. "But it is not my fault," you say angrily or with self–pity. "It does not depend on me." Yes, that is how you think and that is what you believe.

Here, however, is the high truth: When you are incarnated, you are concealed behind a mask, which makes you forget your true identity, your true and divine "I Am" that you really are. As long as you are unaware of your effect on reality, that includes your beliefs, thoughts and feelings, you will be influenced by external reality. **The victim is always an object of influence, while the aware human being is a source of influence. Plain and simple!**

Ilana: Dear and beloved Master Akiva, I am highly aware. I take responsibility for creating my reality; I search for meaning and for the symbolism inherent in every external circumstance. Nevertheless I sometimes feel that negative energies stick to me and disturb me. I strive to identify and neutralize them in order to regain full balance. Surely there are many who are aware, but do not have the energetic tools I possess? They are passively influenced instead of actively influencing. Why is that? What can be done to eliminate it? I remember that we discussed the issue, but maybe you could clarify and add new material?

MASTER AKIVA: There is nothing new under the sun, but new sun–protectors are always coming onto the market. Some people use them because they believe they are effective, for they are concerned about the harmful effects of the sun. Others feel safe and do not smother their skin with protective creams.

Both will be tested on their inner beliefs. Their fears are the reason why they lose their balance. However, the one who is afraid of radiation, but has no doubt that the ointment will fully protect him, will experience exactly that. The ointment will be a source of security. But the one who is unafraid will not be harmed, either, so long as he truly believes he is safe (both consciously and unconsciously).

Now, back to the subject, he who is utterly unafraid of negative energies or unaware of their existence and is constantly in complete balance, in good spirit and a positive thinker, will not be affected by these energies at all. A person who is apprehensive about negative energies and experiences fear, anger and criticism, will create for himself the experience of incorporating negative content. If it is done consciously, he will experience their influence, if unconsciously, his balance will be disrupted.

If one wants to be the source of influence instead of being influenced, if he does not want to attract negative energies, he must cleanse his inner content, maintain and stabilize his balance. This includes protection of his aural bodies as well as his physical body. It also includes assuming responsibility for all his thoughts and emotions.

Is it possible? Certainly! Is easy and simple? Not in the plane of reality you are at. definitely not in the world of duality, which is based on the fierce judgment of good versus evil, love versus fear and even hate, which is anger mixed with great resentment. In this reality, you judge others all the time.

Is judgment love? No. Is it "love thy neighbour as thyself?" Of course not! Anything that is not love and even contradicts its essence is negative energy. Absorbing this energy within you has consequences. You cannot take in this energy without creating blocks in the flow of your channel.

ILANA: Sometimes we experience these negative energies even when we are alone. Where do they come from? Do they emerge from thoughts?

Master Akiva: even when you are by yourself, you are not really alone. Energetically, there is no divide between you and "others," whether they are spiritually close to you, or acquaintances, neighbours, in fact humanity as a whole. Hence, there is a constant mutual influence of energies and frequencies.

The way to avoid the influence of negative energies is to fill yourself continuously with a wealth of positive energies. When you are filled with love and light, nothing evil or dark can penetrate! When you are devoid of light energy, you would absorb any kind of energy roaming around you. Take responsibility for your inner content, your energies; dispose of all fears that can influence you.

It is not that you are at fault if negative energies penetrate you. (Guilt is an emotion that forms an energy block and may cause physical and psychological illness.) But you are responsible for the content that flows through you. Therefore, you can disengage the source of energy that disrupts your inner balance and causes you emotional turmoil and discomfort. You can even close the leak by filling up and renewing your reservoirs of light and love.

Ilana: Thank you for the clarification. Now I have better understanding. It ties into my discussion with my pupils last night.

I now request a short break to digest the material and ensure my balance. Thank you.

I am back. I thought about the formula for removing negative energies. It has been serving me and my patients very well. Its effect is instantaneous. As if by magic negative energies are removed and balance is restored. For the benefit of my readers, I'll repeat it here. It removes energetic parasites, the evil eye, curses and sorcery. Here it is:

Breathe deeply through the nose. Hold it a little in your chest. Exhale through the mouth and declare three times:

"All that is in me, around me, below and above me, in all bodies, all layers, all dimensions, all incarnations – which is not light, balance and love – depart from me now!"

After each declaration, breathe to bring light into the body through the nose and exhale darkness (disruptive elements).

It immediately releases nervousness, stress, apprehension, anger, sadness, self–pity and all negativity within and even what we perceive as being outside and not associated with us. According to Master Akiva, we have allowed them access. Now I understand this formula better, since what makes us feel good is the balance that contains love and light. Dear Master Akiva, please take over and proceed with the discussion. Thank you.

MASTER AKIVA: You see dear Ilana, everything, including the maintenance of your physical, emotional, mental and even spiritual balance, relates to implementing the principle of: "Love thy neighbour as thyself."

You are an instrument containing pure, unconditional love. This love is felt as a balanced, pleasant, relaxed, non-judgmental, respectful and enabling ensemble of feelings. This expanse of love spreads to include your fellow human beings, regardless of status, nationality and their relation to you. The expanse of love attracts to you the experience of love and a frequency of harmony. If you depart from it or before you enter it and become aware of its power and beauty, you distance yourself from its effect. Then you find yourself in the zone of fear, darkness, where light is utterly absent.

ILANA: Dear and honourable Master Akiva, isn't the concept of light and darkness characteristic of the philosophy of duality? Isn't there a concept above it, which we can perceive as reality?

MASTER AKIVA: Dear Ilana, an excellent question. This also relates to Liad's inquiry, directed at me last night. How you perceive reality, corresponds to the manner in which your inner belief system produces your experience. Your mind and understanding cannot capture what your consciousness does not have.

While you are embedded in the board game Earth, which has its own rules and regulations, you are players who act and are acted upon. Just as a chessboard is made up of black and white squares, you are in a state of war and you behave accordingly, you experience the root chakra, which is based on the principle of fight or flight. It causes you to attack or defend. You cast accusations or else you are filled with guilt feelings of your own. This affects the field of energetic consciousness that currently operates in your time and space. However, those whose instrument is ready to accommodate the high consciousness, have the ability and access, from the level of **"love the Lord thy God with all thy soul and with all thy strength,"** (Deuteronomy 6:5), would have access to the high plane whence divinity is seen in its entirety and which contains comprehension of creation as a whole, whose nature is both co-operative and symbiotic.

ILANA: I feel that in order to accommodate the knowledge and convey it accurately and cleanly, I should transcend duality perception.

MASTER AKIVA: So be it! Dedicate today to inner work of transcendence above separateness, above the illusions of the ego, to the understanding of **the Law of One.** Later today we will meet and proceed with our task. Meanwhile it is also recommended that the readers take a break, put down the book, breathe in the knowledge, ask for expansion of consciousness and ask to accommodate the knowledge of the one: "Our God, one God."

Say:

"I request to transcend duality.
"I request to know the One.
"I request to accommodate unity."

Now, you are invited to read aloud **the *Shma* prayer** (see text immediately below, citing Deuteronomy 6:4–9) and let the knowledge instil in you the energy it contains:

"Hear, O Israel: The Lord our God is one Lord. And thou shalt love the Lord thy God with all thy heart and with all thy soul and with all thy might. And these words, which I command thee this day, shall be in thy heart. And thou shalt teach them diligently unto thy children and shalt talk of them when thou sittest in thine house and when thou walkest by the way and when thou liest down and when thou risest up. And thou shalt bind them for a sign upon thine hand and they shall be as frontlets between thin eyes. And thou shalt write them upon the posts of thy house and on thy gates."

Breathe deeply and ask to be in tune with the frequency of the prayer. Declare:

"I request to be in tune with the frequency of the prayer, 'Hear, O Israel.' "

The frequency will activate codes within you and will enable access of the message to your consciousness.

After every request, after every declaration, remember that you should take deep breaths to provide the energy passage into your heart and all the energy centres in your body.

Blessed be in your eternal being, which enables the expansion of your consciousness and of all those who opt to be clean channells of the message of unity, "consciousness of the one," which is past separateness and duality. Here I Am, Master Akiva, the bearer of the flag of, "Love thy neighbour as thyself." Thank you dear, Ilana, for choosing to participate in the process and to anchor the knowledge.

Lesson 23

Release of Creativity; Beyond Duality

ILANA: Good morning wonderful guides, higher self, Archangel Metatron. Good morning dear and wonderful Master Akiva. I would like to proceed with our discussion. Before we do that, however, let me say that today I got up quite late. I was seized by a fear of ending the book; a fear regarding publication and distribution. In fact, I far prefer the creative process of writing. I wish a well established publisher would believe in me and my work and publish my book under highly advantageous terms. I would like to have a literary agent. In short, to avoid the executive activity. To sit all day and channell is much more exciting for me. What do you think, dear and wonderful Master Akiva? Are you ready to arrive and communicate with me?

I have this apprehension that yesterday was our last discussion and that the channell is shut, it was however just an apprehension. I'll breathe and let it evanesce. The time is 09:00 (a.m.) and that is a wonderful time for a channelling.

MASTER AKIVA: Dear and beloved Ilana, release your apprehension that someone would "rob" you of your favourite toy, your last scrap of bread, and, in general, anything that belongs to you and that is dear to you.

Your channell is permanently open and many light entities, even seraphim and heavenly angels, desire to deliver messages through you. If and when our discussion is bound in the book of light that is before us, you will release the creation and give it life, so that it will materialize through distribution. You have a problem with holding on to your material and that is blocking its distribution. Please dear, I beg of you, check that tendency with your energy tools. Thank you.

ILANA: I have examined it energetically, using the third hand laboratory (hand based energetic sensation method I have developed based on Reiki) and, to my surprise, I found what you have said to be accurate. Of course, I believe your statements, but I did not know about this tendency. When I am aware of it, it is much easier to heal and release it. As it turns out, I do not want to consciously let go of what is stored in my subconscious.

The way to heal it will be as follows:

I summon the **violet flame and its angels**. This is the flame of transformation. I ask to give away the fear and transform it into an urge. While undergoing the healing process, I will breathe deeply until I feel that the constriction in my abdomen is released and my breathing becomes deeper. This is an excellent means of transforming any kind of fear and anxiety.

Another excellent way to release fears is through working with the **Angels of Karma**. One may call upon them and request their assistance to transform limiting beliefs, negative thought–forms or fears or to heal a relationship. The way to work with them is as follows:

"I call upon the Angels of Karma and request healing and complete karmic release of [name the fear or limiting belief] in all bodies, all levels, all dimensions and all incarnations, here and now and in my entire being. Thank you."

Repeat the request three times and then ask for a sign.

I feel the release of an unconscious fear from my energy content and certainly from my conscious beliefs.

I am checking, by way of energy sensing, whether I fear publishing. The answer that comes up is, "No." Do I fear distribution? The answer is, again, "No!" I consider whether there is another fear in me of which I am unaware, one that could potentially block the distribution of my books. I will be glad to receive the absolute truth. The answer that rises in me is: "Dear Ilana, you have great faith in yourself. Your self–esteem has greatly improved. Your self–image, as a spiritual teacher of the path of love and light, compassion and transformation is pure and cleansed. Therefore, there is no reason to block the flow of books and their consequent effect on the awareness of the public who thirst for the knowledge."

I feel quiet and calm now. I ask Master Akiva to proceed.

MASTER AKIVA: Dear and beloved Ilana. Your guidance is vital. Do not ever belittle your self–worth. Naturally, it is tied with great humility because of the source you communicate with. You are an inseparable part of the source. You are not merely a pipeline – as you tended to think when we wrote our first book (The Dawn of Consciousness Rising – Keys of Personal and Planetary Enlightenment). You were apprehensive about receiving the names of the sources of your channelling, so that your ego would not be blinded. Accordingly, all the light entities working with you in close co-operation in this plane and the sublime planes, agreed to call ourselves, for your sake and your sake alone, dear, the Guidance of the Light. In your second book (The Gate to Sanctity – Conscious Creation), you assented to write the name of the source who is communicating through you, though you did it rather tentatively. But your self–worth as a stand–alone light entity, currently present in a human body in the service of the world, still needs improvement and reinforcement.

You have belittled yourself, clung to anxieties and the fear that you might not be worthy to channel such important, even holy messages.

Since then, you have come a long way. You have learned to acknowledge your self–worth, your many qualities, your abilities. You have grown a great deal, you have undergone significant transformation. The layer of your personality has been embedded in your soul, the higher self and has interlinked with the high will. You have relinquished your personal desires and refined your personality. Now, in your body, your energy and all of your being, you serve as an envoy of the light; an emissary of consciousness with all its value and significance, but, at the same time, you choose simplicity, humour and warmth in your interaction with others. Your sense of humour and friendliness help you remove barriers and penetrate hearts. Your energy is gentle yet potent and you influence those around you, in fact you have an effect on the whole world.

Every person who has developed from a spiritual evolutionary aspect, who carries high frequencies, *affects the entire cosmic tapestry*. After all, humanity is cast as one whole and there is a reciprocal effect at the spiritual, energetic and telepathic levels.

A person needs to know himself, acknowledge his self worth and yet understand that he is a messenger of the Creator of the universe, that he is a spark among countless divine sparks. Humility and self–acknowledgment are the way to prepare your instrument for reception of the high worlds in the purest and most sublime fashion. I would add that boasting about your abilities, be they spiritual, mental or supernatural, points to the ego and its desire for self–recognition.

Simplicity and modesty, combined with awareness of self-worth and knowledge of your sources, are the way of the soul. It is vital for channellers and those who communicate messages, whether they be statesmen, executives, the clergy, teachers and indeed any person with influence on others, to strictly maintain inner cleanliness and practice self-examination, What are the beliefs that guide them, what is the manner of their thinking, how do they regard others? Examine their actions, notice their manner of speech. One must never publicly disgrace another. It is unacceptable to tarnish another's reputation. Slander and disparagement must be completely avoided. One should shun excessive judgment and spurn self-aggrandizement. Inner purity should be meticulously maintained by internalizing light's essence and by utilizing the principle: "Love thy neighbour as thyself," and, "That which is hated by you, do not do unto another." Remember to apply these principles in your daily life.

A person who is a clean channell is recognised by the purity of his deeds, the simplicity of his conduct, the warmth of his expression. One who has knowledge, even if it is spiritual and of great importance, but condescends to others, is guilty of the sin of hubris, he is in tune with the channell of darkness, devoid of love and ruled by the ego, its desires and by a lust for power.

ILANA: Dear and wonderful Master Akiva, some people appear nice and possess great personal charm but they are in tune with ego and frequencies of darkness. Though I can see it, they may delude others. Moreover, they have book knowledge and can quote credibly in the language of light. They know how to hypocritically bless with light and love. How can one know who is he facing without tools such as channelling, intuition, knowledge and so on?

MASTER AKIVA: Dear Ilana. You present your query as if it is evil to be a channell of darkness. There is actually no good or evil. Both paths teach, both enrich the soul and impart experience. Both paths offer essential lessons. There are those who are destined to learn by negotiating the path of darkness, even encountering channellers and influential agents who are in tune with such frequencies. Others, like you for example, are expected to learn by way of the light. It may be that in previous/parallel incarnations they have already been through the path of suffering and torment of the ego, which we would term darkness – for it lacks awareness from the soul level (consciousness of light). If they have no need to separate the light from darkness, they will refuse the opportunity to do so. There is no need to save them. They are simply expected to learn on their own, from their own experience, on the path they are traversing.

The courses of light and darkness work in tandem. Angels are sent to both paths and souls choose them for their evolution. Some souls, usually the more experienced ones or those from higher planes, prefer one path to the other. They specialize in that path and, eventually, at the appropriate time, they become emissaries. The masters of the dark side are instrumental in producing the dramas on Earth that teach and point out the path of consciousness of "love thy neighbour as thyself."

Think about basic training. To integrate the boys into a military framework and make real soldiers out of them, they have to be trained. They must learn how to use weapons, improve their physical condition and appreciate the importance of cohesion as a group. To this end they are sent on exhausting expeditions and sometimes they endure hazing, which is perceived as humiliation. Are the platoon commanders bad? Do they force them to perform difficult tasks for no reason? And could the soldiers, who suffer physically and emotionally, skip this phase? Certainly not! It is necessary, in order to turn a boy into a warrior.

The same applies to many lessons imparted on the path of darkness. The needs for control, ego, fear, hardship, agony, even the lusts that have to be satisfied, are of great importance. In order to learn the lessons, a team of teachers has to be assembled. Therefore there are people who serve as teachers, unbeknown to them of course. They teach the lessons of hardship, even suffering, through which their tormented pupils learn how to escape their influence. They learn truth, clarify their actual desires and define their inner boundaries, acquire assertiveness, attentiveness to intuition, release of fears and so on.

ILANA: Nice. Yesterday I had a patient who was livid with her employer. According to her, she had sex with him and he exploited her. She says that she did receive the benefit of his services but she still felt she was the injured party. I knew that there are two sides to every story. The truth, as she perceives it, is not necessarily the way her employer sees it. The high truth is that he was there to help her get in touch with her truth, her desire. He came to teach her to believe in herself and not to fear people in authority who have domineering energy. I tried to explain to her that there really is no victimhood; it is all spelled out in the soul agreement. I feel she did not get a handle on it. I understand that this is the concept of the One, of trans–duality: to see that, really, there are no good guys or bad guys, these are only roles. No doubt, looking at it from the employer's viewpoint, who I understand is married and has a family, she is the villain of the story, because she seduced him and has been exploiting him in her own way.

The two "villains" are allies on the soul level. The woman, characterized by a victim pattern, is one of those people who are unaware they create, out of their beliefs, the reality they find themselves in, some of which (beliefs), naturally, are unknown to them. She did not assume responsibility and did not see how her beliefs had brought her this lesson and the specific instructor who had qualified to convey the lesson. She also has a martyr pattern, sacrificing herself, relinquishing her wishes to gratify others. She claims that she shies away from hurting others, thus often avoids expressing her true desires. I challenged her, stating that she is afraid of getting hurt, that she cannot bear to be hurt by others, that she is afraid of the anger of others when it is directed at her, that she is afraid of not being loved, that the cause is within her.

During the channelling it became clear that she has been carrying these patterns and fears from previous incarnations. She has given up on herself and sacrifices her own will, subjugating herself to others. Consequently she is significantly weakened, has no faith in herself, is not assertive in the least and sometimes she is even unaware of her real needs and her truth.

It is clear to me that in order to learn and understand, she is in need of a lesson, one that can only be taught by a "darkness teacher." I explained that when a student finds certain materials difficult, he may develop hatred toward the instructor who is not awarding him a passing grade. By blaming the teacher he avoids taking responsibility.

The way to learn such a lesson is through spiritual insight, understanding that it comes to teach us and making a conscious decision to be free of its oppressive effect. This can only be done through forgiveness: Forgive the other and yourself, for having been drawn into the situation. Understanding what the lesson has taught you about yourself will help achieve a solution and allow you to depart from the lesson.

I was asked: How do you know the lesson has ended? What if one party understands the material while the other does not?

The answer is: The feeling within! If you no longer feel anger, hurt, bitterness or any negative residue and furthermore, if you can see the benefit of the lesson, than you are done with it. It does not matter whether the other party comprehends the lesson or not. If you do not engage yourself in his drama, your energy will be set free. You are no longer part of the game; you continue your journey elsewhere.

I understand: One – transcendence of duality.

I release myself of all judgment, of the darkness and everything associated with it.

I ask to have myself released from all inner arrogance as well as aversion thereof.

I choose to be linked with the path of love, which is acceptance of all there is, for all is God and His magnificent creation!

Master Akiva: You did well. This is how people should conduct themselves: **Notice the dramas around you and the individuals involved in them and stop making judgments.**

ILANA: Dear and beloved Master Akiva, suddenly a very important question arises: What about intentional injury to another? How do we avoid judgment in such a case? What about teaching morality? We cannot not, God forbid, condone murder, crimes, injustice?

MASTER AKIVA: Dear, there is the truth of duality, which is perceived as law on game board Earth. It is indeed composed of dos and do nots. **You must keep the Ten Commandments with all your strength of will and with all your soul. Beware of transgressing any one of these Commandments!**

Yes, crime is bad. The lawbreaker must be punished to atone for his transgression. There is certainly a vital need for all justice systems. Moral principles must be taught. All of this is correct. There is the good and proper way of "love thy neighbour as thyself." There is the evil path of immorality, anger, revenge, malevolence.

People must learn to choose the good way, the way of law and order. People must learn, sometimes the hard and painful way, all the roles of the game of life. However, there is the high truth of the soul's plane, which is trans–duality, the consciousness of the One. At the moment not everybody is capable of understanding and tuning into it. I am referring to the game of life: A game where aware and evolved souls erase their knowledge, choosing to take upon themselves the rules of the game of duality. They place their beliefs in plots and learn good and evil. This truth may be comprehended by high spiritual insight.

For technical reasons we will stop the communication at this time. This would be a good time to read the material and internalize it.

Thank you and much love to you. Here I Am, Master Akiva, the harbinger of the message of unity, the consciousness of One and "Thou shall love the Lord thy God with all soul and all thy strength," and the message of" love thy neighbour as thyself." Thank you dear, Ilana, for the enabling the transmission. There is no coincidence, all is conducted from above. Remember and contain this always.

Lesson 24

The Holiness of the Holy Land
The Peace Process

ILANA: Good morning wonderful guides and Master Akiva, I would like to proceed with our discussion. Thank you.

MASTER AKIVA: Good morning to you dear, Ilana. I thank you for being kind enough to get up (early), though it was rather difficult for you. Indeed, you demonstrate self–discipline and persistence, which are necessary for pursuing our joint endeavour and in order for you to perform your task and mission. You please me. We will go on with our discussion about duality and games of light and darkness.

People tend to behave like other people. They do not want to be unusual for fear of being ostracized and shunned by society. People influence each other all the time, using telepathy waves and frequencies, in addition to the mass media, which is so accessible to you. This mutual effect causes people, even those who are peaceful and possess high and subtle frequencies, to react to what is occurring in their territory.

When people do not understand the nature of the overall reality - although nowadays a lot of information

is readily available - they get carried away by popular conceptions.

They are told that the security situation is volatile, that the economy is unstable, that society is afflicted with violence and they believe it and act accordingly. They become defensive or go on the offensive. They are brainwashed by the media. They lose their high ideals, the vision of the Promised Land, the Holy Land, the Land of Milk and Honey. They focus on their personal and material wellbeing and by doing so they become cut off from their roots and some people emigrate. Others experience a sense of bitterness and regard themselves as victims.

You have spiritual energetic ties to the Land of Israel, the land of the forefathers. The earthly land of Israel is joined with the heavenly land of Israel, the land promised to Abraham and his descendents forever.

Some people need to go abroad to earn a living. These are necessary and legitimate reasons to leave. But there are those who live in the Holy Land harbouring bitterness and anger toward their native land, its institutions, the military and the whole of society. They are angry with the state and what is happening in it.

Those with a victim pattern tend to point an accusatory finger and blame outside agencies. They do not accept any personal responsibility and do not understand their accountability for what is taking place around them. They prefer to sit and complain, sink into depression and remain mired in self-pity. This is typical of those who utterly lack self-awareness about their real identity and their ability to create the desired reality.

These people are manipulated like puppets on a string by others who aspire to control and maneuver them.

Sometimes those with a victim pattern, blame themselves. Their permanent negative emotions will cause them to develop all kinds of physical and other ailments and afflictions.

Often, their low level of awareness and lack of comprehension of their true nature will lead them to employ conventional solutions, which are also devoid of personal responsibility. Since they are unaware of the interaction between the psychological and biological aspects of the self, they fail to realize that they have the power to influence their own thoughts, emotions and beliefs. Accordingly, they will seek advice from others who think as they do. They will go to physicians and receive medications to treat their symptoms. Since the root of the problem lies within, they may experience temporary relief. However, new syndromes will probably emerge. **In order to gain real healing, it is necessary to heal the root cause.**

This fits not only body–psyche problems, but also the

conundrum of the Land of Israel, the land of the forefathers. At present you are trying to remedy matters with a physical barrier of separation, by sealing the border between you and the Palestinians, by utilizing the security apparatus. You are also attempting to engage in direct talks with some of the elements who threaten your existence. The second approach is good but it does not touch the root of the existential issue: The controversy between Israel and its neighbours, the basic quarrel between Jews and Palestinian Arabs.

The solution must be a root solution, deep and fundamental. It has to include spiritual understanding, mutually acceptable to both sides. Each nation must align with its spiritual vision, its idealism, realizing that without mutual acceptance and understanding, without acquiring the value, "Thou shall love the Lord thy God with all thy soul and with all thy strength," and "love thy neighbour as thyself," in both nations, real peace will not be possible for a long time.

The stark karma between the two nations scuttles all attempts at negotiation. Furthermore, the division of the enemy into those who are acceptable, as opposed to those who belong to the axis of evil with whom no negotiations may be entered into, is childish and unwise. In diplomacy one should not act out of emotions such as, vengeance, anger, deprivation or hate.

Ideally, such consideration should spring from a desire to seek truth soberly and starkly, but with supreme vision and faith.

But first, the common denominator of all human beings must be activated – faith in one God, faith in the natural instinct of human beings to desire peace, to strive for the vision of "every man under his vine and under his fig tree."

The universal desire to earn a living, provide food and education for one's children and enjoy the fruits of material wealth, can pave the way to real peace, in conjunction with the values of "love thy neighbour as thyself" through charities and mutual assistance.

ILANA: Dear Master Akiva, I agree that an in–depth solution is needed. But I think political and military moves are necessary, because as long as such consciousness does not manifest on both sides, we must respond to what is aimed at us, right? How do we solve this discrepancy?

MASTER AKIVA: Your question is important Of course I do not oppose military or political moves, if there are compelling reasons to fight and defend what belongs to you, go and do it! But remember that in order to resolve the situation, which repeats every few years, you need to reach the root of the problem.

First, you must act in the educational sphere, restoring to

the traditional values, the vision of the redemption of the Land of Israel. Bring back the high ideals of the Land of the Forefathers, to which the People of Israel returned after two thousand years of exile, after the Holocaust that took the lives of six million Jews.

People adapt easily to new situations. They tend to forget the past. The history curriculum in schools must be overhauled. The beliefs, customs and perceptions of reality that form your collective experience as a nation must be combined with spiritual awareness, with insight into the sources of religion, with understanding of cultural effects and more.

You must emphasize how collective fear creates events linked to those fears. How great faith and yearning, combined with activity in the physical dimension, can affect and create a new reality.

He who is detached from his history is disconnected from his people, cut off from his roots, disengaged from his spiritual essence. He lacks the ability to draw conclusions and learn from the wisdom of the ancients and the occurrences of the past.

Why repeat the mistakes of the past instead of learning from them and distilling their lessons in all walks of life? See how the State of Israel is continuously engaged in battle with its enemies; why not stop the wheel and observe what is driving it?

It is true that God watches over you and saves you always. However, "in every generation they rise up against us to destroy us." This belief recycles again and again because it is anchored in the law of creating your reality based on your beliefs. The time is ripe to shake off this belief. Re-examine the belief system of the Chosen People.

What is the Chosen People? What are its privileges? What are its duties? What is its role among the nations of the world?

The Chosen People was asked to uphold the Ten Commandments. It was instructed to develop in–depth insight into the divine decrees, which are a spiritual directive to maintain moral values and an orderly society. The Children of Israel were chosen to internalize the Ten Commandments, which speak of instilling love as a value. "Thou shalt love the Lord thy God with all thy soul and with all thy strength," "love thy neighbour as thyself," for you are created in the image of God and a divine spark pulsates within you. Your fellow man, who is created exactly like you, is your neighbour, whether you regard him as an enemy, a foe, a lover or a co–creator.

All human beings are created in the image of God! All of creation has been stamped with the Divine Seal! Therefore, all of creation, with all its creatures, is part and parcel of God. You cannot harm one part of God without desecrating the heavens, without harming

yourself, for you are an integral part of the whole. You cannot possibly separate yourself from all of creation. You have to honour, cherish, love and accept all of creation as the Chosen Creation of the Creator of the universe, the God of whom you are a part. Do not hate yourself, do not criticize yourself, do not fight with yourself. And "do not unto your fellowman what you hate being done to you."

Some of the Commandments are prohibitions, to ensure that you will not doubt their efficacy. But the love pronouncements are stated positively. Incorporate then within you, through your subconscious. Absorb them into all layers of your awareness. They will take root in your higher consciousness as well as in the consciousness of your body personality.

They can exert tremendous effect on the consciousness of your nation and all of humanity. Declare your new and renewed choice, one that will link you to the root of your soul and give meaning and flavour to your life:

"I hereby choose and agree to accommodate the message of Oneness: "Love thy neighbour as thyself" and thereby activate my inner genetic code!" Say it three times with complete intention. After each repetition stop and take a deep breath, to convey the verbal message to all your bodies.

Blessed be in your eternal being, all who are walking in the way of teaching of love, for the time of the teaching of love is at hand.

Here I Am, Master Akiva, the bearer of the message of unity for all of the People of Israel and the nations of the world, ending (this session) with thanks to all messengers who aid the dissemination of the message.

Thank you dear, Ilana, for enabling the passage through you.

Love is the respect of all of creation, to God, the root of your souls.

"Holy, Holy, Holy the Lord of Hosts and we are his angels," calls the choir of seraphim and the golden trumpets resonate and open the gates of heaven for the sake of the union between heaven and earth.

Lesson 25

Acknowledge Happiness

ILANA: Good morning to all my dear and beloved guides; good and blessed morning to dearly beloved Master Akiva. I would like to proceed with our discussion. Thank you. I feel joyous and do not know why. I feel enthusiastic, even without a reason.

MASTER AKIVA: Good and blessed morning to you, dear and beloved Ilana, messenger of God and the angels, priests and sanctified beings. Why would you wonder about your "inexplicable" joy?

Dear, when you are in tune, when a human being is directly connected to his soul, he is under its light, in its full guidance, his will entwines with the divine will and all of heaven shares his joy. There is no need for an external factor for you to feel enthusiasm and even happiness. The whole is always within you. When the heart is open, when faith percolates through you, when you feel you are on a direct path to fulfillment, you are in a place of joy, gratitude and great happiness.

People look for happiness outside themselves, outside their homes. They look to others to make them happy. They rely on the attainment of material desires and the fulfillment of lusts. Their gratitude does not last long. Nevertheless, every activity can be the source of happiness, when it is done with a willing heart and out of utter willingness to be in the experience of being here and now, in the moment.

ILANA: Dear Master Akiva, I have noticed that our thoughts have the capacity of either making us happy or unhappy. Why is that?

MASTER AKIVA: Think of your thoughts as a fleet of trucks. They can transport good and desired products or they can carry trash. You can choose what your thoughts will contain. It often appears as if your thoughts control and manipulate you. That is because you fail to comprehend their significance, their ability to affect your conscious mood and the unconscious creation of reality in your life. You allow them to roam with no control whatsoever.

Every thought has its own frequency, enmeshed with emotions and associations. It carries electrical pulses to the brain, affecting sub-conscious programming and thus affecting your life. Therefore, you should try to be aware of your thoughts and take responsibility for them. Positive thoughts contain high frequencies; they are happy, harmonious and quiet. Negative thoughts contain low frequencies, negative emotions, fears and anxieties and they attract corresponding events.

We have discussed energy defences, I explained that it is an inner approach with specific comprehension and its truth at any given moment paves the way to reach it from the outside. It broadcasts a frequency which forms a channell to accommodate the frequency itself and its contents. To hold positive and healthy thoughts that will create the positive experiences you desire, choose such thoughts.

You can consciously program yourself by using verses of scripture, prayers and positive declarations. Prepare empowering sentences ahead of time, to protect you from negative thoughts of envy, jealousy, slander and thoughts aimed at yourself, whose main content is self-pity or lack of acceptance.

A verse recommended for inner cleansing and healing is: "Restore unto me the joy of Thy salvation; and uphold me with Thy free spirit." (Psalms 51:12.) Another is: "Blessed is the man that walketh not in the counsel of the ungodly, nor standeth in the way of sinners, nor sitteth in the seat of the scornful. But his delight is in the law of the Lord and upon His law doeth he meditates day and night. And he shall be like a tree planted by the rivers of water, that bringeth forth his fruit in his season; his leaf also shall not wither; and whatsoever he doeth shall prosper." (Id., 1:1–3.)

The entire Book of Psalms is a talisman for integrating the frequency of sanctity, for it carries good thoughts and feelings, through expressions of gratitude and glory to God.

A happy person is one who feels fortunate and expresses gratitude for what he has. Happiness stems from gratitude to God, the Creator, for the gift of life. Furthermore, one should try not to disrupt the mind with idle worries and thoughts.

Express appreciation for what is, without complaining or thinking about what you lack. Be grateful for your health. Express gratitude for being close to the Creator of the universe. Let go of your lack of acceptance of what is happening in your life. Let go of your need to control your life. **Worry indicates a lack of faith and a desire to control destiny.**

Worry plants seeds of doubt (regarding the proposition), that all that happens is for your ultimate benefit. Instead of worrying, take action. You can pray and ask for help. You can seek advice. Understand that you cannot control everything. Ask to strengthen your faith in the Creator and in the laws of nature. Learn a method of healing such as Reiki, to send healing and assistance across time and space. **Release the scenario of fear and know that you have created that which you believe and know to exist. You can create out of jealousy, out of hardship. But you can also create the treasures your soul yearns for.**

ILANA: In other words, a happy person is one who does not worry, who believes that everything is happening for his highest good, who believes that all is as it should be, who is grateful for his lot in life, who takes responsibility for his thoughts, does not indulge in negative thoughts and is in tune with his soul and his purpose.

MASTER AKIVA: Happiness is a state of having been acknowledged. A person who accepts all that transpires in his life acknowledges what the Creator has given him and that he has been placed on his "game board" for lessons that have to be experienced. He does not fight or resist. He accepts what God has bestowed on him. He is in tune with the supreme purpose of his soul and walks by its light and guidance. He listens to the commands of his heart. He is happy because he is grateful. At times he will feel joyful, at other times he will feel tranquil. Of course, the vicissitudes of life will sometimes bring him down and make him sad. But if he perseveres, he will soon be restored to his state of happiness. Acceptance allows him to transcend to the soul level and his capacity to attain the light of love will be great indeed.

Emotional happiness is the happiness that resides in thoughts. Physical happiness is usually equated with the union between two lovers. But there is a more splendid happiness, spiritual happiness, which is attained when you accept all thoughts and emotions, the physical state and all of life circumstances.

ILANA: To my mind, some people could be happy in their present situation but they nevertheless suffer and feel miserable. How could you help them?

MASTER AKIVA: Gratitude would put them back on the path of happiness. They need to acknowledge what they really have. They must start to appreciate what they take for granted. Nothing can be taken for granted: Neither freedom, nor breathing; neither the body nor life itself.

Everyone can choose the manner and fashion of his inner dialogue. Pay attention to your thoughts: Are they fraught with anger and grievances? Self–pity? Comparisons between you and others? Read passages from the Book of Psalms or any other inspirational book which has positive content. Recite and sing songs and poems with positive and optimistic words, words of gratitude and love.

Do not allow your thoughts to rule you. Be their master!

Call upon the light and love energy to be internalised in you. Call upon your soul to lead you through your life. Know that the moment of power is in the present and you always have the power of choice. Use it wisely!

Choose to acknowledge life and live happily. Choose to be thankful for everything that exists, without taking it all for granted, without thinking negative thoughts, time and again. Correct negative habits by self–reprogramming.

Everyone can be happy, no matter how difficult his circumstances, even if he is suffering from ill–health or economic hardship, as long as his spiritual well–being is optimal. Spiritual well–being can be attained in an instant if you choose to link with the essence: "Love the Lord thy God with all thy heart, with all thy soul… and with all thy strength." (Deuteronomy, 6:5.)

ILANA: I am requesting a break, so that I can internalize your message.

MASTER AKIVA: It is imperative to contain this knowledge. It is like a sweet fruit: First you see it with your eyes, then you feel it with your hands and experience its fragrance and only then do you taste it and absorb it into you. You said it well. I recommend that you internalize the knowledge in all its layers: the surface and the deep, the mystery and the secret. Breathe deeply and ask to incorporate the teachings, because they are all divine.

Lesson 26

Many Paths – One God

ILANA: Good morning exalted, dear and very beloved guides. Good and blessed morning to dear Master Akiva. I wish to proceed with our discussion. Thank you.

MASTER AKIVA: Good morning dear and beloved Ilana, trailblazer of the path to understanding unity, through, "Love thy neighbour as thyself." Well, time is short. We need to provide a great deal of information verbally as well as at other levels.

You have joined with many other messengers to carry out the mission of rescue and communication of knowledge from distant cultures – *from an ancient future*. These are you in another time, another place, another experience. You are helping yourselves to bring yourselves salvation from wars of annihilation that will otherwise wipe you off the face of the earth. The path to peace is crucial and vital if you are to preserve your race.

This mission has to be undertaken simultaneously on several planes: political, economic, intellectual–philosophical, social. A strategy for peace must be developed, along with the study of strategies for war.

ILANA: Who is the speaker, please? I do not sense the energies of Master Akiva, it is important for me to know who the speaker is.

MASTER AKIVA: Thank you dear and beloved Ilana for noticing the subtle change in the passage of energy. Indeed, it was not I who conveyed the message but an entity from Jupiter, from the Order of Melchizedek; however, you need to understand that I am not separated from other light entities. We operate together, envisioning one supreme goal: **Imparting consciousness and the expansion of awareness on planet Earth.** This expansion is in fact the accommodation of the path of peace through personal responsibility, through your maturity as a race, the ascension of the spirit while you are yet in a physical body, experiencing the illusion of separateness.

If the need – the urgency – arises, other entities join the discussion, some better known than others. Nevertheless, I am the principal speaker, in accord with my mission in creation, i.e., to conduct the message of unity. I am the modern interpreter of the Ten Commandments through the positive decrees they contain. You received this as the message expressed in your book "The Gate to Sanctification – Conscious Creation." For your current readers, let's summarize: Every commandment stated in the positive starts with the statement "Thou shalt love."

I started the conversation by saying that time is short.

The entities whose mission is practical leadership, both individual and collective, also want to communicate with you and convey their messages. This will take place later, if you allow it.

"As the hart panteth after the water brooks, so panteth my soul after thee, O God." (Psalms 42:1.)

We will dedicate our discussion to the thirst for God, the yearning to commune with the spiritual body, the return to the source. Every human being innately yearns for the communion, safety, faith and pleasantness in which the souls in the World of Truth are held secure. Some do not yearn and do not remember, but they feel an inexplicable void, because they are focused on the material, utterly lacking spiritual values.

Those who yearn do not necessarily know what they are longing for. They may translate it into a desire for unity of the flesh – physical love. Some interpret it as a passion for space and freedom. Others transfer the passion they feel to their occupation or to a subject that fires their imagination.

When people are in tune with their essence, the root of their souls, their hearts, they receive a regular flow of the water of life, which quenches their thirst and soothes their yearning.

In this era, a great differentiation is taking place between religion and secularity. Those who walk in the path of tradition are called "religious," while those who do not observe the commandments of the Scripture are referred to as "secular." Each side has become entrenched in its beliefs.

Even among the so-called secular, who do not observe religious practices, there are many who ardently follow the path of "love thy neighbour as thyself." Although they do not practice religion, in their overall insight and their walk of life they maintain the essence of the whole Torah, which requires maintaining one's love of God and of his fellow human being.

"Thou shall love the Lord thy God with all thy soul and with all thy strength," "love thy neighbour as thyself."

Conversely, among the religious, those who have undertaken the burden of the commandments, there are some who keep the commandments superficially and barely uphold the injunction to "love thy neighbour as thyself."

Since you live on a planet with free choice between light and darkness, between good and evil, you may choose the path of religion or a different mindset. Even one who does not fully obey the commandments is experiencing trials, which are important for people who have a different approach to knowledge. Some interpret it superficially, others more in depth and according the mystery teachings. Those who differentiate between religious and secular and expropriate the Torah that was given to the whole People of Israel on Mount Sinai for themselves cannot fulfil the commandments as they should. They fail to understand the essence of God. They fail to comprehend unconditional love and they will not fulfil the verse, "love thy neighbour as thyself."

I am not adding new teachings to the Torah, for you, dear, are not the right instrument for such. I am not here to take away from the religious sector's interpretation of the Torah. Since you are highly devout person, who happens to belong to the secular stream of society, I pass through your channell, through the energies and your personal interpretations. My goal is to bring knowledge to the readers, who thirst for it. My aim is to inform all human beings, beyond the divisions of religion and secularity. My endeavour is to unite the People of Israel. Your mission is to transmit the knowledge of the light to those, who are secular, yet wish to receive the knowledge of the Torah, to receive God, through the portal of the New Age.

Those who respond emotionally to the message should ask themselves: Why do I react this way to a message of love and unity? Am I in touch with genuine love? Do I know what is it? Can I actually love and respectfully accept others, no matter what they believe? It is written: "The just shall live by his faith." (Habakkuk, 2:4.) Truth, faith and love cannot be forced. That which is kept in a man's heart is known only to God, "for man looketh on the outward appearance, but the Lord looketh on the heart." (1 Samuel 16:7.)

In his heart, one may be very righteous, even saintly. One need not maintain a religious–traditional lifestyle in order to uphold God's will. Some people pretend to be dedicated to God. They are punctilious in their observance. They may deceive others but they do not fool themselves and certainly not God.

Modesty and humility are good for man, as are acceptance of the other with compassion and without judgment. Likewise self–compassion is good. One should avoid severely punishing himself and respect the divine spark within. And as he would love and accept himself, forgive and absolve his transgressions, he should equally forgive and absolve his fellow man. He should embrace those who, to his mind, are less aware or know less, with love and acceptance. A compassionate father would not judge his young children for failing to undertake duties reserved for their older siblings. He would not discriminate between his children but accept them all equally and lovingly.

In the same manner, the People of Israel should accept their brethren, no matter what their lifestyle, without antagonism – which annuls "love thy neighbour as thyself" and constitutes a failure to understand the essence of God in, whose image all were created equal, without distinctions of race, religion, sex or nationality. *All* are the children of God and all should smile warmly upon their brothers and sisters. Others are not "baddies" but "buddies." We must honour all of creation and maintain the flame of faith in God. All is God and you must respect all that is in creation with love and respect, for all is the work of God.

ILANA: Dear and beloved Master Akiva, I would like to receive additional material, relevant to all nations of the world, regarding the tolerance you have been discussing. Thank you.

MASTER AKIVA: One's faith is his path to the truth. Every path is a piece of the whole puzzle and when you see it this way, you approach world peace.

The source of all human beings is the same. Actually, humanity is a single component of consciousness, containing an infinite and colourful range of beliefs, opinions and customs. Every religion started out as a channell, a portal to eternal truth, to the one God, the source of the whole of creation. Every religion was specifically suited to the particular era in which it was dispensed and to the souls then walking that path.

People believed with all their hearts in a given religion, until another arrived, carrying away the consciousness of the masses and becoming installed in their perception as the sole, exclusive truth. And so it has been since time immemorial.

You must remember and internalize nature's law of conservation, which is reincarnation. The purpose of all souls is to evolve and attain reunion. For this reason they reincarnate time and again, in order to learn, to undergo trials and to apply what has been learned in previous incarnations. Otherwise they repeat the same lessons again and again in one form or another, until they have learned and incorporated them.

Those who specialize in past life regression, as well as those who recall past incarnations, even partially, know to retell the truth: They incarnate in various religions, nationalities and lands in order to realize the law of compassion and oneness. A soul can incarnate as an idol worshiper, a Jew, a Christian, a Muslim, a Buddhist, an atheist and more. It is linked to the lessons it has to undergo. If you would really understand the law of karmic incarnation, you would understand that, although today you might be a Catholic, it does not mean that in previous lives you were not Jews, Celts, followers of Zoroaster, Muslims and so on. Identifying with your current faith and believing that it alone is the right one, while believers of all others faiths are "infidels," is wrong. It is a belief that creates intolerance toward the other paths, all of which are designed to reach faith in the one God who appears with many faces, under many names. Human beings cannot consciously reach eternal truth, they can only try to interpret it to the best of their understanding. Accordingly, understand this: *All of you are one*! You have forever incarnated and will forever incarnate in various religions. Do not develop identification with your religion. Instead, develop identification with the consciousness of your soul.

Thank you for an excellent inquiry. Be blessed.

Here I Am, Master Akiva, the bearer of the message of unity to the People of Israel and herald of deliverance at this time. And, as you shall keep the decree of "love thy neighbour as thyself," salvation will soon be at hand.

Resolve all disputes among yourselves. Unite as brothers. You are all sons and daughters of God, the Creator of the universe, who gave us compassion and love to conduct ourselves by its light. Love is giving (by the Lord) and acceptance (of human beings) and giving in return (to the Lord).

And thank you dear, Ilana for enabling the transmission of the message and its acceptance. Love to all the People of Israel.

Lesson No. 27

The Victim Pattern

Good morning dear and beloved Master Akiva. While editing our book, I discovered that several chapters are missing, despite the fact that most of the material was written in a conceptual continuum. I have no doubt that this is no coincidence and it was all pre–planned. Should I include here a chapter about the Victim Pattern? I feel I ought to do so. Could you please explain to me, why I have skipped a particular chapter?

Master Akiva: Dear Ilana, I have wanted to teach you and others through you, that there is no limit to time and space! At every point in time you can resume an activity you have halted previously, for any reason. There are no errors, it is only a form of continual experience for the sake of learning. You can place the chapter about the victim pattern here, as part of this particular lesson, which is very important for mankind. The time has come for people to understand, once and for all, their importance and degree of influence in the process of reality creation.

You ask, who is dictating this chapter? My reply is complex: You have written it. You are a high channell of communication, from whom flows knowledge from eminent hierarchies. There is no artificial segregation in the higher spheres, there is no separation in the planes of reality where you reside, in the Earth dimension. The knowledge arrived from God. The knowledge came from the high guidance. I have conveyed the knowledge. It was transmitted by the Supreme Karma Council. It was dispensed because the time of change and transformation has come.

Mankind has to take responsibility for itself, its choices, its belief system. Mankind has to assume responsibility for its part in creating reality and its influence on life on planet Earth.

All the guides, who plot a course of humanity and define its path of action are included. You are currently endowed with high frequencies. You are one of these frequencies. You have chosen to be born in a physical body, to be an emissary who channells these messages. That is the high purpose of your soul. You are fulfilling it with supreme grace. Be glad and proud of yourself, be self–assured and radiate your goodness and the warmth of love unto the universe. We are all behind you, we all are with you.

We are one. We are all in complete communion with God. We re–emphasize the utmost importance of this book. Now, with your permission, please implant the channelling you have recently received. Do not be concerned as to whether it belongs in your next book, for all your books are but one book.

Expand your vision and see all your books, your CDs and yourself as one, as a whole whose purpose is to spread the awareness of light and love, the highest and foremost compassion energy, in every avenue and with all the means at your disposal.

ILANA: Thank you. These statements are exciting and somewhat surprising. Indeed, there are no mistakes! I am glad to serve as a bridge between dimensions and here is the chapter, as I have previously channelled.

* * *

Dear and beloved people,

We would like to remind you that you are powerful creators who, due to manipulative external agencies, were disengaged from their source of knowledge. These are powerful entities, who sought to control humanity for various reasons, including the production and harvesting of emotional energy by inflicting suffering, pain and misfortune. Other reasons are the accumulation of power, competitiveness, pleasure and more.

In order to neutralize you from your source of power, which is the memory of how to consciously create, you have been programmed, like a computer game and an advanced robot. Implants have been placed in your psyche. One significant implant is the victim pattern.

A victim is helpless and can therefore be controlled by a range of manipulations: On the one hand, threats and fears and on the other hand promises and temptations. This sophisticated formula, which is in fact a divide and conquer effect, sowed doubt, suspicion and apprehension in you. You were placed in a state of defensiveness, which resulted in separateness among you.

The victim needs to be protected from an external factor. He does not trust himself. More often than not, he fails to comprehend that he has the ability to alter the reality he finds himself in. He is utterly unaware that it was he, who created that particular reality in the first place, regardless of whether it is pleasant, difficult or intolerable.

The failure to accept responsibility for elements of his existence, is typical of anyone harbouring the victim pattern. It implies a lack of comprehension of and insight into the fact that people have the ability to create their own reality and that their energy, which is composed of thought patterns and emotional configurations, acts as a magnet to attract certain outcomes. They are unconscious of this process, because the events summoned for them by their higher self are lessons whose purpose is growth and personal development. These individuals are unconscious of the fact that it is all for their highest good. They are mired so deeply in their drama that they stumble and sink.

This pattern tends to create guilt, defensiveness, aggression, or, an inability to act, rendering the person helpless. The victim is characterized by self–pity, depression, helplessness and guilt, on the one hand, and, on the other hand, aggressive feelings of anger, rage, vengeance, hatred, suspiciousness and belligerence.

The victim becomes attached to his ego. He cannot view the picture from its widest and highest perspective. He is immersed in his drama. He functions as an actor in a play, who has forgotten that he is just playing a role. He completely identifies with the character he is playing, its feelings, thoughts and actions. He is activated by the script and forgets that he is a person, whose profession is acting. This is dimensional intoxication (similar to the depth intoxication that afflicts divers under certain conditions). You are not one–dimensional, as you mistakenly assume. You are, in fact, multidimensional. You are present in several places at the same time, including your soul and higher self. In a higher plane of your existence you are aware that you are playing a role on a stage. You are aware of the play's purpose and what it is trying to teach you. The purpose is always tied to soul evolution and transcendence of the needs of the ego, accomplished by understanding of the soul and in the process, by taking responsibility for the drama.

When someone hurts you, the first thing that happens is the infliction itself. You feel hurt. In the second stage you may develop self–pity and submerge yourself into anguish, which recurs again and again based on past experience of similar injuries. You may lash out in anger and have the desire to retaliate. Both reactions are linked to your fight-or-flight survival reflex, which has been embedded in you since the dawn of human history.

The forces of nature and wild animals endangered the life of prehistoric man. He needed swiftness, physical strength, keenness and cunning in order to survive. Sometimes he had to hunt down wild animals, while at other times he had to flee and hide. He was constantly exposed to threats and uncertainty. These survival instincts are still imprinted in your psyche and motivate your actions.

In order to connect with the soul plane, you have to know how to transform your ego, which is the purpose of all souls who desire to evolve and ascend. Do not suppress your ego or be enraged by it or deny its existence. Instead, you should understand it, for it contains the essence of your soul's lessons. You must learn to identify the programming that induces your behaviour.

For example, **anger**. Anger is the result of lack of spiritual insight, a feeling of deprivation, injustice or pain caused by injury. Anger is a powerful tool that may be used to alter your situation from helpless victim to one, who is in charge of his life and affirms: "This is it! This is my red line!"

You may be angry at others and at yourselves as well.

Learn to identify the energy of anger and ask to transform it to a higher level, a level that is associated with the soul: **forgiveness**. If you harbour anger, seek to release it and forgive yourselves and whoever appears to have wounded you and ask forgiveness of those you have hurt, consciously or unconsciously.

Note that people tend to get hurt, when things happen in a way they did not expect. For instance, a friend calls you and leaves a message to call her back. Perhaps you are tired or busy, but you forget to return her call and even erase her message. Some days pass with no contact between you. It is certainly possible that your friend will interpret your conduct as ignoring her, as lack of care and as an injury you have inflicted on her and she may develop resentment towards you. People tend to interpret action or inaction according to their utterly subjective inner world.

Another type of such energy is **self-pity**. When you feel despondent, dejected or drained, you are in a passive situation, wholly unaware of the spiritual aspect of your existence. When you identify this sort of energy, first ask to transmute it into spiritual insight, then ask to be in tune with the notion of assuming responsibility for having summoned your own experience. Understand that when you feel this way (self–pity) you are actually in the midst of a meaningful soul lesson, but, you are embroiled in the drama, in an emotional current that clouds your senses, causing you to forget the essence of the lesson.

How do you leave the drama in order to view the lesson?
Imagine yourself in a large ocean wave. Now feel yourself leaping out of it, like dolphin surging from the depths. Breathe the crisp air and look at the wave from up high.

Now ask to be an eagle gliding on the air currents, engulfed in white light, looking down. Ask to rise higher and higher till you find yourself in the answer. The answer is the right one for the challenge you are struggling with.

For example: A woman lost her mobile phone. She remembered having it that morning. Since she didn't leave home that day, she knew that it was inside the house. She turned the house upside down in an attempt to locate the lost instrument. She asked psychic friends to help her. Despite all their efforts and hers, the phone could not be found. The woman was aware that everything has a meaning and that she was in the middle of a lesson, so she lit a candle and some incense and sat in her favourable armchair. She calmed down, closed her eyes and asked to understand the meaning of the lesson. Immediately, the answer surfaced in her mind: communication or rather, lack of communication. She combined the answer with various other issues and challenges she had dealt with that day. Despite the fact that she never recovered the phone she felt satisfied and pleased.

Understanding that you are in the midst of a lesson, sensing the lesson which empowers you, links you with your inner strength, you cease feeling sorry for yourself

and this brings an end to your suffering. Instead, you now seek to solve issues from several different angles.

The woman in the story decided that if she did not find the lost phone, she would contact the insurance company and purchase a new one. Note that the victim pattern had departed. Another woman in her place, one implanted with the victim pattern, would have sunk into self–pity, grumbling and complaining, becoming angry at herself and utterly failing to grasp the lesson.

The lessons are the same, whether you have a victim pattern or not. The difference is in *the ability to cope*. Are you coming from a place of inner balance, with composure and presence of mind, which allow you to resolve the challenge easily and even with pleasure; or do you lapse into self–pity and by so doing deplete your energy. At any event, it is possible that the difficulty will be solved. Conversely, if you fail to figure out the lesson, the problem will recur later in one form or another.

In order to restore your vigour, in order to be conscious creators who create from a clean place of light, love, faith and joy, you must ask to be free of the victim pattern. As a matter of fact, you do not need to ask at all, for in asking there is an inner centre of weakness and inability to perform by the self. **You have to declare and to do!**

Since you reside on a planet of free will and choice and you are free to be either in light or in darkness, since you are powerful creators, choose!

Be proactive, not reactive. Declare: "**I choose to relinquish the victim pattern, to remove it from myself, from all bodies, all levels, dimensions, incarnations, here and now and in my entire being. Thank you.**"

The declaration should be made resolutely and powerfully and repeated three times. Breathe deeply through the nose. Hold your breath. Assimilate it into your emotional body. Then exhale forcefully through the mouth.

Also make the following declaration: "**I choose to be fully in communion with my soul guidance.**" Make this affirmation three times as well. **Request and choose to be untangled from your ego and to transcend it.**

As stated above, the victim pattern is easy to control. For that reason, dominating agencies are interested in maintaining it within you. A saying such as, "It is good to die for our country," is characteristic of the quality of sacrifice, whose importance you were taught to appreciate. You learn to sacrifice yourselves for your fellows and for lofty ideals. Such notions are noble and have intrinsic value. But you should know how to be in tune with your inner truth and be attentive to the command of your conscience. Remain centreed in your inherent strength rather than becoming victims who experience their existence from the murk of muddy emotions.

Wash away the deposits, cleanse your emotions, clean up all the bodies – the physical, ethereal, emotional, mental and spiritual.

Affirm your choice to relinquish your karma.

Be here in the present. Here and now. Multidimensional. In the core of your power. Tell your selves: "**I am that I am, I am not just this physical body.**" Know how to create from a position of responsibility, without guilt, without anger, without fear.

Know how to forgive, how to love, how to smile and understand that you are players on the stage of the game of life. Know not to identify with all dramas, especially those from the past. Get in touch with the soul and observe the entire picture in its widest aspect.

The victim pattern connects us to the course of hurt. When you rid yourself of the victim pattern, you are empowered to request and declare your transfer to the course of heart.

MASTER AKIVA: The process is of great significance for personal evolution. Its importance is that much greater, when the evolution of human society as a whole is at issue. This process brings comprehension at the deepest possible level, of the verse: "Love thy neighbour as thyself." There are no victims, there are no guilty parties, there are no dramas. Everything is one big stage–play designed to teach and rouse all the actors, bringing about their full and perfect wakefulness.

When you have accomplished the process of liberating yourself from the victim pattern, doing it with great and focused intention from the soul plane, you will be able to unite your physical body personality (ego) with your soul. You will be able to observe your lessons as individuals and as a nation, as humanity as a whole, through the eyes of the soul, through the eyes of God.

There will be no divisions; there will be no place left for differentiation. Inner and outer borders will be dissolved and peace will cover the planet. Peace will be the privilege of each and every one who would walk in this path, the course of the heart.

Blessed be in your eternal being and goodness and grace shall be your lot forever.

Here Am I, Master Akiva, in the name of the light guides, the angels and God's glorious and illustrious messenger. And thank you dear, Ilana, for your incisive attentiveness to your inner guidance, to which you have submitted when necessary. Be blessed.

And through my words I exude the frequency of unity; I emit the energy of pure love, which is giving–accepting–giving.

Lesson 28

Beliefs of Energy Centres

To See the Lesson: the Path of Heart – the Path of Hurt

ILANA: Good morning dear and wonderful guides, good morning dear Master Akiva. I would like to proceed with our discussion. Thank you.

MASTER AKIVA: Good morning Ilana, my dear and beloved scholar. Today is the 28th continuous day of our sessions. I would like to address a question you had sent me telepathically: Is there a correlation between the fatigue and lack of energy you have been feeling lately and the fact that you have been channelling for such a long period and rise so early?

My answer is: No! It is not related to the channelling. Quite to the contrary, the channelling makes you happy and gives your day added meaning. It has to do with an energetic expansion you are undergoing. The channell that you are is being adjusted for long distance reception, for longer time. By long distances I mean very high frequencies. For that activity you require much rest, to renew your reservoirs of physical energy. The physical body has to adjust to the intensity of the frequencies, so it feels difficulty and sometimes you are fatigued. Please do not interpret this fatigue as psychological, mental or spiritual.

I would like to digress for a moment and relate to your unprofessional interpretation, which is how we would relate to it humourously. You tend to interpret everything that happens to you by analysis, classification and filing, according to its emotional content. You classify events as happy, sad, hard, exciting and so on, according to what you are feeling, but sometimes your interpretation is incorrect. You relate to a powerful emotion and enhance it with an erroneous interpretation. For instance, if you are excited about something, you call this feeling excitement, which can either be good or bad, based on your expectation. At other times you interpret the excitement as fear, for both are experienced similarly: rapid heartbeat, restlessness, impatience, etc.

Sometimes, you feel sadness arising from within, even from unknown regions. These regions were formed in past experiences, either in your current life or previous ones. You may even receive it from the air, because some sort of energy is affecting you. You may receive it from other people and when it penetrates you, you identify with it and make it your own.

As you may recall, everyone has a mutual effect on everyone else due to the connection among you and between you and the world.

All humans are capable of feeling all emotions. Emotions bring corresponding thoughts. Since you constantly interpret your emotions, you may be caught in momentary sadness, become carried away and sink into waves of sadness. This, in turn, could sink you further into self–pity and from there it is a short distance to the victim pattern, where one is helpless and lacks effectiveness.

Of course, when joy is the issue, the same phenomenon applies, as well. But in such a case there is no difficulty experiencing them, due to the cycling of positive emotions.

Negative emotions shut you down and contract you, because the light of love does not reach the candle of your soul, the core that holds life and is formed by the connection with the soul. Positive feelings enable and amplify the flow of the light of love, thus they are very healthy for you and facilitate your ability to make your dreams manifest.

Instead of saying, "I'm sad," "I'm in despair," "I'm angry," try saying it this way: "I feel sadness," "I feel despair," "I feel anger." Precision of speech helps ensure that you do not fully identify with the negative emotion, because the "I" is a divine spark materialized in a physical body, spirit in the flesh, containing all emotions and all thought–forms. The choice of holding on to a particular emotion sheds light onto aspects that are in need of the light of love. Try to follow the emotion. Where does it come from? What are the thoughts that adhere to it? You can identify with your higher self and radiate the light of love onto the emotion. Let it soak up the energy and dissipate it. **Choose to identify with your higher self, which is always in a state of happiness, in a total spiritual union.**

It is also possible that your energy was blocked, which gives rise to a pattern typical of closed chakras. For example, **when the base chakra is blocked**, it will bring up the fight or flight pattern. You will automatically engage your mind with various existential concerns: worries about money or survival, health concerns and anxieties about your life in general. When you are flooded with these fears and with corresponding thoughts, breathe deeply. Perform a deliberate connection by activating your power of imagination and bringing it down to earth. Choose to live. Imagine the energy centre, which is a red sphere at the tip of your tailbone, being filled with red light, turning counterclockwise (matching the movement of Earth). When this centre, which links you with activity and execution, with the force of life, vitality and physical potency, is operating properly, the negative thoughts you were flooded with will dissolve. You can also help yourself by using positive affirmations (accompanied with deep breaths) to transmit the energy to all your other bodies (physical, emotional, mental, spiritual).

A block in the sex chakra, whose colour is orange, will bring with it feelings of want in relationships, a negative self–image and a need for some addiction.

A block in the solar plexus. This chakra's colour is yellow. A blockage could engender sadness and other unpleasant emotions. It is part of the emotional body, which also includes the heart chakra. Its effect on emotions is highly significant.

A block in the heart chakra, whose colour is green, would bring sadness, inability to feel joy, even depression. Feelings of sadness bring up thoughts of sadness and that is an endless cycle that forever recurs.

A block in the throat chakra, whose colour is blue, characterizing a frequency of truth, would cause a failure to connect to the truth. One suffering the blockage would not know his true desires and will certainly be unable to express them in words. He would then feel frustrated, angry and steeped in self–pity. It is possible that his self–confidence could destabilize. His self–criticism will be very harsh. It should be pointed out that long–term blockage in this chakra will cause frailty in that area and possibly pain and disease.

A block in the third eye chakra, whose colour is violet and is located in the forehead between the eyes, impede the ability to utilize consciousness with the power of the imagination, the intuition, overly intellectual and even obsessive thoughts,. A block of this chakra can cause a blockage in the entire centre of the head, resulting in fatigue, lack of attentiveness and confusion. These would, naturally, be accompanied by negative thoughts and apprehensions.

A block in the crown chakra, whose colour is white and is located at the crown of the head, would block the linkage between you and the universe, between you and spirit. It might cause blockage of faith and many seeds of doubt would be planted. The failure to connect to the source of the soul would cause a sense of loneliness, fear, loss of direction.

A block in the golden chakra, located a few inches above the head, would cause a disconnect between you and your guidance, a lack of connection with the cosmic truth and lack of spiritual insight.

All blockages will arouse beliefs that are associated with them, the thoughts and feelings typical of that state. The solution is always energy cleansing and reopening the energy centres (the chakras). This activity should be accompanied by positive declarations, which are crucial for activating and reprogramming all of your organic and energy systems – which are you!

ILANA: Thank you, dear and beloved Master Akiva. Actually, I am aware of this knowledge and use it accordingly. For technical reasons I have to take a break right now. I'd be grateful if we were to resume our discussion this evening. Much love.

MASTER AKIVA: I am in accord with your request. Now, please carefully note everything that happens in your reality till we meet again. You may be surprised. Much love, I Am Master Akiva, the bearer of the banner of unity for the People of Israel, bestowing the message, "Love thy neighbour as thyself." Blessed be in your eternal being.

ILANA: Good morning dear and beloved Master Akiva, I would like to proceed with the subject of our discussion. I'd like to discuss identification, attachment, holding on. I am grateful for continuing the discussion.

MASTER AKIVA: Dear and beloved Ilana. Rest assured that there is neither time nor space and it is all happening here and now. Even if you left the conversation for a while, you can always return to the exact moment in time where we halted our discussion.

We have been discussing beliefs of energy centres. We discussed the essence of the energy centre. Some belief systems are associated with possessiveness and the fear of releasing the past, a kind of fixation pattern. These belief systems lead a person to experience suffering. The reason is that he turns away from his heart. He is not attentive to his heart. Instead, he is trapped in fears. They may be fears of abandonment, of great want. When the heart is released, when the energy of love pulsates in it, beliefs of freedom, of joy, of enabling and of flowing are conducted through it. Free–flowing love energy activates positive secondary beliefs and ensures an improved and pleasant life.

Conversely, when a person chooses to identify with the energy of want, which is the energy of darkness, he is immersed in fears, which activate secondary beliefs that create his reality. These are creations of trouble, sorrow, pain and torment.

I would like to discuss the heart path as opposed to the hurt path. This communication was given to you in the past, dear and beloved and you are invited to place it here.

To See the Lesson – Heart Path, Hurt Path

MASTER AKIVA: Dear and wonderful people. You call upon yourselves predicaments of various sorts, in order to solve them! If and when you solve the problem, you will understand the subject being taught.

Well, your higher self is your teacher. It has at its disposal a comprehensive view of the whole picture, made up of the totality of your trials and experiences. It is aware of all your development programs, your supreme purpose, destinations, potential directions, meaningful events, courses, etc. All these are designed to bring about your growth and evolution.

While you are in a physical body, you are experimenting with something similar to a game, a challenging, adventurous, fascinating game that presents you with various obstacles designed to develop your survival skills and learning capacity.

For your souls it is indeed a game. Souls do not take into consideration the emotional side effects of their trials and tribulations. Feelings of fear, sadness, despair, anger and the like will not factor in their decisions, as they choose the game board for themselves and mark the goals they wish to attain.

Know that each and every problem carries its own solution, arranged as an essential feature of its fundamental structure. In a problem, the solution is hidden from you perception, until you solve it. A problem, even if it casts a cloud over your life, can be seen as a message conveying a lesson presented to you by your higher self. Its subject is always aimed at your highest good and is part of your path of growth.

People are motivated by two main paths. One main path affecting all humans is the **path of hurt**. This path initiated in the karma of all of humanity. In the Book of Genesis in the Bible the story is told of the first murder: Cain's murder of his brother Abel. The reason for the murder was jealousy. Jealousy contains pain, the hurt of being rejected, cast off, not loved as another is loved, being unworthy.

The path of hurt causes anguish, war, trauma and disaster,

both at the personal and the national and international levels. It is typical of those who carry the victim pattern within them. The victim is not responsible for what is taking place in his experience. He is helpless, angry and retaliatory, all at the same time.

The other path, equally well known, is the **Path of the Heart**. This path is piloted by love at its highest level, the essence of compassion. This essence accepts and contains all events and emotions without judgment, evasion or discrimination. It accepts everything simply and naturally, with love and understanding. It understands that all trials and tribulations are lessons, designed for the gain experience and learning. At its essence, compassion comprehends that since everything that happens has its reason and necessity, forgiveness is essential for every hurt, whether intentional or accidental. The path of the heart has no accounting, it does not take revenge nor does it hold any grudge; it is not a victim. This is a path of strength.

Heart versus hurt: Two diametrically opposite paths, whose aim is the same: change through communication. Both serve to **activate** and catalyze chain reactions and lessons.

The **path of hurt** is the source of distrust, suspicion, isolation, vengeance, anger, conspiring to do harm, deviousness, manipulation, inconsideration, cruelty – whether to yourself or another – lack of acceptance, aggression, intolerance, malice and emotional insensitivity. All these are the result of a place, which as a consequence of hurt and pain, creates for itself a suitable way to cope. At the root, before these qualities have formed, there was a feeling of love that was injured. Layers upon layers covered it and created predicaments that must be dealt with. Handling such challenges occurs both on the micro, personal plane and on the macro, universal plane.

Those with a victim pattern typically do not accept responsibility for what is occurring. They display a lack of knowledge and understanding that people are endowed with the ability to create their reality and that their energy, their patterns of thoughts and emotions, attract various scenarios. In particular they are unaware that the scenarios summoned for them are lessons from their higher self. The purpose of these lessons is growth and evolution. Such people are not aware that it is all happening for their own ultimate good. They are immersed deep in their drama, trudging through it and even sinking in it. This culminates in accusations, both of the self and others, a need to be defensive, a need to attack, even an inability to act at all, ending in utter powerlessness.

A victim feels self–pity, depression, helplessness, guilt and on the other end of the spectrum, aggressive emotions of anger, rage, vengeance, hatred, suspicion and belligerence.

The path of hurt is dictated by the ego, the lowest part (in frequency) of the overall identity. It contains a summing-up of the lessons of the soul. It is activated by threats to its existence and it deals with challenges by doing battle or by escaping (base chakra – fight or flight). The ego is distinguished by games of honour and games of power and it is innately manipulative, playing on a number of emotions.

In contrast, qualities of generosity, forgiveness, compassion, love, tolerance, giving, accommodation and acceptance, compromise, good-heartedness, sensitivity, empathy and gentleness, all have their source in the **path of the heart**. These qualities develop as a result of linking with an insight into the whole soul, transcending the role-playing on Earth's board game (arising from games of honour and games of power) of the ego, which has a need to prove itself. This path is the choice of a mature soul that has learned its lessons from the path of hurt and has opted to observe the scene from a high vantage point, that of the higher self. This path has no identification with the victim pattern. Rather, it is one of taking responsibility for all scenarios of reality creation, whatever they may be.

It is worth noting that not everyone who possesses these positive qualities is automatically free of the victim pattern. Sometimes, the opposite is true. Likewise, not everyone who possesses these qualities is necessarily linked with the path of heart. Many on the path of hurt develop noble and inspiring qualities. But at the same time they may possess other qualities such as self–denigration and a lack of sufficient love and appreciation for themselves. Often they exhibit resistance to egotism. They interpret self–love as a negative quality that is injurious to others. However, they elevate the quality of self–sacrifice, at times to the point of self–injury. They certainly have a victim pattern and the need to please others is very strong in their personality.

Both paths join and combine forces. There can be no forgiveness that is not preceded by an injurious act that necessitates it. Generosity is ineffectual if there is no need for it. The paths are interwoven like a double helix.

You may choose whether to be controlled by pain, whose roots are buried in your distant past. Pain, whether conscious or suppressed, is located in the depths of your sub–consciousness, in your emotional body, in your thought–forms, even in your physical body. It is within your power to alternatively be operated by and operate, your heart.

We wish to discuss now **difficulties caused by what is in the "past."** The word is in quotation marks because neither your emotional nor your mental body recognises such a concept as "past." Every scenario, every sliver of memory, is available for immediate access, complete with the attendant emotional experience: anger, sadness, despair, guilt and so on. Of course, positive feelings such as exuberance, happiness, joy and love, are accessible as well.

Since all events are within your reach and since, when you examine a given memory, you in fact restore and re–live it, you need to deal with the suffering that is rooted in your past, whether in this or in a "past" life. All timeframes occur concurrently. All life forms exist here and now in complete interaction.

Sometimes, the source of emotional pain is not in your current life, the one on which your consciousness is focused. You may feel a flooding from a parallel dimension, i.e., a past incarnation. The lessons of the past pursue you from one reality to the next, from present to future, until you fully resolve them.

First, you need to know that the problem contains its own solution. The solution will be accomplished on several planes. One is the spiritual solution of insight, for all is drama designed to anesthetize. Then, there is the energetic solution, the transmission of energy of light and love, which is a healing essence. Next, a karmic solution is offered, a cleansing of the karma among all parties, including individuals, places and situations.

* * *

The Healing Path

Call up your most painful memory. Give it, imaginatively, form and substance. Is it vibrating? Is it prickly? Is it rough? Torn? Take out of your emotional body, which is located in the area where your heart and ribs are, the form in which the memory (which is lively and filled with feelings) is held. Imagine that you are approaching a light–fall (akin to a waterfall). It is blue light and it cleanses and purifies the memory. Wash the memory bubble. Then, wrap it in a resistant bubble, a sort of a transparent pearl. The bubble is made of material that does not allow emotional leakage from the memory. Connect the pearl you have created to an energetic channell of spiritual comprehension. Imagine that a pipe of white and golden light enters it and fills it up with substance. Now send the pearl to your higher self, from which it will produce the required insights.

Next, consider all your other bodies: Send healing light to the emotional body, from which you uprooted the bubble. Fill the cavity with the pink light of love and compassion. Let the light seep into the physical body and affect the mental body as well. Ask for and create karmic healing for all bodies, at all layers, in all dimensions, in all incarnations, here and now and in your entire being. Imagine a great light entering and loosening all the ties and threads that connect you to others, places, events, which are in your pain–throbbing memory. Agree and choose to forgive all those concerned in the past, including yourselves.

The subconscious – this place serves as storage for all your memories and experiences. Project the blue light into the subconscious, specifically to the place where the painful memory is located. You can also project white light to the whole subconscious itself. Intention of healing creates healing.

Once the lesson is understood, there is no need to repeat it, even as a powerful emotional experience that provides you with violent feelings, the kind you sometimes prefer to experience rather than listless boredom. People tend to become attached to their memories, using them as a source of emotional amusement. Assume responsibility for the memory you are entering. Every time you dive into a memory in the deep recesses of your past, there is danger. The danger is that you will draw back into yourself those thought–forms and energy formations, which called up the unpleasant experience in the first place.

Take responsibility for your memories and thoughts. Sometimes the information reaches you by way of dreams. You dream about a difficult, even traumatic experience you have been through. You enact and repeat it, possibly in a different version and with different actors. When you surface it to consciousness, then you can treat the memory, which was repressed for one reason or another.

Treat dreams in the same manner, cleansing and purifying them and ensconcing them in a bubble to prevent the leakage of emotions and facilitate its transfer to the higher self. Always ask to understand your lesson. Most of your understanding is located in your highest layer.

Let's take an example: Someone has betrayed your trust. You need to understand it positively. The understanding is not that you should not trust others, but that that person reflects to you that he was not true to himself. **People are mirrors for you. They always reflect a part of you and your beliefs.**

Inevitably, after you have observed and compared the paths, you will opt to relinquish the path of hurt and move onto the path of heart.

The way to arrive at the path of heart - to come aboard the soul plane, to transform the personality – is by incorporating the soul into the experience of the mundane. It is important to spiritually understand role-playing and dramas, whose purpose is learning and experience. It is crucial to connect the four aces of awareness – love, truth, faith, personal responsibility. The path traverses a comprehensive process of forgiveness, release of all guilt feelings, of all beliefs in being a victim, of all lack of responsibility regarding what has happened, of all anger. This is the path to purification, raising frequencies and ascension. You can ask to connect with it and before doing so, carry out all the requisite procedures.

ILANA: I would like to know who was it I have channelled just now.

The answer comes up: "Metatron and the Karma Council."

Lesson 29

Fears and Their Transformation into Urges

ILANA: Good morning dear and wonderful guides. Good and blessed morning to dear and beloved Master Akiva. I would like to proceed with our discussion. Thank you.

MASTER AKIVA: Good morning dear and very beloved Ilana. Your mission is crucial in my eyes and the eyes of all your guides, who number among them the Galactic Karma Council. The knowledge transmitted here is of great significance. Well, this morning you encountered several difficulties in starting your computer. You have persevered and coped and wondered what did it come to tell you? Later, you looked further into your mind and found certain "viruses" not only in your PC, Right?

ILANA: Certainly. I pulled out fears that have floated up, most of them are fears of whose existence I was aware, but I thought I had released them. Some, in a sense, are new. They all come under one definition: Empowerment. So it seems to me. I understand that there is no coincidence and that will be the subject of our discussion. Is that so?

MASTER AKIVA: There is no coincidence, for all is planned. Human beings err to think that coincidence exists, since they clearly see the energy circles and karmic connections woven between all events, whether they are likely to materialize or not.

ILANA: By probable events, do you mean that there are potentials for actualization of all scenarios, that they all have the potential to materialize, whether they are positive and desirable or negative and undesired? If it is all in existence already, where is the right to choose?

MASTER AKIVA: That is the intent. Imagine a blue sea dotted with an infinite number of islands. You are rowing in a sailboat and you are free to visit any and all of the islands. You could choose to settle on one of them or several, based on your freewill choice. All the islands are your yet–unfulfilled potential. They are categorized as non–physical probabilities until you reach one of them and opt to land on it.

When fear navigates your boat, you inevitably choose an island based on the criterion of fear. You might choose the nearest one, even if it appears rocky and desolate, because you are afraid to row to more distant islands, even though they are more fertile and lush with juicy tropical fruits.

Fear is a highly significant factor in navigating the boat. It can be compared to making choices in life. When you remove the fear, what is left? It is an urge, which is a message from your soul to do what's important for you to accomplish.

The way to fulfil your positive and most desired potentialities, in fact, strive to actualise your dreams, is inner cleansing and the elimination of all your fears, worries and anxieties, which are the doubts and lack of faith in yourselves. For clarity's sake, know that you are highly advanced software, operated by genetic codes found in your chromosomes and DNA.

These codes are found in your brain programming and interwoven with the sub-conscious, which could also be referred to as the stock of your memories and beliefs. That particular control gadget programs your future, based on your past interpretations and present beliefs. When you are filled with faith, zest, vision and a desire to accomplish something it means that you do not entertain any fears and your vision will become a reality.

When you harbour fears, they too are capable of being projected into your reality. Fears are the viruses that neutralise all that you desire, everything that fits your conscious goal. You may not be aware of some of them. They may be from previous incarnations, the dawn of your current life, even ancient memories stamped into your genes, whose source is the atavistic experiences of your forefathers, even of the entire race. These are existential fears based on the need for survival. They are fears conditioned on defending and protecting your lives and your property or alternatively, on a predisposition to attack in order to enlarge your share.

The way to recognise these fears is to ask to get to know them without apprehension and without any... fear! Fear has no reality and if you disarm it by detaching it from the keen emotions that accompany it (because you believe so fiercely in its existence), you would be able to rid yourself of it.

In order to identify fears, you have to be in tune with your inner truth. You have to be brave and very sincere with yourself. It is not a shame to be afraid. However, you can decide whether to be afraid or be in charge of your experiences, to determine your reality and even plan your future. You may decide to dismiss it from its position as the founder and determining agent of your experience, both present and future and most certainly from your past memories, replacing it with a more positive factor. This could be a belief, which provides you the right inclinations for action, removes the various elements of fear and attracts to itself that which you desire.

We have discussed the path of fear and its opposite, the path of love. Know that fears come from the path of fear, whose energy lacks consciousness and, thus, is termed darkness. Darkness is characterised by the inability to clearly see in it what you can easily detect in the light. When you consciously experience fear, you will discern that you have entered its path. Once you understand that, you can choose to stay there or leave it and shift to the path of love. When you have a conscious diagnosis, you can alter whatever you wish to change. When you are unable to identify it and lack a diagnosis, you will not be able to fit the remedy to the disease.

When you are afraid and want to be released from your fear, after you have identified it, of course, breathe deeply, then declare a new choice of joining the path of love, which is the path of light. Affirm:

"I choose to be in the light and only in the light!"

Breathe deeply and affirm it three times.

You have to intend it with all your might, so that the affirmation can become a skylight through, which you will pass from a state of darkness to a state of being illuminated by the inner light – love!

ILANA: People do not always know that they have beliefs based on fear. They see themselves as realists and rational, when in fact they are pessimistic and view things darkly. They think they are anchored in reality. They fail to understand that they are motivated by fear–based thinking. How do you explain it in a way that would be acceptable to them? And, in general, how do you identify fear–based beliefs, which are not fierce emotional and physical fears?

MASTER AKIVA: An excellent question. All people should develop their awareness and comprehend that they create reality; that they affect its formation through the creative energy within them; energy which they have been accommodating in their inner system of beliefs, thoughts and feelings. Scientists have already arrived at this understanding. It would be better for those pessimists to let go of their way of thinking and convert it to – water.... In other words, a substance that flows and incorporates the new facts, which have been discovered: **Creation of reality!** The knowhow has been in existence in all facets of time, now however it is more accessible.

People should take apart their beliefs and break them down into their components, like a children's jigsaw puzzle. Check and see if it is based on love, which is light, faith, high soul–truth (always based on love, acceptance, enabling, free–will choice). Examine whether it is based on the concept of personal responsibility for creating reality. Or, is it a compilation of fears piled on top of other fears, like dominos. If one domino were to fall it would create a chain reaction that would take down the whole structure, which is based on unity.

ILANA: I suggest a new occupation: dis-assembler of beliefs. Like a highly trained computer tech or watchmaker or even a surgeon, he will pick out a belief and take it apart. He then will discard whatever is rooted in darkness and fears and preserve that which is based in light and love. What do you think?

MASTER AKIVA: Indeed a worthy proposal, though entertaining for both of us. Suggest it to the Academy and no doubt you can teach it well. Laughter is healthy and it also promotes creativity.

I should point out in this context that laughter is wonderful for neutralizing fears. There is a well–known technique in the East, where you look at a fear, give it shape and appearance and simply laugh at it to its face, until it shrinks, explodes and vanishes. Dear Ilana, since you are in tune with the concept–cluster of our presentation, you have spontaneously extracted a very effective solution for fear and its transformation into an urge.

Think of a fear that dwells inside you and contracts you. Give it a form – it can be a creature of any shape. Give it dimensions, colour, texture, smell. Now use the power of your imagination, with which you have created the image and make it disappear. You could use laughter to make it blow up, you could focus on it a ray of light radiating from your third eye (located in your forehead between your eyes), you could project balls of light from the palms of your hands. You can envision it burning up, crumbling and melting. This is also an excellent way to dissolve doubts, which are a block to faith and to high creativity at the soul level.

ILANA: Fine, so let's say I have identified fear in me, even if it seems weird and irrational and I understand that I need to dissolve it. Do not I need to fill the resultant void with reinforced faith? Light? What do you think, dear Master Akiva?

MASTER AKIVA: Thank you for that important addition. Well, it is indeed desirable to imagine light being sent to the place where the fear had resided and to add a positive declaration which is contrary to the fear, to turn it into an urge. For instance, fear of the dark. This may be a double–edge fear, physical darkness in which you cannot see, in which the imagination starts to create horror scripts, as well as darkness in the sense of lack of consciousness, ignorance, as in the Dark (Middle) Ages. After you have acted to neutralize it, declare something in contrast, using positive language. You cannot say, "I am not afraid of the dark," for this is a negative declaration, unsuitable for reprogramming the sub–conscious. It only responds to positive statements and does not compute "no."

Accordingly, say: "**I am safe and secure.**" "**I am always in the light,**" and similar statements.

Another example is acrophobia. The in–depth explanation is that it is fear of falling and crashing, spiritually as well as physically, loss of life. Say: "**I am safe and protected in high places.**" In fact, every physical fear represents a deeper spiritual fear. Try to dredge up the source of your fear. If and, when you retrieve and release it, it would be like releasing a cork, which, once removed, will cause a large chain of related fears to be let loose.

ILANA: Nice. I am mainly interested in the spiritual aspect of physical fears. I have a memory coming up now, of a treatment I provided a few days ago. This person is suffering from an ailment that causes loss of control over the sphincter. His quality of life has greatly declined and all his actions are regulated by fear that causes him to stay near his home. When I conducted a channelled communication, the following came to light: The source of the fear is a traumatic experience during the Holocaust. Then, a second layer from a dominant incarnation in Japan came up. There he was a man of great power and control over himself and others. I saw that fear of loss of control is what has caused the difficult trial in the current life – total loss of control over his sphincter.

MASTER AKIVA: Indeed, it is true. Every physical fear has a spiritual aspect. You will do well to observe and ask yourself: Does it contain a fear of death or even a fear of life itself. Some people harbour in themselves both of these, apparently contradictory, fears. These fears really paralyze them. They are afraid to experience, because they are afraid to die. But, they are also afraid to live. These are examples of root–fears, each of which would grow a chain of additional fears.

For instance, fear can cause a person to be afraid to leave home for work. He knows that in order to earn a living and for sake of his self–image, he must work, but he harbours subconscious fears that work is slavery which he equates with loss of freedom and independence. Slavery physical hardship, torture, death. He will then experience a long process of searching for work. He will regard himself as unemployed. He may secure a job but then, a short while later, he will leave it, either on his own accord or by being laid off.

In every area of your life in, which you are unable to make a dream come true, be sure that parallel with the desire, there is an energy pipeline that is saturated with fear and scuttles that which you seek. Therefore, mapping out your belief system would make it possible to adjust accordingly.

ILANA: Thank you. I see now that our current lesson ties with our previous one, which I thought was too short, that I did not dedicate enough time to it. It turns out that there is a link between fear–based beliefs, located in energy centres and the subject of identifying fears and their transformation. If so, this was an immediate extension of the former lesson.

MASTER AKIVA: Certainly. A lesson can be short or long in physical terms, but intellectually it would include that which you need to know and which you are capable of digesting. So you were not wrong when you did not continue with the lesson last night. All our lessons are one intellectual chain, where we discuss the path of love and its significance.

Since, for technical reasons, you have to end the lesson, know that there is no coincidence, there are no disruptions and whatever we must bring to completion will be done in a different time frame. Be at peace with yourself and be happy with your doing. You are well guided and even the fears that rose up in you before our communication were an integral and vital part of the whole.

I Master Akiva, the bearer of the message of unity by way of "love thy neighbour as thyself," am sending the blessing of my love to you and to all the readers of these, our words. Let there be will that all fears shall be released and faith will replace them. Amen and amen.

ILANA: Thank you for this interesting and important lesson.

Lesson 30

Personal Responsibility
Deciphering the Language of the Universe Unity

ILANA: Good and blessed morning to all my wonderful guides, superb and blessed morning to dear and amazing Master Akiva. I would like to proceed with our discussion. Thank you.

MASTER AKIVA: Good morning dear and exalted Ilana. Great joy is rising within me and you, too, in anticipation of our meeting. You felt this morning, despite your difficulty in getting up, that it has become harder for you to give up these spiritual encounters. You have seen what a habit can accomplish, when it is the result of perseverance, dedication and devotion to a supreme goal: transformation of the personality. The moral is to desire. Simply to desire yet always, at the same time, to act!

Activity is the key in all areas of your lives!

Some people always maintain that they have nothing to worry about, although they do not understand why. You need to remove worry, which blinds the eye and introduces negative thoughts into your creative software. But it does not relieve one from activity and implementation. Things have to be made manifest and transformed from theory into reality. You need to know how to distinguish between what should be left to the spirit, to God, the angels, the guides and the entire host of the universe and what you should do yourself, by your own hands.

ILANA: But how would we know what we should do and what we should relinquish to the spirit? Could you please clarify?

MASTER AKIVA: Of course. The term "will" incorporates "personal responsibility." When your car breaks down, what do you do? You could cry, complain or pray for help. These are emotional, rather than practical reactions. You should keep your emotions, thoughts and actions separate and carefully choose what to hold onto in any given circumstance.

When your car breaks down you must assume personal responsibility and understand: "I have created the situation." Nothing happens to you randomly. These are all lessons from your higher self, intended for your highest benefit and for your growth. They are designed to teach you and prepare you to cope in a practical sense. They come to fortify and strengthen you, to demonstrate to you how your inner being, perception and attitude pave the way and enable the external occurrence to approach you.

Indeed, your body–personality (ego), your daily awareness,

does not want your car to break down, because now you are faced with problems of transportation, inconvenience, financial expense and so on. Your lesson, however, relates to decoding and comprehending a message sent you from your higher self.

Whatever transpires in your existence is a message from your higher self, which allows the subconscious beliefs, which are integrated with the lesson plan developed by your soul, to emerge in the outer world and materialize in the physical dimension.

You should relate to everything that occurs as follows: Accept personal responsibility and declare, "I created that, although I did not consciously do so. It is unpleasant for me to experience that, which I created, but it is for my highest good and it is offered to me as a test that I have to pass successfully."

a. See the message in what is materializing and try to decipher it! For if you do not understand it, more messages will be transmitted, not necessarily in ways that are pleasant for you. Remember, there are no coincidences. It is all the outcome of planning by all of creation's powers and you are an actor in a play.

b. At the same time, you have to take viable action. You have to release the emotions which could affect you in several ways. One is self–pity, typical of those who possess the victim pattern and fail to comprehend the measure of their responsibility for creating their reality by being angry with themselves or casting blame on another. All these feelings will be summarized as: "Not the right answer" in the following test. **The test is internal and "the right answer" refers to: What do you think about what has happened to you? What do you feel about it? What do you do, in practical terms, in order to solve the problem? Of course, it is crucial to decipher the message.**

Let's get back to the example of the broken down vehicle. You need to ask yourself: What does the vehicle symbolize for me? In this case the answer would be: the capacity for movement in life, even life itself. Pay attention to the nature of the mishap. Do you have a blown tire in one of the wheels? Where is the wheel located? Is it in the front or in the back? Is it on the left or on the right? If it is in the front, it symbolizes the future; if behind, the past. A blown tire is symbolic of a fear that paralyses you and prevents your progress. Left and right represent yin and yang, masculine and feminine. The right is always the male, which is doing, acting and giving, while the left or feminine side, represents receiving, acceptance and intuition.

Another example: your computer broke down. Ask yourself: What does it symbolize for me? Why did I create this malfunction? Well, the computer stands for your way of thinking. Do I have in me "viruses" – self–destructive programming comprised of negative thinking? It is also possible that a person needs rest and is withdrawing inwardly, because by sitting too long in front of the computer he is diverting his energy into it?

To summarize: Nothing in life happens by chance and all glitches, accidents, diseases and trouble, as well as joyous and exhilarating occurrences, of course, bear a message and meaning for you. If you succeed in figuring out the messages sent to you, you will feel more in tune with the spirit, with your higher self, with your soul and all of creation. Your consciousness will be awakened. Your intuition and inner attentiveness will be boosted. It is a highly recommended condition of being. You can also regard it as an entertaining game, decoding universal messages. And why shouldn't you engage in a little playful interaction between you and yourself? It will keep you happy and preserve the innocence of childhood; it will refresh you and keep you youthful. You need to know when to be serious, when to let loose and celebrate and even when, to act foolishly, all in balance and the right measure, of course.

ILANA: I looked through the window that faces north and, to my excitement and surprise, I saw that in some places the light rays radiated downward. The thought crossed my mind that these are light ladders: A wonderful and gorgeous sight. Could you please decipher it for me?

MASTER AKIVA: Nice. This is exactly what I am talking about. First, notice every detail. Second, know to feel and even get excited about it, as little children do when they see something for the first time. And why is that? Because this excitement and enthusiasm connect you to your soul; it is the soul that is excited and moved. The excitement connects you with inspiration and gratitude, which opens a portal towards love, to waves of joy, which in turn connect you to God, the Creator of the world and all its many wonders. As it is written "The heavens declare the glory of God and the firmament shows his handiwork." (Psalms 19:1.)

And, indeed, dear Ilana, you saw the heavenly splendour of light ladders sent from the high heavens, forming an opening for the ascension of pure souls; angels who spread the knowledge and the teaching of the light ascending and descending. This phenomenon occurs daily, mostly unseen. Some who notice it would say, how nice, look, rays of light or else they would completely ignore it. Those with a poetic and artistic nature would be awed by it and would interpret it well, according to their inner perception.

In your case, you need to realize that you yourself function as a light ladder and through you, souls reach destinations and people get in tune with their higher selves, their souls and their objectives. You, too, had a light ladder sent to you by very high, senior guides. Every one of you who has raised his consciousness serves as a ladder to those behind who are affected by him.

It is the mission of some individuals to function as light

ladders in creation. They are not aware of it at all, but that is of no consequence (terms and definitions such as light ladder, are but words that colour the essence, the truth). The mission of those light ladders is to disperse clouds of dark mood and pessimism and spread hope and the awareness of peace, through joy, mutual respect, sanctity and "love thy neighbour as thyself."

Incidentally, there are actually quite a few openings for the job of using humour combined with seriousness and any reader who desires such employment merely has to submit his candidacy. The requirements are: An open heart, compassion, fulfillment of "love thy neighbour as thyself," and "thou shalt love the Lord thy God with all thy soul and with all thy strength." It should be pointed out that a high degree of self-awareness combined with modesty is also required. The better you acknowledge your worth, the more precise and connected to your soul you will be. A person who does not appreciate his own worth and is often stern and critical with himself diminishes the effect of his soul within. By so doing he shrivels the apparatus, his temple of the soul and the personality – ego, dominates him. His consciousness is lower than that of a person who respects and appreciates himself, thus allowing the forces of creation to be conveyed through his heart, his thoughts and, of course, his deeds.

"Love thy neighbour as thyself," requires love and acceptance of the self, which necessitates compassion,

not self-criticism that is piercing to the point of self-destruction.

ILANA: if I understood correctly, the subject of our lesson today is: "**Deciphering the language of the universe and its messages, taking responsibility for all creations.**"

MASTER AKIVA: Correct, you have summarized it well. The supreme goal of our lesson is to point out unity: The relation among all scenarios, all occurrences, problems, lessons, in fact all of life's circumstances in relation to the higher self, guidance, all of humanity and God, of course.

ILANA: **The unity.** Could you please expand the discussion about that? What is unity, how would we understand and sense it? I recall that I requested to be initiated into the "**Consciousness of One,**" beyond the perception of duality.

MASTER AKIVA: And, indeed, you were initiated and now the concept is more readily embedded in your awareness. Everything is tied with everything else. God has created the world and placed of Himself in all of creation. He placed His sparks in all kingdoms on the planet, the corporeal and the spiritual, the ethereal and the astral, the kingdoms of flora and fauna, humanity, earth, the elements, the crystals and anything and everything you can perceive. Humanity is interconnected in a tapestry of life, a karmic mesh which is similar to a spider's web. When one thread is damaged, it causes a chain reaction in all the other interlinking threads and these in turn affect the threads they are connected with and so on. Therefore, when one person hurts another, whether he is a friend or an enemy, he himself will come to harm. That is the meaning of the verse, "that which is hated by you, do not do to another;" it depicts, in the negative, more conventional way of duality, the term, "Love thy neighbour as thyself."

All of humanity is tied by threads of life into the grand tapestry which collects and accumulates the karma of each and every human being. This tapestry is beyond time and space. It contains all of humanity from the moment of creation, along all times and eras. It holds all souls, whether they are incorporated in the material dimension or not. The tapestry is multidimensional. You cannot fathom its beginning or end, for it is infinite. Not only does it contain the Kingdom of Humanity, but all kingdoms are interwoven with it. Consequently, every human being affects and is affected by it. Every living creature is a piece of this supreme, infinite jigsaw puzzle.

Because your perception is limited, it is beyond your capacity to discern the tapestry of unity. It is therefore recommended that you expand your perception! Ask your higher self to provide you with visions and messages through the channell of your imagination. You may even understand that you do not comprehend, but agree with the logic of the concept.

The **unity frequency** is conveyed through my words. Therefore, let us try something:

Breathe deeply. This is the initial point of entry into a spiritual procedure, the connection with the soul and your high guidance. Now try to expand your perception. Ask to contain the unity frequency within you. Do it this way:

"I choose to connect with and contain the unity frequency in me forever!

"I hereby ask and acknowledge that the connection will occur in all bodies, all levels, all dimensions, all incarnations, here and now and in my entire being. Thank you."

After making these statements with complete intent, breathe deeply in order to accommodate the frequency being transmitted to you. Repeat the procedure with total intent three times. Do it for eight days, continuously.

Possibly now, maybe later, you will understand the verses: "thou shall love the Lord thy God with all thy soul and with all thy strength," and "love thy neighbour as thyself."

Here I Am, Master Akiva, the bearer of the message of truth and light, love and unity to the whole nation of Israel and all nations of the world. Blessed be dear Ilana in your eternal being. Thank you.

Lesson 31

Money – Connecting Heaven and Earth
Poverty Consciousness – Consciousness of Abundance

ILANA: Good and blessed morning to all my wonderful guides, good and blessed morning to dear and beloved Master Akiva. I would like to proceed with our discussion. Thank you.

MASTER AKIVA: Good and blessed morning, dear and so very beloved Ilana. I would like to support and bless you for your sanctified activity in promoting the consciousness of the human race. Know that you teach many and are very influential. They, in turn, affect others, who come in contact with them. Your circle of influence and that of your predecessors and those working in parallel with you, is growing and growing.

Some people are afraid of the light, of truth and they feel unworthy of love. They pretend they want help and are ready to receive treatment, but in fact they are not ripe for it and are unable to be immersed in the frequencies of light within. That was your experience last night and it left you feeling anxious. Remove it. Shake off all feelings of guilt.

You did your best. Your intention can affect the order of creation, human karma; you are very powerful. This is linked to your great compassion and the pure love with which you perform your blessed mission. Your ego, the personality of the body, was very surprised by the result of the treatment, but not so your soul, which summoned the lesson.

Know and from now on tell your patients, that results will not necessarily happen instantaneously. First there is an inner process that must take place within the person. He has to accommodate and adapt the frequency, so as to internalize what is said and of course, simultaneously, take responsibility for the flow of his energy. He must carefully choose the thoughts and feelings he believes in and to which he directs his energy.

It is true that most of your patients immediately feel their energy centres open up in response to your treatment. Even that specific woman felt it, as she had indicated. However, her fears brought her right back to the initial point she was seeking to leave. Angels and other light entities participate in the treatment and you are never alone when you conduct it. This is the reason for the highly enjoyable sensation, when a connection occurs with the soul. No angel or light entity and certainly not you, our emissary in a physical body and the conveyor of frequency to the patient (who is a vessel, receiving it), can compel a human being to accommodate the frequency and internalize the message.

There is a clear division between you, the emissary and channell conveying the frequency and the patient, who is a vessel. He can accommodate only as much as he has the capacity to hold. There are some cracked vessels, dear, who are unable to hold on to the light frequencies. They are barren soil so far as spiritual and energy matters are concerned. So you should feel at peace with what you do, be proud and satisfied, receive those who come to you with love and compassion and accept what may come. Not everything depends on you and your power of intention. There are other factors, including the karmic lessons and duties the patient has to learn in his own way. If he chooses the easy and pleasant path of growing through light and love that you have offered him, so much the better. If, however, he does not opt for that path, he will remain on the path of fear, which is suited to him and furthers his learning.

It is not for you to judge which path is good, which path better suits his needs. You must release the discomfort and guilt brought about by your apparent failure. It was actually a distinct success and the woman will experience it in a more distant future. Accept the payment you are entitled to with gratitude, even if the one making the payment does so with little enthusiasm, introducing her fears and manipulations into the process.

This applies to all readers who provide treatment, in all areas that involve providing service and assistance to others. Despite your goodwill and talent for providing help, there is a greater and more sublime power than you and that power is God. Commit the following sentence to memory: "**Thy will be done**." You function to the best of your ability, but some things do not depend on you but on the karmic choices made by the souls of the people you encounter. There is a lesson to be learned here, which reflects inner beliefs, some of which may be negative, even fears that you are unaware of. The patient does you a great service by coming and undertaking a role in your reality.

Remember to assume responsibility, for it is all your creation. First, accept what is happening. Second, tell yourself: "I have created this." Third, ask to understand the message you shall have received. Of course, this does not include self–blame or the blame of others, but it should reflect to you beliefs that you hold within. Once you understand why you have enacted the drama, during which you were "asleep," you should forgive all the actors, yourselves included. Also thank whoever assisted you in the play, including yourself. "It is all happening for your highest good," is the profound meaning of the sentence.

ILANA: Thank you, dear and wonderful Master Akiva. I would like to point out that when someone responds with gratitude it is pleasant to accept money from him. It feels fair to accept it after pure giving, in other words, it is an exchange that is pure love. What I experienced yesterday – a person who pays unwillingly, even manipulatively – takes all the pleasure out of it.

People fail to understand that money is energy: accomplishing energy. When they make a payment while still attached to the money, out of a sense of great lack, reluctant to pay for what they agreed to purchase in advance, they establish a perception of poverty. When they pay with gratitude and love, knowing that they deserve and are entitled to the service they received, then they link with the consciousness of vast abundance. The universe will restore to them the money they spent, many times over.

I have learned this out of the process of creating reality and naturally I implement it in my daily life. I think, dear Master Akiva, that you should discuss the issue of money, giving and receiving it, consciousness of poverty and consciousness of plenty. This subject interests many people.

MASTER AKIVA: Willingly. I do have some expertise in this area. If you recall my personal story, it is well-known that I was indigent and destitute, in material terms, until I was 40 years old. Spiritually, however, I was conscious of great wealth. After I learned the Torah and became a luminary, my economic situation improved considerably. I was able to purchase for my faithful and beloved wife the jewel, "Jerusalem of Gold." This is actually recorded in ancient writings.

As I learned the mysteries of the *pardes* and the secrets of creation, I understood the lack of distinction between heaven and earth, which were created jointly. I observed that "as it is above so it is below." I learned the importance, sanctity and beauty of money, which is the manifestation of man's yearning at the material level, which is a direct projection of the spiritual level.

Many people distinguish between spirit and matter and sometimes even see contradictions between them. Some of the current perceptions have their roots in ancient sources, which attribute supreme value to ascetics and extol the importance of abstaining, physical suffering and want, as paths of spiritual empowerment. There is truth in this, for when man lacks bread and a roof over his head, when he loses his material assets; he then turns his gaze to the heavens with a supplication for help and salvation. As it is written "Then they cried unto the Lord in their trouble and he saved them out of their distress." (Psalms 107:13.)

In times of trial and crisis, the Children of Israel and the other nations of the world always called upon God, on powers greater than themselves. Self-affliction and abstinence were commonly accepted ways of attracting God's attention, grace and mercy. From time immemorial, belittling oneself was regarded as acknowledging the supremacy and potency of the deity.

Well, this perception need no longer govern your approach now, in the new age, where frequencies have changed and new paths have been paved. The belief that God reaches out to help those who are tormented and call for His assistance, is linked to the Path of Fear. It conforms with the victim pattern, whose owners are unaware of the tie between their inner world (the subject–matter of their beliefs, thoughts and emotions) and the external world (everything that happens to them). Those following that path were in need of this calming notion. When one believes it is so, he facilitates the creation of the assistance he prays for.

However, there is an easier way, more suited to those with high frequencies and those who are connected to and have internalized their **Master Frequency**. This frequency reminds them of their role in and responsibility for creating their reality, that which they are experiencing. This frequency shows them that there have never been victims, neither of other people nor of destiny. They know that they are eternal souls, linked to higher–frequency worlds with the assistance of their higher self, which is connected by karmic threads to all of humanity and all of creation and therefore they have permitted certain probable scenarios to take place.

These scenarios contain prospects for personal growth and transcendence past the body–personality (ego)'s patterns. They include a lesson plan summoned by the souls themselves. These are formed from the patterns of their own beliefs, most of which are most certainly subconscious and consequently they are unaware of their contents.

Individuals with master frequency understand that all is

always created for their highest good. This good is not usually understood while you are in your physical body. Sometimes, with the perspective brought about by the passage of time, one can see the good that has transpired since the occurrence of the event.

For instance, people do not see what can be good about a disease, disaster, separation, bereavement and mourning. They complain and become annoyed. They are offended by statements such as, "it is all for your highest good," "there are no coincidences," "that is the soul's choice, its karma," etc. This is not about good and evil, pleasant and unpleasant or suffering. It is about the supreme purpose that souls have set for themselves on game board Earth: Evolution through formation of difficulties and their ensuing resolution. Souls desire transcendence while in a physical body. Transcendence includes sublimation, release of all fears and passage from the path of hurt to the path of heart, from fear to unconditional love.

Such love embodies complete acceptance of all that happens. Therefore, this love has, integrally build in it, an utter lack of judgment. It manifests in the transcendence of duality, which classifies everything as good versus evil, black versus white, permissible versus forbidden. What is good in the eyes of one person is not necessarily good in the eyes of another; in fact, the latter may even regard it as evil. What is permissible for one is not necessarily permissible for another, in fact it may even be utterly forbidden for him.

What a non-observant person may do could be forbidden to a religious person. What is permissible for a member of one nation may be denied a member of another people. Allowed and disallowed can also change at different times. Things that seemed right and good in ancient times might be prohibited at other times.

Take polygamy, for example. In Biblical times it was customary to marry more than one woman. Today it is illegal in many cultures, nonetheless, there are some places where it is still permitted. Whether it is good or not, allowed or impermissible, depends very much of course on whom you ask. The truth is subjective and subject to interpretation, as is the whole concept of duality.

Money, too, can be perceived in numerous ways. You hold many beliefs about money, some of them are negative. If you ask people about their perceptions regarding money, you get answers such as, "money does not grow on trees" (in other words, it's hard to get), "money corrupts," "it takes hard work to earn money," "money comes, money goes," meaning that there is no certainty it will always be in your hands. Some people maintain that money is not the most important thing, what really counts is health. Indeed, myriad beliefs abound regarding the subject.

Some people associate labour with servitude through their sub–conscious beliefs. Quite often work has negative connotations, denoting the investment of immense effort, not necessarily out of a sense of pleasure.

Some are of the opinion that money should not be charged for performing 'spiritual work.' (Even some therapists feel guilty and ashamed when charging a fee for their work.) Thus, if they are obliged to pay for therapy or consultation, they do so resentfully and angrily. These individuals, whether they are therapists of patients, have the notion that no money should be charged for something "pure," as if money somehow spoils the spiritual purity. They make a complete distinction between what they call "matter," and what they term, "spirit." They do not really understand the nature of money, its value and importance in the mutual exchange of giving and receiving. Many spiritual people make this distinction and consequently their economic situation is of the poor variety.

In reality, money is nothing more than a symbol of the spiritual energy of performance and realization. Money links spirit and matter, facilitating the purchase of what is needed by the soul for its physical existence. Money allows an energetic exchange of giving-receiving-giving in a manner that has been agreed upon in advance.

Money puts a price (value) on time, ability, investment and a given product. Many feel themselves unworthy of this "energy" of money, though they want to possess it. Your self–image and sense of lack of self–worth are tied to whether you enjoy the money at your disposal or not.

Your attitude toward yourself determines whether you readily release money, your 'accomplishing' energy, with pleasure and joy, allowing it to fulfil your dreams and fill your needs or whether you hold on to it with fear and limit your spending. Maybe you fear that your money will run out and soon you will not have any more.

The knowledge of creating reality has become accepted and widespread in your era. In other words, all of your inner content – your beliefs, thoughts and emotions – affect the creation of your reality. It is invented through them. Of course, these beliefs dwell in your sub–conscious mind, which could directly contradict whatever you consciously desire. It is easier to access the conscious than the sub–conscious, which is why people must take direct responsibility for what they think at any given moment.

When people spend money and immediately fear that they, won't have enough for their basic needs, they project their fear on their future reality. Their sub–conscious mind is then imprinted with the concept that money is equated with fear of deficiency, fear of poverty, fear of survival, fear of suffering and death. Whenever they obtain money, they will feel unsafe. And whenever they part with money, these thoughts and feelings will emerge. Actually, this is a fixation and a trap, planted in the consciousness of poverty.

Consciousness of poverty relates to scarcity, to threats to one's survival, threats to life itself. It is linked with low self–image and the development of an excess of negative thoughts and feelings. This consciousness is tied with the path of fear and its implications appear in every aspect of life. It can affect physical health, emotional stability and mental balance. It spreads fears and concerns which will materialize in the fullness of time and become firmly fixed in the consciousness.

Money is a symbol which enables your consciousness to work through it, to implement and actualize all your conscious and unconscious beliefs. It is therefore very important.

Many doctrines maintain that money is not the essence. The underlying logic is that money is not a goal in and of itself; it is a means for attaining your goals. This does not imply that you should separate money from spirit, assigning to it a quality of sheer "matter" and calling it dirty, corrupting and so on. Money is the means by which you can fulfil your dreams.

Consciousness of abundance enables you to understand the value and importance of money, out of love for yourselves, love for life and an understanding that you are worthy and entitled to fulfil all your desires. In order to link with this consciousness you must alter your self–image. You must erase the old programming of poverty, lack and the need to settle for less. You must completely release all fears associated with money.

Some people want to be rich. They consciously make positive affirmations, as we will learn in the chapter on Creating Reality, but subconsciously, the old beliefs that reside in them may foil their aspirations. These beliefs may be composed of the fear of possessing wealth, fear of losing their possessions, as is written," He who has much wealth has much to worry about," the fear that a lover would only want them for their money and so on. Many are also afraid that money would distance them from their spirit, making them arrogant and proud. There are those who, in former lives, squandered vast sums of money or were suddenly impoverished and found themselves with nothing and their consciousness has been imprinted with the trauma, ever since. They prefer not to have a great deal of money, then to have it, lose it and end up with nothing. Some people, notably monks, nuns and the clergy, have arrived at their current life after taking a vow of poverty in a previous life. This causes them to hold negative beliefs about money and make a substantive distinction between spirit and matter.

When a conscious and powerful desire to create reality exists together with a subconscious conduit to the contrary, the weight in creation will be tipped in favour of the concealed forces of the subconscious. The power of fear is greater than the power of conscious desire. So the way to actualize your conscious desire is to release all conscious and unconscious fears that arise from your previous experiences, including the most ancient ones. Connecting to the heart, to the path of love, is the most effective way to accomplish this. The path of love embraces and dissolves all fears that stem from your lack of awareness of your power to create your reality.

If you want to link with the consciousness of wealth, take responsibility for your thoughts. Abundance, of course, includes love at all levels of life: the physical, emotional, mental and spiritual. Abundance is about good health, about an exceptionally pleasing quality of life, about a sense of value, about a sense of the meaning of life. It is about, "Love thy neighbour as thyself," implemented to the full.

Money is not abundance; it is, however, tied with the path of abundance.

In order to improve your economic situation, which, spiritually, is so vital and important, for it is written: "If there is no bread there is no Torah," you should immediately transform your conscious approach to money.

Ask to release all limiting beliefs. Ask to assume responsibility for your awareness. Tell yourselves:

"I deserve vast amounts of money."

In order to reach that state, you must improve your self–image. You will do so by accepting yourself as you are at present, without judgment and without destructive and unnecessary criticism.

"I love and accept myself as I am, here and now."

Only then will you know how to appreciate and even love, money.

"I love money and appreciate it."

This part may be hard on many of you and you may sense an inner contraction and discomfort, when saying this sentence. Well, with exercise and spiritual understanding you will succeed.

After comprehending that you are on the path of love, that you are entitled to money, which is a wonderful and certainly spiritual accomplishing energy that joins spirit with matter, know to give and to receive love. Know *not* to become attached to money through apprehension or miserliness.

When you spend money, tell yourself:

"I pay with love for the services to which I am entitled. "Money returns to me in abundance. I love to give and to receive money."
Also, **"Money comes easily to me."** And, **"I always have money when I need it."**

While you are making these affirmations, breathe deeply and imagine it. Convince yourselves of the truth of the new belief. Entrench it in your subconscious. At the right time, you will know that it is so and that it will happen in your life. Express gratitude for the money you have, be glad for your share and by so doing you will increase it.

Do not focus on what you still lack, but gratefully cherish what you have, even if it is very little. Stop comparing yourself with others and stop being jealous of what they have. Look into yourself and understand that real wealth is found within you.

People seek money in order to be happier, healthier, more serene and more secure. You can have it all in the blink of an eye, instantaneously. Just breathe deeply, connect with your soul, with your inner fountain of abundance. Enhance the gratitude, love and joy and reinforce your faith. This is the right attitude for those who have a master frequency and take responsibility for creating reality.

Remember, love is the key!

Love yourselves, love the money, give lovingly and generously, accept with love and generosity. Allow the flow of the cycle of giving-receiving-giving and do not impede it. Implement "love thy neighbour as thyself" in money matters, as well.

As you love to receive money for services, labour or as a gift, know also to give it to your fellow human being who needs it. Instead of thinking that you are short of money, think how much good it would do for the person or institution to which you have given the money it needs.

Do not associate money with fears, but give out of love, generosity and gladness. Your subconscious will then, in your reality, implant in you positive beliefs of giving and receiving money that will, in time, bear fruit.

These are my words for today. Here I Am Master Akiva, the herald of the message of unity for all of the People of Israel and the nations of the world, "Thou shalt love the Lord thy God with all thy soul and with all thy strength," and, "Thou shalt love thy neighbour as thyself."

Thank you, dear Ilana, for experiencing the right lesson and for learning to accept it and produce pearls from it, for the benefit of all. Blessed be in your eternal being.

ILANA: Thank you and much love, dear Master Akiva. Since taking personal responsibility for the creation (of my reality), I have learned to see negative beliefs in me and to release them with the assistance of the Angels of Karma, to understand the value of the lesson I have summoned. I feel wonderful. Thanks to all those who have participated in my creations, thanks to all the human beings who are messengers of the spirit, even if unconsciously. Thanks to the Creator of the World.

Lesson 32

Soul Name, Reincarnation

ILANA: Good and blessed morning to all my dear and beloved guides, good and blessed morning to dear and beloved Master Akiva. I would like to proceed with our discussion. Thank you.

MASTER AKIVA: Good and blessed morning, Ilana dear. How are you these days? Long time no see… I understand that you are fed up with channelling and your ability to accommodate has diminished somewhat.

ILANA: Yes, dear Master Akiva. I have to digest the material and achieve physical balance, which is of crucial importance in my book! Besides, I thought that we have a sufficient quantity of material for one book.

A couple of days ago I received my soul name or my galactic name or my star name or something like that, what could you please tell me about that?

MASTER AKIVA: Congratulations my beloved and talented student, for getting in tune with the root of your soul. In every incarnation a person gets a new name, usually one that is related to his soul's root. It is adjusted to the will of his parents, to the prevailing notions of his times and culture. The parents receive messages from the fetes while it still in the womb, regarding its soul name. Their interpretation is not always precise and consistent with the soul's expectation, but usually they come very close. Consequently, it is common that the letters of the soul name will appear in some kind of sequence in the newborn's name.

ILANA: I thought so, especially when, in my dream, I was handed my soul name. In the dream, as the star entity told me the name, I felt a shiver and a most powerful shudder in my shoulders and I cried with excitement. I repeated the name all night long, so I understood that is of great importance to me and that it is a key. A key to what, Master Akiva, what is the significance of the soul name for us while we are still in a physical body?

MASTER AKIVA: Dear Ilana, a soul name is the key to understanding the overall, grand, cosmic identity which is you yourself. It is your power name. With your soul name you can come and go in and out of high shrines. It is your "entrance card" and an approved–in–advance password. Of course, each soul has the hierarchy it belongs to, the shrines it attends and at which it is welcomed. No one name is the same as another, yet they are all equal; all souls are equal. Be that as it may, the soul name is the individual code and deciphering of your soul's achievements and its superior purpose. It is the cipher for decoding messages from high worlds.

When a person is given his soul name – which, incidentally, he cannot designate for himself – it is an indication that he has evolved, he has reached a galactic level; he is in touch with all of creation, with all his selves.

ILANA: I received my soul name on a Saturday. The following day, Sunday, the date was 9.9.2007, which numerologically is 9.9.9 and combined it is 9. On that same day, a Reiki masters' course was held. We were nine altogether. I wore blue and lit blue and white candles. By the way, I lit the blue ones first. Liad, who is familiar with the Mayan calendar and lives by it, told me it was my galactic birthday! There, my glyph is: "Blue Galactic Storm." It turns out, that the blue frequency I adorned myself with was rather intuitive. Likewise, the blue candles. I find it rather charming that I received my soul name on my galactic birthday. Liad also told me that the stars in the sky were arranged exactly the same way as they were on my birthday. The coincidence is astonishing! I believe that the name was a birthday gift from my guardian angels. I would like to know who the entity who disclosed the name to me was. I remember her as a young feminine looking woman, maybe it was I myself?

MASTER AKIVA: Dear, this entity comes from your celestial home world. She has magical and creation consciousness. She is a marvellous achiever and is a very close soul connection. It could be said that she a sister soul. You have forgotten your noble legacy and she has come to bestow a key on you, in the form of the memory of your heritage.

ILANA: (In the dream) we have met her father, a very authoritative man.

MASTER AKIVA: Of course, as a ruler and eminent king it is but natural that he would reprimand his daughter for violating a well–established moral imperative. There are laws of creation, you know and human beings, even godlike entities, cannot just do what is right in their own eyes. There are inviolate tenets. The logic is that one creation should not be mixed up with another, to avoid releasing an evolutionary creation into the world, that would compete with humanity. Cosmic laws are very important. Your friend, the feminine entity, actually violated these laws when she released an ancient, different, creative effort from the trees (of the evolution we are familiar with in this reality). Think about what was just said regarding cosmic laws and (about the verse) "every man did that which was right in his own eyes." (Judges, 21:25.)

As I have explained previously, a cosmic name connects you to your true essence, to the nature of the multi–dimensional reality of your soul. The name is a key, putting you in touch with ancient knowledge on one hand and ultra modern knowledge on the other. That is because there is no time and space, it all happens in one vastness.

ILANA: I want to connect with my knowledge! I want to recall and remember everything! I believe that I am ready to know the truth. If I have obstructions, I am ready and willing to let them go. I ask the Angels of Karma to release me from whatever has been blocking me from knowing the cosmic truth while I am still in my physical body, of course. With your permission, dear Master Akiva, I am bringing this communication to a halt. I am not focused. Thank you.

MASTER AKIVA: Get yourself in balance, raise your frequency, keep, it high and at the right times we will proceed with our discussion. I am always here, at your service. I wish you a good and wonderful year and the same to the whole People of Israel. Thank you.

ILANA: Another day had passed, it's morning again. There is neither time nor space. I now feel I am in a high, clean, pure and cleansed frequency. During the night I had dreams of great anger and when I woke up I regretted them. I conducted a healing and fell asleep again. I woke up feeling a great sense of purity, so I have most likely succeeded in my task. Will we proceed with our discussion about the soul, dear and wonderful Master Akiva?

MASTER AKIVA: Dear and beloved Ilana, after [the Jewish] New Year's Festival, we will work together on editing our new book, which is sanctified. It is vitally important that it will be published soon, this year. People write books for years, but you were blessed with a book that was written in just one month (plus a few days). You are a talented woman. This is the fruit of your accomplishment in past lives.

ILANA: I would like to have an explanation about those past incarnations. Is it true that it all comes to pass in parallel? If so, how could we, in past lives regression, in hypnosis, remember former existences, but not concurrent or future ones? Could you please clarify the matter? Thank you.

MASTER AKIVA: Ask, my daughter and I shall answer. Everything exists and is located in eternity. All times (past, present and future) spread a gigantic, infinite network that covers all dimensions, which are all here and now. Time[35] is a definition of the third–dimension, which your perception divides into length, width, depth and time. In the higher dimensions, where I am, the picture is different and more dimensions are included. Our perception is not four–dimensional. We can perceive in a non–linear manner divided into time segments of the past, the present and what will occur in the future.

ILANA: I feel blocked in some way. As if my channell is clogged. I cannot perceive what my perception cannot conceive. However, I choose to skip over this obstacle. I am requesting expansion of my consciousness, increase in awareness, a tuning into high perception, the ability to

---

35 According to the Theory of Relativity, the universe is four–dimensional, composed of the three spatial dimensions (length, width and depth) that we know. Einstein added a fourth, time. The four were termed "space–time" and they are inseparable. Thus, every change in space will have an effect in time and vice versa. Every point in time is called an event and has four coordinates (t, x, y and z). From Wikipedia: "Space–time."

accommodate, digest, comprehend and further transmit the knowledge. I ask for help from you, from Metatron, from the Angels of Karma and from my own high being. I will now go into meditation and while doing so I ask that you open that which needs to be opened and introduce the required knowledge. Is my request reasonable and correct?

MASTER AKIVA: You are an instrument of spirit. Your will is interwoven with the High Will and with divinity. Enter the process, open all channells and I will be with you.

ILANA: My request is to unite with the highly developed aspects of myself.[36] I am aware of three. I have felt the different energy of each one. My energy was the same as my soul name, which looks like an angelic being and is related or is close to Kuan Yin.

I understood that my perception of my incarnations is based on the duality perception of good vs. evil, of lessons and learning. I asked for initiation into the perception of the One; to comprehend everything at the level of unity. And, indeed, I saw how everything is one. An image of a huge residential building entered my mind, each level representing a timeline and all interlinked with everything.

I asked to know the overall purpose of all incarnations, but as yet I have not received a response. I am still waiting. I am patient. On second thoughts (I am smiling) I actually

---

36 Self – parts of me from previous – parallel – incarnations.

have the answers: I am enlightened, I have all knowledge. That is how it is in oneness. Now, where I am focused – in separation – I am not aware of that. But, with the power of consciousness I intend to join it all and experience it here and now.

MASTER AKIVA: Let it be known to you that the supreme goal of all incarnations is evolution toward oneness, in order for the soul to accumulate experiences and trials, for it to expand and contain the great light, God. Every incarnation is a karmic system that contains lessons. It includes experiencing all patterns of your beliefs, some consciously, others not. These beliefs guide and activate you as if they have programmed you. People tend to think that they control their beliefs, but in reality it is the beliefs that create their perceptions, activities, deeds and their evolution.

ILANA: Dear Master Akiva, it sounds as if the beliefs are... intelligent!? What you say is rather strange, very surprising and novel. Is it true?

MASTER AKIVA: Dear, all your bodies are composed of energetic networks, a sort of wireless nerve–system, transmitting pulses and signals. These trigger and initiate activation codes. Beliefs are such network system. Beliefs have intelligent awareness of their own. Incidentally, the same applies to every cell and organ of the body. The whole body is aware intelligence linked to various kinds of intelligence. For example, your blood is intelligent, your lungs are intelligent, your heart is intelligent and so is every organ and system of your body. Let's expand the dissertation, your aural bodies – the emotional body and the mental body – also called the intellectual body – are intelligent. So is the spiritual body that contains all your complex and high communication with all of creation and which holds the conduits of your communication with the high and exalted God. They are all intelligent.

ILANA: If beliefs control us, how can we change them? How could we create a different reality? This is not clear to me.

MASTER AKIVA: Dear, what are you if not a cluster and array of your beliefs? You are not made up of a single "I" but of many parts: sub–personalities. Each sub–personality holds beliefs, customs, habits, desires and passions. These passions may be contrary to those of another sub–personality. This condition is the cause of your inner conflicts.

Let me clarify further: Sometimes you find yourself attracted to somebody. You may want to enter into some kind of intimate relationship with him, either a long term partnership or a brief romance. One sub–personality desires the person, but it is quite possible that another sub–personality opposes the idea, because it is contrary to its beliefs. For example, it tells itself that the person is unworthy, not sufficiently wealthy, not handsome enough, not tall enough, lacking certain criteria. Your moral personality may tell you that he is a married man and therefore not available. It may warn you that he is not trustworthy and will undoubtedly break your heart and it would be pity if you were to get hurt, so it would be better for you not to enter into any relationship with him. Sub–personalities conduct dialogues, arguments and even conflicts among themselves. The dominant personality will prevail.

Now, since the belief system is intelligent it is magnetic and it causes events to happen in your life. You can enter into a dialogue with it. You can hold conversations with your belief system. To make it easy for yourself, since you need some degree of personification, you can give a name to the belief system that deals with a particular issue. The name represents a sub–personality. You could give it a form, a nickname or a mission. Indeed, every belief system or cluster of belief systems that have joined together, has a specific mission, connected to the supreme purpose of the incarnation, the overall purpose of the soul itself.

For instance, you have a belief system for relationships. They are beliefs of vulnerability: "If I am in an intimate relationship I will ultimately be abandoned, betrayed and hurt. I will suffer, I will die!" This is a rather extreme example, but beneath every belief there is another, related belief. Now, looking at the example before us, we perceive a formula. Relationship death: Death of the free body–personality (ego).

Ordinarily, a person would not be consciously aware that

he has such beliefs. The belief system would camouflage itself; it would suppress its deepest fears, the ones it is not able to deal with, whether directly or indirectly. The defence mechanism (which we have previously analysed), will produce pulses transmitting danger signals. The body–personality will find rationalizations and excuses for not being in a relationship, why it is not in an intimate partnership. It will even believe the rationalizations provided by its logical mind. But in reality, an intelligent belief system is manipulating the body–personality, finding it appropriate to protect itself from pain, disappointment, even death, which is the worst eventuality for the body–personality.

ILANA: Very interesting. I suggest we call the belief systems by their names and give them images, as if it were some sort of a play. Are you actually saying that each one of us is a complete stage–play composed of many actors?

MASTER AKIVA (with a smile): Indeed, it is so. Not only is "the world a stage and we are all actors," but each one of you is a stage crowded with actors, secondary players, entire production teams!!!

Let me clarify the example. Consider the woman who desires a relationship (a favourite subject), who is not in a relationship and fails to comprehend why. I would suggest the following: If something does not transpire, it is because you have an intelligent belief system that believes it preferable that your wish should not come true.

Giving it a name and an image? You could invent it. Use your rational, spiritual imagination channell. Give it a name that befits one whose task is to prevent you from being in a relationship. Now start questioning it. Who are you? What is your name? What is your task regarding me? What are your beliefs? Why do you believe I do not have any use for a relationship?

ILANA: Actually, I once did something similar. I did not know it was about an intelligent belief system, but I related to it as a previous incarnation. I gave it an image and an identity and started questioning it about its beliefs. It turned out that it was a powerful, commanding entity that opposed relationships and regarded them as weakening and unnecessary. I learned that unrequited love was the fruit of its endeavours. However, I have a question: Let's say that I have discovered an intelligent belief system. I have given it an identity, examined it about its beliefs, talked to it. How would I convince it that it is my conscious desire to be the one to determine the outcome? How would I cause it to fade or to change?

MASTER AKIVA: I really like your question. Look dear, the belief system has its own intelligence that ties in with the supreme will of your soul. It is no coincidence that a person contains his own unique beliefs. Therefore, you could be in tune with the supreme will of the soul and project the supreme vision desired by the soul.

ILANA: Okay, but how exactly? Could you please, dear and beloved Master Akiva, grant us the knowledge about the process of transforming our belief system? We need precise instructions. Thank you.

MASTER AKIVA: Certainly. I shall gladly fulfil your heart and soul's wish, whose supreme purpose relates to the transfer of knowledge for the transformation of mankind, for healing and unity. **Here is the process for transforming an intelligent belief system.**

Breathe deeply through your nose. Imagine a golden rose and sense its fragrance. Hold your breath and then exhale it forcefully through your mouth. Do this three times. Next, imagine a large golden conduit of light. Ask to enter. It will connect you with the supreme will of your soul. Affirm as follows:

"I choose to be in tune with the supreme will of my soul!
"I project the supreme will of my soul to all the belief systems contained within me."

Now imagine a wide, white, three–dimensional screen. Project your desired vision onto it. If it is not contrary to your soul's supreme will, you will easily be able to imagine it. You will feel enthusiasm and joy. If it is contrary to your soul's supreme will, if it is not for your ultimate benefit, the vision will become cloudy and disappear.

Say:

"I give my belief system a task... (to accomplish the supreme purpose of the soul, to create harmony and abundance in my life, to bring into my life fitting and suitable relationships, to maintain my good health and so on....)"

Speak to your belief system, manifesting as an entity. Befriend it. Send it love and light, by projecting light upon it and delivering love from your heart. It is truly effective and can alter the beliefs it contains.

This ends my talk today. Do you have any more questions, dear and most beloved Ilana?

ILANA: Now that I know my soul name, the one I was given in my dream, how will I benefit from it? I have a feeling that it is a secret name which I should not disclose. Is that correct, based on your understanding and knowledge?

MASTER AKIVA: the soul name, the spirit name, is most secret and sanctified. The secrecy is related to the fact that you can summon a person's energy with his soul name. The soul name has great power for getting to know the complete identity. There is immense importance to maintaining the secrecy of the name. Even in cultures where the spiritual name is given, it is only revealed to the tribal shaman and those closest to you. You were also given an external name, which is your "false" identity – your body personality (the ego)'s name. You have an inner name which serves you in initiations of the spirit and your journey of consecration. Solemnly safeguard the holy name given to you as a gift, for the time has come.

Blessed be in your eternal being. Blessed be all who come to your abode. Blessed be the People of Israel unto all generations.

Here I Am, Master Akiva, the bearer of the message of love and unity of all the People of Israel and all the nations of the world.

The time is at hand for the awakening of mankind!!!

Lesson 33

Release from the Bonds of the Past Freedom

ILANA: Good and blessed morning to all my dear and beloved guides, good and blessed morning dear and beloved Master Akiva. I would like to proceed with our discussion. Thank you.

MASTER AKIVA: Good and blessed morning, dear and lovely Ilana. I would like to heap compliments, congratulations, good news, joy and satisfaction on you. The subject of our discussion will be: The past and its ties to the present. There is a double meaning to the word "ties."

ILANA: Yesterday I experienced an interesting chain of events, I uploaded a poem and generated a forum discussion on the effects of the past and its importance in the present. I then checked my mail and found a communication from someone who feels that she is caught in the past and unable to forgive her ex–husband. She found me when she was doing a Google search on learning how to forgive. I posted her mail (anonymously) at the forum, in order to raise the issue. It tied in with the poem I had intuitively posted earlier. I then decided to channell Lady Kuan Yin on the subject of forgiveness, while on the forum. She said that there is no need to heal the past, just to accept it. But whatever is still unsettling in the present requires healing. I would be grateful if you would discuss these matters. Thank you.

MASTER AKIVA: Well said. Well, at the high level there is no separation. The division of time and its components is characteristic of the human experience in this dimension. From a higher perspective, all times are here and now in one perfect dynamic, probability-oriented unit. What you call past, present and future, is one continuous present. The present is composed of components resembling a huge jigsaw puzzle, each piece interlocking with the others. Each is composed of a slice of memory and a dream slice. Your emotions and thoughts bridge the gaps between aspects of time. Emotions are the conduit which allows the experiences you have gone through, as well as those you have not yet experienced (although you probably will), wash over you. Emotion ties together all aspects of time. Events which have been engraved in you, which have singed you and have embedded their memory within you, are still tied to you by bonds of thoughts and feelings. When this is the case, it means that you have not yet completed the process of learning and integrating the soul lessons for which they were summoned. Every event that you interpret as bad actually has its source in light.

Remember dear ones, for your soul - who has chosen for the sake of its lessons to participate in certain dramas - there is neither good nor bad, only a lesson about making choices. With the distance of time, with a perspective of years, you are able to appreciate what you have gained from a particular lesson, even though at the time you may have suffered great hardship. The lessons that leave their mark on you are of the utmost consequence in your lives. They shape your personality, forging and consolidating your beliefs.

You believe what you experience with all your senses and bodies. If you would search within yourself, to discover your belief system about a particular issue, it would only be through trials and events that you would know how to clarify it and justify and stabilize your beliefs.

Beliefs create reality. This is difficult for you to understand, especially when it relates to what you call the past. You are capable of comprehending how willpower, determination, perseverance and maybe a dash of luck, can bring fulfillment of your desires. You are prepared to accept that intended awareness creates reality. But you are unable to project this same understanding to events that have occurred in your conscious awareness, leaving a residue of burns, scars, even infected open wounds.

It is difficult for you to see that you have created a problem for yourself, that you have brought it about and now you find yourself in a deep hole. For, you ask, why would I do such a thing?

It must be emphasized that the body–personality, which

we call ego, does not consciously wish to punish itself. It tries to avoid unnecessary obstacles. It wants to satisfy its needs and its urges, to fulfil and its dreams. It finds expression in accumulation: of property, status, people to be close to, comfort, knowledge, etc. Essentially, your body–personality is searching for love and the security and comfort that love provides. This search is conducted in accordance with the specific belief system that guides the person, coordinated with the preferences and needs of the body–personality. The real needs are of the soul, which resides within the body–personality and seeks to guide its choices. Due to freedom of choice, it is possible to choose. The body–personality may achieve the supreme goals of the soul the easy way or the hard way. Both are beneficial and will bring the person close to the goal he has set for himself, the supreme goal of the soul, which is to open man's eyes and show him his power in the grand scheme of creation. "You create the reality. Rouse yourself and wake up."

Much channelling has been provided on the subject and the knowledge is still in the process of penetrating human consciousness, which prefers not to accept personal responsibility, blaming the external world and remaining blind to the existence of an inner, direct connection between the internal world of man and what transpires and is projected to his external world.

You are familiar with the phrase: "As above – so below."

I would like to add another crucially important and vital element: "As within – so without." Those who feel a lack of inner balance project it out to their external world and they thirst for what they lack. Such a deficiency would be reflected in their economic situation, relationships, health and so on.

As you may recall, we have discussed the self–image and its importance in creating the reality you desire. This self–image includes imagination, which is visualization through the eyes of the mind. It can include external features, economic or social situation, the condition of one's health, a state of serenity, suffering, apathy or even lack of feeling.

Maybe you feel satisfied in certain areas, because your self–image is in a state of being whole and you accept what is and are at peace with it. (It is of course possible that in other areas you feel a lack and focus on what you desire in order to fulfil it.)

Know that the act of focusing, in and of itself, is a process of creating reality! When you focus on the whole, you maintain and even amplify its wholeness. Conversely, when you focus on lack, you grant it license to grow and expand, through your creation energy. Whatever you give your attention to is fed by your creation energy and is enabled to grow in your life.

Ilana: Dear and beloved Master Akiva. At the intellectual

level, the insight is familiar. It is the analogy of the glass that is half full or half empty. But it is hard not to think about what you are in need of. For instance, if a man lacks a mate, how could he not think about it? When a person needs money, how could he not worry about it? Theoretically we can have the knowledge, yet be utterly unable to implement it. Could you please explain to us how we could create the desired whole?

MASTER AKIVA: Imagination and faith have the power to create the lack and also to utterly eliminate it! With this power you can break the bonds of the past, which have created the difficulties whose overripe fruits you are biting into in the present. The fears that you drag with you, the fears that originated in your past experience, are what prevent you from rapidly advancing toward your goal.

Imagine the following:

A man wants to purchase a horse so he can gallop like the wind. He will feel free and powerful and he will rapidly reach his destination. There are two individuals here. One will find the horse, mount, grip its mane and hasten to his destination. His fellow, who has just been released from prison and is still shackled, will have a hard time mounting the horse, after he finds one. He will trudge along, dragging behind him the heavy weight of metal. He still feels like a prisoner and he carries many fears with him. Will he be able to reach his destination as fast as the man who is free and therefore light? His way will undoubtedly be longer until he removes the chains of the past which greatly hamper him.

Past fears and memories are just that. In order to release them, you have to use the gifts of imagination and enacting, which you have developed so well, although more often you use them to imagine doubts and qualms.

Do you feel that certain experiences and events from the past disrupt your ability to fulfil a particular need in the present? Well, first identify your target. Second, mark it with a circle. Third, become an arrow released at it, but only after you have removed the fetters that impede and hurt you.

To accomplish that, let's do something to allow us to release the bonds of the past. Take a deep breath... exhale through the mouth... Do that several times until you feel a release and relief in your chest and abdomen. Now see yourself with your hands and legs chained and bound. You are in a prison cell, but you do not see the bars. Know that you are both the inmate and the prison guard. You are granted a pardon and now you may be released. All your transgressions have been forgiven. The question is: Can you forgive yourself for what you have done or what you, in your own mind, think you should have done yet did not dare do? Without such forgiveness, you will not be able to purge the prison's karma.

Remember, it is all jointly created by all the souls who have opted to play a part in your drama.

There is no victim and there is no victimizer, there is no evil, there is no good, they are all merely stage parts in your play. Just as you would not be angry at characters in a play onstage in a theatre, there is no justification for holding a grudge and being angry with the characters who are playing in the drama of your life. Similarly, there is no reason to hold on to anger (toward yourself) and to feelings of guilt, which can cause all kinds of bodily ailments. It is these feelings that punish you, creating reservoirs of want in your lives.

Forgiveness is essential for release. Therefore, let's have a cleansing process of forgiveness. It will be done with the power of intent, the right of choice, allowing the release of the negative karma of lack. Declare this:

"I choose to enter a process of total forgiveness.
"I ask forgiveness from whoever was hurt by me.
"I forgive everyone who has ever hurt me.
"I forgive myself for all that was done and that which was not done, in this life and other lives.
'I am asking for assistance in the process of forgiving and request that it shall take place in all bodies, all levels, all dimensions, all times, all incarnations, here and now and in my entire being. Thank you."

After every declaration, breathe deeply through the nose; bring light into your body, to wash away the feelings of pain and the illusion of separation. When you exhale through the mouth you blow out all that is unnecessary, burdensome and oppressive for you.

After inhaling and exhaling several times in this manner, you will feel much lighter and more relaxed. Now is the time to include imagination. See you bound in chains, wearing worn and torn prisoner's clothing, locked up in a solitary cell. A heavy steel door bars your exit to the world.

Now imagine in your mind's eye a large, white, luminous hand presenting you with a big golden key. First, agree to accept it and to be free. Next, unleash all cuffs and chains and be free of them. Use the key to open the door. The key fits! Next, take off your prisoner's clothing. A new, clean, cloak is awaiting you. Wear it. You have turned into the corridor and it has many doors. Most of them will lead you back to prison while others will take you beyond the walls. Define your goal. Where are you heading? Who do you wish to meet on your way?

Declare:
"I choose to go free and be a free human being.
"I choose to be thankful for everything I have (fill in the blanks)
"I am entitled to freedom and to fulfil all my soul's wishes here and now!"

Leave behind all memories of hardship, pain and confusion, which impede and block you, preventing you from making headway and accomplishing your conscious wishes.

Now say: "**I release the bonds of the past!**"

Breathe deeply. Repeat the declarations three times with great intent.

Find the door marked: "**Freedom!**" Stand in front of it. What prevents you from really being free? Leave behind all thoughts and feelings that limit your inner freedom. Breathe deeply and declare: "**I am free.**" Do it three times.

Now place your palms, one palm against the other (Namaste gesture), near your chest and say in your heart: "**Thank you for my freedom!**" Raise your palms (still in a Namaste gesture) up, above your head, pull them apart and release what is superfluous…. Breathe and sigh aloud, feeling relief and release.

Open the door marked "Freedom." What do you see in front of you? Is there still something that obstructs your passage? If so, cast it aside. Proceed. Nature is spread before you in all its glory: A green concourse, numerous paths, flowers, trees and springs. You now arrive at the white waterfall which flows from a high cliff. The waterfall cleanses you. Enter and immerse yourself. Let the water wash your hair, your body. Great white light penetrates with the water and cleanses you within. Release all that is superfluous: Guilt, anger, sadness, impotence, faithlessness, doubts and trauma.

Repeat the declarations concerning release from bonds of the past. Then say: "Create in me a clean heart, O God and renew a true spirit within me." (Psalms 51:10.) This is an appeal for great purification, out of intent to link with God, to be one with the plane of the soul and with the soul itself, here and now, while in a physical body. This declaration expresses your deep intention to be released from bonds with the past: whatever has tarnished your feeling of inner purity, whatever has overclouded the tie between divinity and materiality, between spirit and substance. It is an intention of inner unity created at the purest possible place. Repeat it three times. Use the declaration now and again to feel cleansed of burdensome guilt feelings; from a sense of sin, which is a deviation from the feeling "I am worthy," and "I am one with the whole of creation."

ILANA: Thank you dear and beloved Master Akiva. **Could you explain here the term "karma," which you have used? People do not understand it and its ties with the past.** Thank you.

MASTER AKIVA: Dear and beloved Ilana, as I recall, we have already discussed this, but for the sake of your readers I will clarify the term. Karma is a connection of spirit, energy and destiny, which, in a practical sense, affects the results of your experience.

All humans are tied, one with all others, by bonds of karma. This includes family karma and soul group karma. Ties that are pleasant and beneficial are called "positive karma." Other ties are unpleasant, burdensome and difficult. They are called "negative karma."

Since all planes of time are interconnected, karma links them together. There is actually no separation between what has happened, what is happening and what will happen, is it good or bad. You do not, of course, have a choice as to what "has happened," but you have a choice as to what is happening and what will happen. You can untie and sever bonds of negative karma linking you with others, with events and with life situations, which are hard on you. But you may leave the negative karma in place and permit it to meld your life through its patterns.

People are usually unaware that karmic choices are made in order to correct past life situations. Many ties on the relationship – romantic and economic planes, every type of relationship and in fact even the choice of a place to live – are direct results of previous karmic choices.

Karma may be defined as a curriculum in a particular behavioural format. The Karma Council is responsible for administering karma. The Council is made up of the most senior among humanitys guides. They are discarnate entities. Some of them have incarnated and experienced human existence, but others have never dwelled in a human body. Among the council are angels, known as the Angels of Karma, whose role is to assist with the souls choices. The format of the lessons is specific for each human being, according to the needs of his soul prior to its incarnation. Therefore, *all* that he encounters and experiences in his life are karmic soul lessons. Everyone who has an effect on him, whether positively or negatively, as he subjectively interprets it, will be a person with whom he has a karmic soul agreement.

ILANA: I have noticed that people assign great importance to karmic connections on the personal–relationship level. I have encountered people who say that a channeller has told them that they have known their mate or the one they are in love with, in a previous incarnation and that they are in a "karmic relationship." Could you please relate to that?

MASTER AKIVA: Sometimes the understanding of karma is taken out of its context. The fact that you met someone in a previous incarnation and that he played a certain role for you, be it rogue and enemy or alternatively mate and lover, does not prove that is the role he will play this time around in your life.

The fact is, everyone you encounter and interact with probably met you in one incarnation or another. Souls come back for one another, in order to play different roles. It is possible that a beloved soul has come to play your son, daughter, father or mother in this life. Or it may have come as a male or female friend, an employer or a neighbour. Roles change, but karma remains the same. If the association between you was positive and satisfactory, it will be the same in the current incarnation as well. But if the relationship was fraught with difficulties and obstacles, the same can be expected to recur in this life.

You reincarnate to mend relationships, release the karmic debt between the participants, sever the bonds of the past and fulfil soul agreements. These are agreements you have sealed in order to learn and understand a particular subject in depth. Every such issue requires testing. It may be pleasant, difficult or painful, but as long as you fail to comprehend, internalize and implement the lesson being taught, it will be repeated, either in this life – maybe with a different "actor" – or in another.

Before true forgiveness is accomplished, karmic release remains impossible between you and the one who has caused you pain or anger. Your karma, produced through inner hologramic imagery, will return time and again. It may recur with other individuals and even in different spheres of your life, but karma of lack and pain must be created again and again until its cause is released and healed.

You have no control over what has happened and what will happen, but you have the key to change and control what is happening now! Here and now you can always choose to ask for forgiveness from all the participants

in the drama, including yourselves. **The path of forgiveness is the key to your release from the yoke of the past, the template of karma.** This is the only way to freedom, to unburden yourselves of the patterns of slavery which incarcerate you in manifold dramas, each containing similar or even identical features.

As long as you do not find it in yourselves to forgive, you will not be in a place of deliverance. As long as you do not feel worthy of forgiveness, your self–image will incorporate guilt, which causes you to punish yourself. It is worth your while and highly advisable to focus your intentions (of forgiveness) during holidays, for they are portals of special energy.

To sum it up: To be free of a bond you must surrender your psychological need to re–cycle dramas in your imagination. You must forgive yourself and everyone else who has participated in your drama, whether it is the person who hurt you or the one who was hurt. Either way he has touched you and left his mark and you have been tied together in a karmic bond.

ILANA: Thank you dear and beloved Master Akiva for the excellent lesson. I still would like to understand, I do not have a mate and I feel the lack. What should I do?

MASTER AKIVA: Fill yourself from within. *Focus on all that you have.* Feel inwardly that you truly deserve a mate.

Release the deep–rooted fears that remain hidden within you, based on your past experience which, of course, was brought about by karmic agreements. Fear is the source of lack. When one feels needy and worried and afraid, he must first release the fear.

Remember this formula:
First of all: Accept what is, which you have created, even if unconsciously.
Second: Pour unconditional love on that part that feels the lack. Accept the self as it is in a given moment; increase the springs of faith, cancel the doubts. Act instead of worrying! Focus on what is and not on what is not.

That is all for this time. I thank you dear, Ilana, beloved and dedicated emissary, who has enabled the delivery of a vital process for the benefit of all the People of Israel and the nations of the world. Here I Am, Master Akiva, the bearer of the message of unity and love, "Love thy neighbour as thyself." "He who makes peace in the heavens will bestow peace upon us and on the whole of Israel and we shall say amen." (An excerpt from the ancient, Jewish prayer *kadish yatom*.)

Lesson 34

The Purpose of Life
"That which is Hateful to You Do not Do to Another"
The Parable of the Egg

ILANA: Good and blessed morning dear guides, dear Master Akiva. I was asked a question, which I, too, find interesting, about the purpose of life. Someone sent me the following e–mail:

"Usually, I am happy with my life and I find meaning in it. During the last few days I feel I am withdrawing. It is in the form of negative thinking which pierces and poisons me… there is a common theme accompanying these thoughts, which is: loneliness and lack of purpose and meaning to my life, as it is at present. I feel I am attracting great need to myself. I do not even like writing this, but I feel that I need to get out of this state and understand it."

This is a woman who is aware and usually thinks positively. I identified with her feelings. I request Master Akiva's assistance. Thank you.

MASTER AKIVA: Dear and most beloved Ilana. Here I Am, Master Akiva, in the service of the great light, the entire Angelic Kingdom, light entities, God. All of creation is standing behind you. I will tell you a secret: The moment you are exposed to criticism directed at someone else, it is you who goes into a state of piercing self-criticism. When you criticize and judge a person, you become connected with his stores of judgment. You then see yourself as that person sees you. That woman has been exposed to the arrows of criticism by her family as well as others with whom she is involved.

I now address that dear woman (and any reader who can identify with what is being said): You, with your criticism, have lowered your high frequencies, which are the carriers of happiness, compassion and unconditional love! Your need to be right is causing you to engage in an inner fight for your brand of justice. Your negative thoughts about others are an excellent conductor of negative thoughts aimed to you. They are activating your self-destruct mechanism of annihilation and extinction! It is a bit harsh, true; but it is the bitter, naked truth.

To remove the veil from your inner point of compassion, you must connect with complete lack of judgment and find within yourself the forgiveness that will eliminate the arrows of criticism you have absorbed.

ILANA: Thank you dear and beloved Master Akiva. Truly amazing! Apparently it is very simple to implement this. Do you have a suitable healing procedure? I am examining this new function, the **point of compassion.** Very nice.

Energetically, I can see that there is such a thing. I notice that I can determine whether it is open or closed, whether it is functioning or not. Interesting...

MASTER AKIVA: Indeed it is so, dear and beloved. The purpose of all life is simply love and compassion. The moment you are detached from these qualities you fail, first and foremost, to direct them toward yourselves and then toward God's creatures, at which point the purpose of life is lost.

The purpose of life is always crucial for the soul. The purpose of life includes acceptance, compassion, kindness and love. Criticism is in no way associated with the meaning and value of life. In fact it casts a shadow over life.

There are of course further aims and preferences of other souls. In principle, they are based on what is necessary for the soul for its development. It could be influence, power, abundance, etc. However, if a person is looking for purpose in life and intends to experience happiness, the above qualities (acceptance, compassion, kindness and love) are the ones he needs. They find expression in the verses: "Thou shalt love your God with all your soul and all your might," and "love thy neighbour as thyself."

If you are not immersed in love and compassion toward your fellows but, on the contrary, you find reason to burrow into and trample their shortcomings by gossip or even just in your thoughts, you will become cut off from others. You will become wrapped up in the energy of lethal condemnation. You will wallow in the very same energy that you are directing at another,

The parable of the egg: Imagine that someone wants to throw the contents of a rotten egg at his enemy. He holds the sticky, mucky substance in both hands and hurls it, but then what happens to his hands? They become smeared and foul–smelling. Furthermore, he may not even hit the object of his rage. Perhaps his aim is bad or his enemy has fled.

You cannot use negative energy against someone else, without that same energy adhering to you and affecting you, inwardly. You contain your emotions, thoughts and beliefs within you and they affect your actions. You have a **well of creativity** from, which you draw what you need to create your reality. It can become polluted by negative energy. Your creativity will be affected by the urge to commit evil that has entered you and spoiled the pure water within.

You cannot curse without becoming a conduit of cursing. These curses will rebound upon you, harming you and those near and dear to you. Alternatively, one who bestows blessings becomes a channell of blessings, which provide great abundance and blessings in his life. *Whatever energy you use will take up residence within you.* You cannot aim the poisonous arrows of criticism at someone else without piercing and poisoning your own flesh.

"That which is hateful to you, do not do unto another." Now you can internalize the message and understand: You cannot hurt another without getting hurt yourself. You cannot bless and heal another, without receiving blessings and healing yourself.

Whatever you do to your fellow man will happen to you. This is not punishment; it is not based on the definition of sin. (The concept of sin implies the idea of missing the target, the essence.) This is because of the unified nature of creation, due to the karmic ties which enclose energy within it, energy that contains your inner essence. These ties envelop all of humanity.

Your justice is very important to you. You are guided by your need to be right as regards your thoughts and deeds. You may sometimes be drawn into a quarrel or even a conflict, whether it is external or internal – within yourself. On the one hand, you will heap curses on the object of your wrath, while inventing rationalizations and excuses.

Dear ones, please stop the quarrel! End it forever. Who is angry? Who is humiliated? Who seeks vengeance? The answer is: the ego - the body–personality, which is motivated by the basic fight or flight survival instinct, which is embedded as a template in the base (root) chakra.

Instead of being angry with others or even with yourself, which is a distinct possibility that stems from feelings of guilt, ask to comprehend the lesson at a higher level. What is reflected to you from the person you are in conflict with in thought or deed? Remember the Law of Mirrors: others reflect back to you the beliefs you hold within.

Remember the dramas. Remember that every drama involves participants tied together by a soul agreement. They are all actors in a stage play, produced by their soul for the sake of their growth and for their highest benefit. The purpose of all the dramas you experience, is to play out and demonstrate what you house in the storerooms of the subconscious: Old costumes, maybe even mouldy, composed of beliefs, thoughts, emotions and images. You do not like the drama? Well, take responsibility for your part in its creation. Change the script by first changing your inner attitude. Purify and cleanse your thoughts, your feelings. Do this through the energy of forgiveness, which will resolve the quarrel, regardless of whether it is an inner or external conflict. Forgive yourselves. Forgive your neighbours, ask their forgiveness. Only forgiveness can smooth things out.

Perhaps you have squabbled, internally, with another person, in other words, within yourself. "Externally," you did not even talk to him, either because you were afraid to hurt his feelings or because you were afraid of a confrontation or for some other reason. What happens is that, energetically, you are in fact quarrelling with him. He will perceive your inner feelings towards him and respond accordingly. Maybe he will distance himself from you, even if he does not know the reason. He may even develop animosity towards you, which may or may not be expressed outwardly. Every act, even if it takes place in the hidden chambers of your inner world, affects your external experience. And, as I showed in the Parable of the Egg, it is you who becomes soiled by criticism, anger, hatred and so on, as dictated by the power of your imagination.

Healing occurs, first of all, by absorbing healing energy inside of you. Relax, let go and request healing. Only through repose can you accommodate compassion and recuperation. Incidentally, inner conflict automatically causes great imbalance, which will manifest bodily–physically, as well as psychologically–mentally. You may feel ill and develop ailments. You will certainly experience a flow of negative thinking, which will clog your energy centres and bring down your frequencies.

Know that in your high frequencies you hold compassion, love and joy, which combine to form happiness. In contrast, low frequencies are packed with negative thoughts, which bring in their wake negative feelings and may cause stress syndromes in the essential systems of your body.

ILANA: Dear and beloved Master Akiva, may we please receive the healing procedure?

MASTER AKIVA: Dear and beloved, from my statements you

can ascertain the healing procedure – which is inseparable from forgiveness. However, I can clarify the point further. We will enter an energy process of healing and purification to release and discard needless and damaging inner baggage.

As always, we start by taking a deep breath, through the nose, as if you are sniffing the pleasant scent of a rose. The fragrance is entering your body, activating the clogged energy systems, healing and re–balancing them.

Now, exhale through the mouth all your negative thoughts, feelings of fear, sadness, anger and oppression. Repeat the process several times until you feel relief and comfort. Healing through breathing is the key to altering your state of consciousness. You can use it in every situation, every time you think or feel imbalance, negativity and even a lack of purpose in your life.

The energy process for cleaning your, well of creativity. We will now resort to the imagination. You are near a well. It is your creativity well. Look into it. Look around it. Look into the water. Is it clear and pure or does it seem cloudy, full of toxic gas, malodorous? What colour is it? How does it taste? Is it sour; is it bitter or maybe salty?

There is a pail tied by its handle to the mouth of the well. Draw up some water. Let's assume that a poisonous substance has polluted the water. You may not see it, but you should know those negative, dark thoughts and bitter, oppressive feelings affect everything you create.

We will now cleanse and purify the water. A great, white, light–filled angel approaches. Between the palms of his hands is a shiny sphere. He hands it to you. Throw the sphere into your well of creativity. See how its light spreads through the water and purifies it. Look into the well and see the transformation that is taking place. Using your power of creation, you can add various essences to the water: love, compassion, abundance, happiness, inspiration and enlightenment. Add whatever you wish to experience, using your imagination.

Now drop the pail down the well and draw water. Look at the water. Its colour, smell and flavour have changed. You are in tune with the essence of abundance, love and compassion.

Remember to take responsibility for your thoughts. Know how to rid yourself of negative thinking, which pollutes your well of creativity. The well attracts your conscious or unconscious wishes. When you think negatively about another, remember that you are doing it to yourselves. Therefore, use your inner feeling to understand the association between your thoughts and emotions. Understand the connection between your inner feeling and your source of creation. Perceive the link between that source and what is happening in your life.

Know to forgive and let go of every quarrel, whether within or without. Walk in the path of love and you will taste its fruits.

The purpose of life is simple. The purpose of life is accessible to everyone. The purpose of life is the unconditional light of love, which is giving–receiving–giving. What you give another, you give to yourselves. Give goodness and you will receive goodness. If you give evil, that then is your choice.

In summary: "That which is hateful unto you do not do to another." "Love thy neighbour as thyself!"

Here I Am, Master Akiva, the herald of the message of unity for the good of the House of Israel and the nations of the world.

Lesson 35

A Heavenly Union
Relating to Homosexuality

ILANA: Good and blessed morning to all my dear and beloved guides, good morning dear and beloved Master Akiva. I would like to proceed with our discussion. Thank you.

However, before we start, I would like to note that congratulations are in order. Twenty one years ago today I gave birth to my son Joab.

Last night I suffered a choking attack. I rose from bed unable to breathe. My mouth was completely dry. It was horrible. I silently asked for help. It took a few minutes, so it seems.

My son, Ido, called me to remove a wasp that had entered the room where he was playing. Also, there was a dying cockroach at the entrance. I showed signs of a hypersensitivity reaction. I wonder about the choking I experienced. What caused it? What was its purpose? What is the sign in it? What should I become aware of? Besides, lately I have had hardly any treatments and this is raising economic and existential concerns. Your assistance please, dear Master Akiva, help me and talk to me. Thank you and much love.

MASTER AKIVA: Dear, beloved and lovely Ilana, emissary of angels and of the Creator of the universe. My desire – our desire – is that you should notice that nothing can be taken for granted. Breathing, a natural activity which is taken for granted more than any other, can stop suddenly. There are no preparatory lessons for it. Therefore, you must live every day fully. Live each day in soaring consciousness, as high as you can go. Live every day in goodness, pleasantly, with love. Live every day in gentle compassion toward yourself, your body and your fellow human beings upon the face of the earth. Live every day as if it is your last, as if the final exam is due that day; every day, minute, hour.

ILANA: I accept your words with love. Nevertheless, do I have a health problem I should know about? Am I asthmatic? I do not want to die by choking or in pain.

MASTER AKIVA: Dear, beloved. For this very reason, the maintenance of your physical body and its energetic, emotional, mental and spiritual contents is important. As far as the spiritual is concerned, your content is lovely, clean and very rich.

ILANA: Is it related to the aversion and criticism I felt when I saw, on the news, a man who boasts of using mind control on heads of state? His method of treatment appears to be that of a charlatan. Maybe he represents an aspect of me that can do similar things? Does he represent the physical manifestation of dark energies? Was I under a dark attack?

I do allow dark energy to flow through me, when I am mentally and emotionally in tune with it. It is made possible by judgmentalism and disgust.

MASTER AKIVA: The person you have referred to, whose name I intentionally will not mention, is in fact a great emissary of the light, but he is operating from an extra-large ego, out of his desire for control, fame and power. This is why he has joined the forces of darkness. Be that as it may, he does have keen command over various energies and immense capacity for influence. Incidentally, you, too, have this ability but you restrain it, because you are in tune with the laws of morality. In one of your incarnations, however, you were just like him.

Many are tempted to employ the knowledge and power entrusted to them by God for their own ends. It is hard to say where the thin line that separates proper and improper use passes. It is linked to the inner limits and to the gauge of truth and morality, which is sometimes planted in you.

In the case of this particular individual, there is a double standard. He has no link with universal integrity, but he is, nevertheless, linked with a truth bigger than him; with his truth, the truth of power and control. He should not be judged but accepted with compassion.

People look for a strong, charismatic personality, one with influence, who will mesmerize them and heal all that ails them. People love to admire, on one hand and to despise and condescend, on the other. That is because they fail to get in tune with true love for themselves and their fellow human beings, when their self-image is not validated and is at low ebb.

Those who do not take responsibility for their reality, failing to understand that their health is primarily their creation, will fail to understand the cause of their illness and will not be healed. They may temporarily feel relief. Maybe certain symptoms will be eliminated; however, I can assure you that other afflictions will take their place. When the body houses negative energies, composed of emotions and thought-forms, it will create these experiences from them.

That therapist, who is highly celebrated (due mostly to self-promotion), is not aware of these facts. And even if he were, helping others for the love of God is of no interest to him. The aggrandizement of his ego and swelling of his purse has his full attention.

You have already encountered therapists who do not work for sake of Heaven, but for personal gain. You are utterly innocent of such tendencies. Therefore, be joyous and happy with your lot in life, for it is great in the Kingdom of Heaven. Clean hands and purity of heart are the greatest accomplishment a human being can achieve in his material existence, in the here and now.

ILANA: Indeed, I do not want to judge or criticize him. No doubt he is doing his best, according to his understanding and he is coming from his truth (which, clearly, is not my truth). I understand that he is playing a role (he really does look like a character in a stage play) for many individuals, for himself and whoever sent him. And a role is just a role. No doubt he is acting his character very well. There is no question that the goals he is seeking are not the goals of my soul. His accomplishments are not what I would choose to accomplish. But every goal is good and worthy for a given soul. All in all, experiences are lessons for all souls.

I therefore accept him. I understand his ways. I respect his deeds. I release all critical emotions, which emerge, to be honest, from arrogance and the thought that "I am better, purer and spiritually wiser than he is".... It is true, I do harbour such thoughts.

MASTER AKIVA: Dear and beloved Ilana, my pure soul, I will, willingly and easily, assist you with your entanglement. Look, self–acknowledgment does not necessarily come from a place of judgment, arrogance or a sense of superiority. You can and should recognise your value which is very great and highly important in both the Kingdom of Heaven and the material realm. Nevertheless, you must accept other beings, no matter what lessons they have created for themselves. Acceptance is the key for you, dear and for all the souls walking behind you, next to you and ahead of you, who are faced with the need to be non-judgmental. That is the path of compassion. It is devoid of *any* judgment. It is not the only path. The paths of law and grace are not unworthy either. Mercy, justice, law enforcement, lawgiving, all serve one supreme goal, encouraging humanity to ascend the ladder of consciousness, until they reach understanding of the divinity within, which manifests in the spark that governs you, creating you as a very advanced program that constantly learns and improves itself. There are transformations upon transformations during countless incarnations, each according to his ability to accommodate, at the rate desired by the soul cluster that is associated with him or her. Each one of you is associated with a soul cluster, which, collectively, is fed by the fruits of its combined experience. That is your soul group.

ILANA: Somebody at the forum wants me to ask you what love is and what is a match (of a couple). I think that, as regards love, we all know the answer more or less. Love is everything. It is the manner by which creation is conducted. It is the essence of giving–receiving–giving; the essence of enabling, accommodation, generosity, calm. I find the word, "matching," unpleasant. There is an artifice about it. What is its interpretation and meaning (though, please forgive me, this might be utterly unrelated to our discussion)?

MASTER AKIVA: Dear, a match is a connecting. You take two seemingly separate elements and join them together in one bundle. Matching can also be done in groups, as is done when celebrating the harvest and four plant species are tied together so that each brings into the connection its own unique qualities and attributes.[37] Together, as a group, they possess the sum of the characteristics of each component.

The question, of course, was about human coupling. When two people join together a coupling occurs, when they couple, a new human being is formed. Coupling is having sex. To be a couple means to be in a relationship, which we have already discussed. People who have joint purposes and desire to experience them together, even in a sexual connotation, form a relationship. As to the term, "a couple from heaven," which you are asking about in your thoughts, well, indeed, there is such a thing. When there is a perfect match between members of a couple, when their genetic makeup is specifically adjusted to carry codes of continuity, of a dynasty, then such a coupling occurs.

ILANA: Now is the time to bring up Ariel's question, which was addressed to you at the forum. He wants to know your opinion about homosexual relationships. Are they permitted or forbidden? Are sexual relationships intended exclusively for procreation? Could a "match made in heaven" be homosexual?

MASTER AKIVA: My children, God has made for you many

---

[37] Here Rabbi Akiva is referring to the four species used by practicing Jews during the celebration of the Jewish holiday of *Sukkoth* (Tabernacles). For more, see http://en.wikipedia.org/wiki/Four_Species.

senses, more than you have discovered so far. Each sense can be employed in various ways. Indeed, you are commanded to enjoy all your senses. Sex is a magnificent way to express your love, your union, being in a state of mutual giving and receiving, which is pure love. Sex is of course a means of procreation, but it is certainly a legitimate means for sexual release, for the renewal of vitality, for the pure pleasure of joining your bodies together. Orgasm is very important. It breaks down negative charges, stress and obstructions in your body.

Sex is a charged subject, because it can be associated with abuse, exploitation, rape and subjugation. Nevertheless, it can be used well, for pleasure, dedication, creating offspring and great joy. Sex is the most natural way to achieve contact among you. Observe the animals and even the plants and insects, which fertilize one another without inhibitions, pangs of conscience or fear.

Some sexual interactions take place in the energy of fear, when a weaker person is dominated by someone stronger. Other sexual relations take place in the energy of love, which has a vector of giving–receiving–giving. Intention and manner of behaviour are what determine whether a sexual interaction is a good experience for you or not and perhaps even disruptive of your natural balance.

As to same-sex relations, my response is the same. If it is based on mutual consent, for the sake of pleasure and union, there is nothing wrong with it. However, if inappropriate and wrongful means are used: seduction, control, punishment, intimidation or rape, they are damaging to both participants.

ILANA: In the book of Leviticus, verse 20:13, it is written: "If a man also lies with mankind, as he lieth with a woman, both of them have committed an abomination: they shall surely be put to death; their blood shall be upon them." There is an injunction against a man having sex with another man, i.e., homosexuality. Yet you allow it. I do not want to provoke a controversy. Please clarify and explain.

MASTER AKIVA: In different eras different societal needs resulted in different legislated norms. When the Ten Commandments were handed down to Moses, who was leading a nation of emancipated slaves, they had not yet internalized true liberty and certainly had not yet assimilated a proper measure of personal responsibility. Thus, numerous limitations had to be imposed externally. All the laws and commandments were enacted for the purpose of achieving overarching goals.

Today humanity is capable of accommodating new rules. People can interpret the law in a more aware and enlightened manner, differentiating between laws linked with the path of fear and those associated with the path of love.

In this Age of Aquarius, each person can draw his own truth from himself, from his direct connection with God. It must be understood that what once held true may have been interpreted on the basis of prevailing tendencies, opinions, the fear of contravening prohibitions and the desire to walk in the path of righteousness.

Naturally the method of teaching kindergarten children differs from that applied to elementary school children, high school students or adults.

Know and remember dear ones, that the truth has many facets. You cannot accommodate it right now, only interpret it. Every person interprets his own reality according to the specific interpretation of the truth he possesses.

It is true that great rabbis, Torah scholars and Cabbalists are able to interpret the express will of God and it is good and transcendent. Nevertheless, it has been said, "The Torah has seventy faces," thus there is an opportunity for in–depth interpretation.

My key to deciphering is the verse, "Love thy neighbour as thyself." When you love yourselves and honour and respect your neighbour in exactly the same fashion, your interpretation rises, step by step and enter the path of what is permissible. The moment you take the dark paths of fear, where you see numerous warning signs, you enter the road of that which is forbidden and you have to adhere to the restrictions.

"Allowed" and "forbidden" are merely interpretations. You may allow yourselves something that would be utterly forbidden to another. It is not a matter of right or wrong/inappropriate, it is merely an interpretation. Are you interpreting from the light or from darkness? Are you interpreting from pure and unconditional love or, alternatively, from fear? That is the deepest secret.

ILANA: Are you then allowing the verse, "Every man does that which is right in his own eyes"? For your statements may be interpreted in this fashion and that is an opening for great chaos and transgression in the manner of Sodom and Gomorrah, God forbid.

MASTER AKIVA: Thank you dear and beloved Ilana, for clarifying the matter. Yes dear, interpretation can be distorted to the point of rampant corruption and lack of morality. You can see it in your government, law enforcement authorities and even in the military, long considered a shining example of purity and integrity. Can you see why the commandments given to Moses in Sinai have to be enforced? This is precisely the reason!

I am talking about human evolution, which is approaching the point in the heart, the point of compassion, the path of "love thy neighbour as thyself," which is pure and unconditional love.

When people are at this juncture, their interpretation may

be more flexible and more in tune with the truth, seen with compassionate eyes that have been opened, from a place of true attentiveness in the heart, guided directly by the soul, which is an immediate conduit of the Supreme Will, of the exalted and lofty God Himself. However, if people are not at that point, they must be led with the whip of fear and flogged every time they deviate from the straight and narrow. The straight path is the path of love and light.

Stringent laws were designed to lead humanity to the path of compassion, caring and identifying with the weak. It is a path of mutual respect, of brotherhood and companionship, of unity, as opposed to the isolation of the ego, which rules you most often when you are unaware. The path of darkness and fear is the path of the ego, that seeks to take for itself as much as can be taken, to accumulate material gain, status and power.

The path of light and love passes through ties with the soul, which is connected, as the active divine spark within you, to true and pure love. This implies giving from the heart, acceptance of what is and that which is granted, whether it is a heavenly decree or a creation for which you are responsible.

Reciprocity is the key. Just as you love yourself and aspire for your highest benefit, so you should be merciful to your fellow man, your neighbour, in whatever role he undertakes on the game board Earth. When you are considerate of him, then the verse, "The just shall live by his faith" (Habakkuk 2:4), meaning that all beliefs incorporating mutual respect are worthy, shall be fulfiled.

ILANA: It seems to me that we are in a twilight zone where some of humanity is still walking along the old path, immersed in the old energies of fear, while another part is awakening and starting to walk in the path of light and love. Therefore, there may still be a need for restrictive laws, designed to enforce truth and justice through fear.

MASTER AKIVA: You are correct, dear and beloved. However, there are some who have learned to interpret the highest truth at the level of "love thy neighbour as thyself." Their role (and you certainly are numbered among the emissaries of the path of light and sublime compassion) is to spread the knowledge, to bring to light the new interpretation of the high truth.

If someone has a flashlight that he can use to see better in the dark, he should also light the way for those walking behind him. That is the role of the light, to make visible, cast light, illuminate the path of love and share it. Darkness, which is driven by ego urges and the need to aggrandize itself, takes and keeps for the self alone.

Light contains the essence of giving. Darkness is conditioned on personal benefit and gain. It may even pretend to be true giving, by flattery and boosting the recipient's ego.

ILANA: Every person is connected with his own truth and at times the truth of one seems like a lie or an error to another, even to the point of mockery and disdain.

MASTER AKIVA: To be sure. You are right. That is the beauty of creation. It has diverse flavours, fragrances and resonances. Each person interprets the truth at the level of his evolution, based on the inner standards he has accommodated.

Some people accept the truth of others without question, because they do not acknowledge their own worth. They fail to appreciate their own insights; they are unaware of their inner truth, which might differ completely from the accepted truth around them. At some point they may learn to distinguish between what is essential and what is of secondary importance and then they will have the courage to finally discover their sublime truth.

Some people are led by others, who want to influence them and establish the standards by which society should function. A small number of individuals attempt to break down walls and build a path. They may seem weird and strange to others and they are likely to run into a range of difficulties regarding their personal identity and social status. They may be mocked by those for whom being like everybody else is of paramount importance. The former have an original way of thinking. They are connected to their inner truth, by which they are guided. They believe in themselves and do not conform to the prevailing beliefs of their society. I would like to emphasize that they are people who are in touch with their morality, conscience and compassion. I do not, of course, approve of lawlessness and those who desecrate love and light.

There is a fear in you, of not being like everyone else. You have to let go of it and desire to be what you are, the way God has made you, in touch with your most sublime inner truth. Commune with the true desire of your soul, your higher self, God Himself. You are apprehensive about being exceptional for fear that you will be scorned and mocked, deprived of the love which is apparently the lot of those who force themselves and their customs on everyone else.

True love, dear ones, is found within you, in your hearts. You do not need to look outside in order to draw it into yourself. Do not expect others to acknowledge your self-worth, but enable and bestow it upon yourself. First accept yourself, your truth, your path and then it will be less important what others might say and whether they accept you. When you accept yourself, you naturally transmit it to the environment, which then accepts you, as well. And if it does not, accept their lack of acceptance with a smile, with compassion.

This is all for today and thank you for all those who brought up questions in the forum of the Temple of Light. I Am Master Akiva, the bearer of the message of unity and salvation for the whole of the House of Israel unto its generations and all nations of the world. Thank you dear, Ilana, for enabling this process and overcoming the fear within you, that caused you to be afraid to raise a controversial matter. Blessed be, you and members of your household, with abundance and good fortune, for you are worthy. Thank you for the wonderful mission you are fulfiling, in that you spread the knowledge of the light and of unconditional love.

"Holy, Holy, Holy is the Lord of Hosts," and we, his angels, the choir of seraphim are blowing the golden trumpets.

Lesson 36

What Is Channeling?
Methods of Prediction – Orientation Tools

ILANA: Wonderful and blessed morning dear and beloved guides, wonderful and blessed morning to you dear and beloved Master Akiva. I would like to proceed with our discussion. Thank you.

MASTER AKIVA: Dear, beloved student who is dedicated and devoted, I am with you. What would you wish to ask of me?

ILANA: A man name Nathaniel arrived yesterday at my forum, the Light Temple. He describes himself as ultraorthodox and nationalist. He has heard about my discussions with you and wants to know if I am a woman with a familiar spirit. What is the relationship between a woman with a familiar spirit, which is forbidden by Jewish law and séances and channelling? He says that since the destruction of the Temple, prophecy has been granted only to fools and children and since I am neither a fool nor an infant.... Actually, I had summoned a religious person to discuss the matter of my communication with you and I was glad he had in fact arrived. Please explain this matter. Thank you.

MASTER AKIVA: Dear Ilana, I would like to address, through you, the student of wisdom, the emissary who has reached you, not coincidentally: Dear and beloved Nathaniel, your path is a lovely one, the path of religion and tradition, the *Halacha* and *Gemara*. That was my path as well and I followed it eagerly, with rivers of faith, delving into the verses and discovering their mysteries.

As you know, the Torah is a great book of mysteries, holy and filled with the crown of creation. People still do not fathom the extent of the treasure of knowledge hidden in the Torah. Usually, it is interpreted plainly (*spat*). In–depth insight (*drash*) is employed to elucidate and clarify. Only a few of those who entered the *pardes* have understood it at the highest levels and emerged with knowledge and new understanding. In all modesty, I was one of the few. I have influenced rulings from the depth of my knowledge and my extensive scholarship. I died and passed on like any other mortal, as is written, "dust thou art and unto dust shalt thou return." (Genesis 3:19.) However, as those well–acquainted with Cabbala, the inner wisdom given by the Almighty to the People of Israel, are aware, the soul is eternal and it returns and reincarnates if its course of learning is incomplete and if it needs to make amends.

The World of Truth is a real place, which pulsates and vibrates at a high frequency. You cannot see nor hear it while you are incarnated in a physical body. Very few humans are attentive enough to accommodate the knowledge that penetrates the temple walls of the World of Truth. They are endowed with a capacity to receive high frequencies, internalize them, understand them and function as relay stations. Their mission is to connect the worlds and convey vital and necessary messages. Some execute their task faithfully, others' performance is flawed. Yet, they all act as catalysts and fulfil their intended task. In different cultures and at different times they have been called shamans, magicians, witches, oracles, soothsayers, prophets, women with a familiar spirit and priests. Over the years they have acquired a negative connotation. Fear of the unknown, of the unexpected, of that which is hidden and of the occult, is a repeated motif in humanity, dating back to the times when man was still a hunter living in caves, in small tribal circles. The danger and uncertainty of those days are etched in your chromosomes. Fear strongly motivates your legislation and commandments: a dread of "Thou shalt not," and "Do not" deviate from the straight and narrow path, due to anticipated of heavenly retribution.

To summarize: Humans tend to fear the unknown. They are also afraid of superior forces. Thus, they fear those who are capable of reaching superior worlds. People have forever respected and feared those with the gift of prophecy.

Now, why was there a ruling, that since destruction of the Second Temple prophecy was given only to infants and fools? It was to ensure that individuals would not take advantage of the aforementioned fears of the masses in order to manipulate and control them, thereby manipulatively twist the spirit of tradition handed to Moses on Mount Sinai. If you consider the impact of the prophecies uttered by Jesus of Nazareth, you can see the logic. He was a good Jew who kept the commandments and I liked him very much. However, his prophecies and messages were taken out of context and transformed into a second Torah, the New Testament. It has been the cause of events that resulted in countless deaths of martyred Jews, destructive wars of annihilation, conquest, forced conversions and the Inquisition, all due to erroneous interpretation of prophecy.

I say that prophecy is not only about the future. It also relates to messages and bodies of knowledge handed down from the heavens, whose purpose is to direct humanity toward a particular path.

And why was prophecy completely banned to everybody, with the exception of infants and fools? That is because their utterances are dismissed as nothing more than "vanity and vexation of spirit." (Ecclesiastes, 4:4.) Infants and those regarded as fools do not care for the norms of their times. Their logic is not limited to what is permitted or forbidden, reasonable or unreasonable. Mentally, they are capable of receive messages.

It was easy to brand those with a spirit of prophecy as fools or even false prophets, in order to ensure that rulings (regarding the Torah) would not be changed in any way.

At the highest level, of course, there is nothing wrong with the various interpretations, for it is all in the hands of heaven. Trials and experiences are not random events but are well planned. There is no coincidence in the divine puzzle of creation. It is all for the sake of learning and evolution of souls. This is why a ruling was handed down not to make even the smallest change in any of the verses.

ILANA: Fascinating. Thank you Master Akiva. Yet, if it is so, why did you dictate our new book? How is it that I am communicating with you? And, in fact, why is this channelling and not the conduct of a woman with a familiar spirit (which was my original question)? Please elucidate for us.

MASTER AKIVA: Dear and beloved Ilana, dear and exciting pupils, I know and recognise each and every one of you! My students, 24,000 of them, are attracted to this text. Your soul, Ilana, frequents the halls of the righteous, prophets and teachers of all of humanity. Not only those who teach in the Jewish tradition. Your soul is grand and holds high and pure frequencies. Your purity is not in doubt. It contains the frequencies of great teachers, eminent souls of light and angels. God Himself has blessed your mission of spreading light and love frequencies through the path of compassion, the path of oneness. We are tied by a soul agreement. I know you from previous incarnations and you were my right hand.

In order to explain channelling, I will give you a parable:

A spring of water is located on a towering cliff. Its water is clear and pure. One day a young scholar climbs to the top of the cliff. After quenching his thirst, he fills a container in order to bring water to his people

He could choose to stay in that place. The spring is clear and pleasant, the fresh air will do him good and angelic beings will come to the spring and share their presence with him. However, if he chooses to go all the way back, he will come to where the thirsty people are, some of whom do not even know they are dehydrated and in need of the wonderful spring water. That is channelling with sublime worlds. Disciples are handpicked according to their degree of purity and their ability to accommodate frequencies.

You, Ilana, as you and so many in your vicinity know and are affected by your frequencies, are numbered among them. Your effect is like that of the frequencies carried by divine spring water. The personality need not necessarily be aware that it carries such vibrations. There are disciples in all sectors and faiths, of all ages.

As to being a **woman with a familiar spirit**, such women enable spirits to speak through them. This relates to a particular frequency and mission. The Torah prohibits it because, on one hand, it disrupts the spirits of those who have passed away, leaving behind the follies of this world and who desire rest. (Do not disrupt their peace for the first three years after their passing!) On the other hand, it also causes errors and is misleading when words are attributed to the dead. This procedure relates exclusively to people who have physically died and not to light spirits.

ILANA: Dear and beloved Master Akiva. Thank you for your explanation. But the question arises: What is the difference between light souls and human beings? Aren't all humans light souls?

MASTER AKIVA: Nice my daughter, an excellent question. I will clarify: Indeed, all human beings are great souls of God's light. However, there are and stages on the ladder of souls. Souls who are at the beginning of their way are referred to as human beings. Then there are the souls of teachers, emissaries and leaders, who have fulfiled their mission and the intensity of light they hold, their measure of expansion and accommodation of God's light, is very great. They are referred to as light entities. They are directly associated with the sublime hierarchies. Sometimes they have no need to incarnate in a physical body and they serve as guides and observers of human evolution, as well as for other species.

ILANA: In that case, according to your definition, I am not a woman with a familiar spirit.

MASTER AKIVA: (with a smile) Rest assured, dear and so very beloved, indeed you are not such a woman. You are not a witch but a pure emissary of light and love. Your soul descended to the world to complete what remains of its healing process and to contribute the pure water of heavens to all of humanity. You are Aquarius, the sign of the new age, a sign of pure giving from superior sources and high ideology.

ILANA: Dear Master Akiva, aren't (the People of) Israel above the zodiac? Isn't astrology a form of idol worship (according to Judaism)?

MASTER AKIVA: Dear Ilana, I am using terms that are common with you, concepts that match your beliefs and those of your contemporaries, regarding the Age of Aquarius. Faith based on the stars is of course idol worship. Whatever gives sovereignty to any element in creation other than the one and only God, Creator of the universe, is by definition idol worship. It is not true faith. Do not get bogged down by unimportant matters.

ILANA: I asked for the sake of my readers, not my own.

Dear and beloved Master Akiva, do you reject the science of astrology? What about numerology, tarot and the like? Are they idol worship? Please clarify.

MASTER AKIVA: Dear and beloved Ilana, dear readers. Believe in God the Creator of the world and in yourselves, as co-creators, who are responsible for creating your lives on the material plane. Those bodies of knowledge, more accurately termed "paths" or "tools," *do not* contradict faith in God. However, used incorrectly, they may deprive you of your strength, your ability to effect change and your freedom of choice. Used as an additional navigational tool, akin to a compass, they are excellent. But, just as you do not make a God of a compass or these days of a GPS device (smile), by giving it the power to decide your destination, make sure you use these tools wisely and responsibly, understanding that they are the tools and you are their owners.

This is the place to warn those who use these tools about the potential danger of karmic interference with the life of a person, depriving him of free will choices. Used properly, with emphasis on supportive recommendations, these tools will serve you well in guiding you toward the path of your life purpose. Incorrectly used, they will bog you down, dictate your course, occasionally clash with your intuition and even challenge your soul's freedom to choose.

I repeat and emphasize: You must let go of any dependency upon external accessories. Navigate by listening to the voice of the conscience that guides your soul. External tools are to be used for supplementary support and nothing more.

You may use the tools of knowledge (astrology, numerology, tarot, etc.) and to some extent even rely on them, but always believe in yourselves – that at any given moment you are creating your reality out of a clear intention to do so.

ILANA: Thank you. I am truly touched. This is very fascinating. By the way, when I wrote 35 chapters continuously, I left two empty spaces (one was for chapter 7) and now the second was written. How wonderful.

A moment please. Dear Master Akiva, you did not deal with the issue of séances. Could you please shed some light on it?

MASTER AKIVA: Dear, a séance is the same procedure described when discussing the woman with a familiar spirit. It is a violation of the freedom of souls. It hunts and captures souls stuck between dimensions, in the *bardo* plane (an astral dimension). Every soul – even the most miserable soul submerged in hell – can manifest itself in a séance. It may have negative effects. I strongly recommend to you not to be hasty. Your curiosity is wonderful. If you want to interweave an association between the worlds and receive exciting new information proving the eternity of the soul, then study consciousness, carry out spiritual growth, learn Cabbala, learn how to create reality, do internal work and link with the plane of pure and clean channelling.

These are my words for today. I am grateful to Nathaniel who was a catalyst for this important message. Blessed be in your eternal being. May only goodness and grace pursue you and you will dwell in the House of the Lord for many a day.

And thank you Ilana dear, the pure envoy of light. Never let yourself be motivated by fear of what others might say or think or the desire for them to love and accept you. Act only according to the voice of your high inner truth!

Blessed be the members of your household for your sake. Amen.

Blessed you be in your eternal being. Amen.

Lesson 37

Treatment of Foreign Workers
Karma on a National Scale

ILANA: Good and blessed morning to all my dear and beloved guides, good and blessed morning to dear and beloved Master Akiva. I would like to proceed with our discussion. Thank you.

MASTER AKIVA: Good morning dear and beloved Ilana. I am at your service. Ask, my daughter and I shall respond.

ILANA: Several times the question regarding foreign workers and the way we treat them, has come up in my mind. (I feel that the question is actually coming from you.) Could you relate to the subject from your vantage point? Thank you.

MASTER AKIVA: "You were slaves to Pharaoh in the land of Egypt. And you were tormented with a heavy hand." The treatment by your country, its statutes and regulations, regarding foreign workers reminds me of the treatment, during the times of the prophet Elijah, of "idol worship."[38] You are, on one hand, allowing these workers to enter the

---

38 The terms "idol worship" (*avoda zara*) and "foreign worker" (*oved zar*) are similar in sound and roots in Hebrew. Idol worship was abominable in Elijah's time.

country and you even need their services and on the other hand, you treat them as slaves, reduce and limit their human rights, take away their pride and trample them underfoot.

First, you should change the term "foreign" because of its connotations. You should also change their legal status. No longer should they be called foreigners, instead, refer to them as sojourners. The Ten Commandments instructs you to relate to the sojourner among you as you relate to yourselves and your family. You may not discriminate against them. Do not pay them less than current wages. Think of the verse, "Love thy neighbour as thyself" and implement it. Ask yourselves how you would feel in their place if you were treated as you treat them.

ILANA: Didn't the fact that we Jews were an oppressed people, a people that suffered persecution, deportations, humiliations, anti–Semitism and genocide during the Holocaust teach us the importance of humanitarian treatment of the stranger who differs from us in some way? It is a rhetorical question. It should have taught us. Why have we, the Jewish people in Israel, not learned? This question, of course, has universal application. Migrants the world over, be they Mexicans in Arizona, Tunisians in France, Albanians in Italy and Sri Lankans in Australia, to mention just a few, face exactly the same prejudice. But now walls have fallen, borders have been opened up and people are supposed to acknowledge what they have in common.

I think that the term should not only be sojourner but "assistive sojourner." It seems to me, that "assistance" addresses the heart, one's compassion and grace. What do you think? It reminds me that at one time some school children were called disadvantaged. It was a stigma that haunted them even as they grew older, forming negative residue in their self–image. Later the term was changed to "deserving encouragement," a worthy alteration indeed.

MASTER AKIVA: Indeed dear, you are asking and even answering, with my inspiration and complete approval (smile). I have already mentioned the importance of accuracy in terminology, the power and potency of words. Every word has its own frequency and carries an associative connotation. As said, foreign worker denotes an illegal alien in your psychic dictionary, with connotations of a lawbreaker and of criminality. Naturally, the corresponding emotional reaction contains fear, defensiveness and the sense that someone who is an alien, a stranger, is an illegal resident to be exploited, yet one to beware of; certainly not a human like yourself.

ILANA: There are in Israel these days numerous foreign workers or more correctly now, assistive sojourners, from the Philippines (of course there also some from Eastern Europe and why not?) Is there karma involved here?

MASTER AKIVA: The Children of the Philippines are descended from the sons of Joseph, Ephraim and Manasseh, whose children were exiled to lands across the seas. Their joint karma with other tribes is what brings them back to the Land of Israel, though in a different role. If you were to compare their DNA with that of the Children of Israel, you would have scientific proof of this.

There is a genetic correlation between the People of Israel and many other nations. You have not discovered all of them. You still do not know all there is to know about genetics. Be that as it may, we shall continue to explain, with your permission, the meaning of "karma of a people," and so our discussion will take a bit of a different turn this time.

Karma of a People. It is the collective lesson–plan that members of a given nation choose for themselves. It is undertaken at the level of the soul. It would be more accurate to say a group soul, clustered around a collective idea in the area of tests and direct experiences of the five senses (or, as a matter of fact, six, to be exact (smile)). There are other senses, as well, but we will focus now on what you know about souls at this time.

The focus on a single supreme goal is a solid ideological basis around which many souls can unite. These souls, of course, have a single root. The root contains the supreme will, their desired developmental predisposition. Even this orientation is planned in advance and parallel with the supreme purpose of additional soul groups, who are from a different root, yet nevertheless are one and the same.

What does it mean? **The source of all souls is one!** It has split into roots. Imagine the roots of a sturdy tree. The roots develop sub–roots, smaller and thinner which, in turn, become thicker and produce new sub–roots. A single tree has many roots!

Such is the Tree of Life. It is the tree of souls. When it is said that you are from a single root, it means that there are similarities among you at the developmental plane, that there is much more in common between you than not.

When, in your hearts, you are near the root of your soul, you feel happy and you are fulfiling yourself. This fulfillment is an inner sensation; you do not need external materials to validate it.

Sometimes, for various reasons, a person becomes distant from the root of his soul. These reasons include, among others, finding one's own individuality, finding the inner purpose at the personality level and so on. When this happens, he does not feel whole, he is filled with inner contradictions and conflicts. It may of course all be part of a plan. At the plane of your reality, the body–personality (i.e., the ego) needs to perform its own inner processes to promote and focus itself, in order to reach alignment with the supreme will of the soul.

Karma of a nation is the collective will of a soul group for a collective experience. It includes learning by various means; Some of them will be pleasant, exciting and positive, while others will be negative. These include war experiences – inner wars, tribal wars, regional wars and global wars. Humanity has a tendency to evolve by way of survival, the way of the root, also known as the base chakra, which is impelled by fight or flight.

The Jewish people have unique karma, which is the source of inspiration to all nations of the world. It is singular, "a people unto itself among the gentiles." This is so in order to preserve a reservoir of genes containing a relay of pure data regarding the evolution of human race. The Jewish people are linked to **all** nations through soul agreements, karma contracts and destiny.

The origin of the Arab nation is in close proximity to the Hebrew nation. Our forefather Abraham is the source that unites both peoples. At present they are at war, engaged in a battle over their status in the world. It is a relic of the war of succession and the power struggle between Isaac and Ishmael.

Every war results in victims and bloodshed. The path to peace leads through compromise and spiritual and political insight, which requires extremely long-term thinking.

You ask how does that tie with the matter of foreign workers? The relation, first of all, is on the human level. You have an opportunity to live with people of another, different – even in its physical appearance – nationality. You have the opportunity to encounter on a human–personal level, members of other nations who were sent to live among you; to be of assistance to you, to reside with members of your family who are in need of assistance and aid.

Instead of raising a barrier to distance you from those who are assisting you, get close to them, take advantage of the opportunity to observe how much more you have in common than not. Note that although you may hold different beliefs, if you get close to them and can observe without being trapped in fear, you will see that there is beauty in their beliefs; they are near to Judaism at its fundamental level. Do not maintain rigid decrees and laws, but "Love thy neighbour as thyself," "thou shalt love God, thy Lord, with all your soul and all your might."

Churches, synagogues, mosques, all share a common goal: to get close to God. To get in touch with the spiritual dimension, to diminish the distance the physical and the mundane put between man and his God.

This is it for today. Thank you dear, Ilana for allowing the extension of the discussion about the subject, for we shall continue and discuss it further. My love to you; I wishing you a peaceful Sabbath. I Am Master Akiva, bearer of the message of unity and light for peace and security, herald of the approaching salvation and revival of the People of Israel in the Land of Israel and abroad and of a message of unity to all nations of the world.

ILANA: Dear and beloved Master Akiva. I was very surprised by the course of the discussion and how it circled back on itself in the end. I see now that when we live with members of another nation, we can get acquainted with them and get to know them as human beings, like us. I can see that we still have to learn lessons of understanding, mutual respect and opening of the hearts. We have an opportunity to mend the karma of a nation. We have the opportunity to develop insight into pure love which is giving–receiving–giving. We have the opportunity to acknowledge with gratitude the assistance we are receiving and to compensate those sent to help us and our relatives. We have the opportunity to exercise generosity, love and kindness. We have the opportunity to bridge the cultural gap between nations. I see with certainty how a label applied to a person, group or nation can alter how one relates to himself, even to his treatment on a national level. I think that to call a group of nations the Axis of Evil is actually a crime! To stigmatize nations and regard them with prejudice is, to put it mildly, not very enlightened. We must take heed of the names we attach to others; we must pay attention to the roles people play in each other's lives, remembering that it is just a role being played. We must not identify with feelings of being disadvantaged and project them onto members of other nations. "That which is hated by you, do not do to another."

Indeed, it all really leads to the understanding of unity on the personal and national level. The learning process of humanity truly is, "Love thy neighbour as thyself." Thank you dear and wonderful Master Akiva, thank you very much.

Lesson 38

The Day of Atonement – Meaning of Soul Affliction and Purification
Soul Rescue
Multidimensionality

ILANA: Good morning dear and beloved guides, good morning to dear and wonderful Master Akiva. I would like to proceed with our discussion, if at all possible. Thank you.

MASTER AKIVA: Good morning and a pure day to you, dear and beloved Ilana. There is no impediment to having a discussion today; there is no transgression of any kind in it. Expressions that are holy and spiritual endeavours are good and beneficial for the psyche. Remove all doubts and apprehensions and you will be able to channell easily and pleasantly.

ILANA: I would like to inquire about the following verses:

"And the Lord spoke unto Moses, saying: Also on the tenth day of this seventh month there shall be a day of atonement: It shall be a holy convocation unto you; and ye shall afflict your souls and make an offering made by fire unto the Lord. And ye shall do no work in that same day, for it is a day of atonement, to make atonement for you before the Lord your God. For whatsoever soul it be that shall not be afflicted in that same day, he shall be cut off from among his people". (Leviticus, 23:26–29.)

"... And ye shall afflict your souls." (Id., 32.) "For on that day shall the priest make an atonement for you, to cleanse you, that ye may be clean from all your sins before the Lord." (Id., 17:30.)

Why are we instructed to afflict our souls?

MASTER AKIVA: Well dear, note the proximity between and similarity [in Hebrew] of the terms for suffering affliction and experiencing pleasure. Note that the responsibility for what the soul experiences is clearly that of the person experiencing it. He is ordered to afflict his soul on this day, as opposed to any other day. In other words, on other days you should enjoy yourself. Pleasure or torment depends on one's inner approach and desired focus. Of course, many people busy themselves with daily affliction of their beings, for they are dealing with the frivolous rather than the essence. By frivolous I mean worries, anxieties, keeping score with themselves and with others. The essence, of course, is to focus on "love thy neighbour as thyself," "thou shalt love the Lord thy God with all thy soul and all thy strength." When the psyche is filled with the love of God it is filled with joy, happiness, powerful faith and goodness, for it is in tune with the fundamental essence of love. However, when it is not filled with the light of love of the Creator of the world, it is sapped of divine light and grace and fills up with worries and anxieties. Consequently, it occupies itself with affliction day in and day out.

To understand torment and material lack, focus on what there is. Be grateful for everything: a glass of water, a slice of bread and a roof over your head. These you tend to disregard and at times you are dissatisfied with what you have. Do not compare the possessions of others with your own. Do not engage in envy or jealousy. Do not focus your attention on what you do not own, on what you do not yet have or feel you must obtain (a given item, etc.) in order to be happy.

When something is lacking, you appreciate it much more once it is back in your life. On *Yom Kippur* (the Jewish Day of Atonement) traffic stops and you are not permitted to use motor vehicles. Once it is over, the restriction is lifted and you are able to appreciate your (mechanical) mobility. On that day all places of entertainment are shut. Afterwards you can be grateful for their availability. If you observe the restrictions that apply to Yom Kippur and refrain from washing, eating, drinking and having sex, you will appreciate much more what you take for granted and perhaps fail to express gratitude for.

ILANA: Thank you. It is certainly an interesting viewpoint. I'd like to ask you about purification. How do we purify our souls? Let me sharpen my question: Many people torment their psyches daily, not necessarily by fasting and deprivation, but with thought–forms of hardship and distress. Are not they, at least theoretically, in need of purification? The torment they undergo does not, in and of itself, purify. Could you please clarify the matter for me?

MASTER AKIVA: The soul affliction of *Yom Kippur* has to do with self–examination. One should examine his thoughts and deeds and listen to the voice of his conscience. He is asked to observe whether and how he has harmed his fellow man or himself or God, through lack of faith and violation of "love thy neighbour as thyself," and, "that which is hated by you, do not do to another." You cleanse your conscience and clear away your karma by concentrating on suffering. This, in and of itself, does not necessarily effects a cleansing, if it does not accomplish the goal and the purification is accomplished by intention. By orientation toward forgiveness and absolution, releasing vows you have not fulfiled, terminating curses and banishments, turning over a new leaf. *Yom Kippur* is similar to the ascension of the soul that occurs after death, when all its deeds are scrutinized. The soul, this time with complete awareness of the personality, chooses to be cleansed of all sins and to start anew.

ILANA: Dear and beloved Master Akiva. I feel inspired to ask about when you were last incarnated. Why is it that you died a martyr, your body tortured with iron combs? It is written that you were at least 120 years old. The question is why did you create, at the soul level, such an excruciating experience? (I feel sadness and ask for your forgiveness.)

MASTER AKIVA: Dear and beloved Ilana. Do not feel sorry for my sake, for I am a free light soul and for each person the appropriate form of death is chosen for his soul and his personality and in order to complete his lesson plan. The superb question you have asked relates to *Yom Kippur*, which was the day of my passing. I desired to have my body and my soul tortured for I wanted to examine my beliefs, insights and truths and to accord the prayer *Shma Israel*[39] its deepest meaning. I lived 120 years in a most turbulent period, the Bar Kochba rebellion. You should know that 24,000 of my pupils died in a plague. I knew of the eternity and continuity of the soul. I had faithfully filled my role as the spiritual leader of the nation. I fulfiled my mission and there was a need that, in death, I should be a symbol, providing a personal example and serving as a role model, so that no one could say, "His death disrupted his scholarship," or, "His old age puts his scholarship to shame." I was at peace with dying and knew that it was the time for my departure from the world. You know that action conveys the lesson and the message better than words. It is

---

39 *Shema Israel* is a verse in the Torah (Deuteronomy 6:4): "Hear o Israel the Lord our God is one." It is the statement of fundamental belief in Judaism and encapsulates its essence. It is recited during the morning and evening services; customarily, it is repeated at the close of Yom Kippur; and traditionally uttered by Jews on their deathbed.

said that one deed is better than a thousand words. Did you perceive the depth of what was just said?

ILANA: I understand that you had the great privilege to keep your word and hold firm to your faith. A while ago I conducted a checkup and saw a fragment of your soul trapped at the moment of your frightful death. I then released it. Was that a real event or did I just imagine it?

MASTER AKIVA: Dear Ilana, you are not mistaken. You are a great and graceful light soul. You have the soul of a great and righteous healer, healing by divine grace. Indeed, there was a trapped soul fragment and you rescued it, for that is your intended calling, the rescue of lost souls, trapped, without direction, confused and in pain. You have brought them to the light and to God's grace. At the time of trauma a soul can lose fragments, which supposedly disappear because they separate from the rest of the soul. Such fragments can remain caught in the experience and undergo bitter anguish as a result of the soul's fate and its pain. These fragments will affect the entity as a whole by projecting their essence, feelings and beliefs. When a person reincarnates, he will feel the loss of parts of himself and even experience their energy, which actually is within him.

ILANA: Can you please elaborate on the subject? Can you provide an image that would better clarify the matter? How is it that a fragment of the soul remains wedged in a given event? Are there not angels who are responsible for collecting it and reassembling it with the whole? Is the soul unable to gather all its fragments before it chooses to reincarnate?

MASTER AKIVA: As you were asking the question the entire illumination leaped into your mind. Since the whole is ever-present in existence and continues to exist in all dimensions and levels, it stands to reason that in a particular timeframe all the events that take place in it continue to occur; all the actors continue to perform their roles. Apparently I was in existence in what you term "past." I was born, I lived, I died. Therefore, I no longer exist, right? That is linear thinking. In fact, following my death, following everyone's death, a transition occurs to another existential plane, a higher–frequency dimension than the physical plane. It may be ethereal, astral or spiritual. There is still no term in your language to explain the process. Even so, you can imagine your entire life experience being played in a continuous loop, like a hologram. Therefore, when you experience a trauma and my death certainly was traumatic to my physical body, fragments of the soul remain there and repeatedly undergo the trauma. Did the explanation make sense to you?

ILANA: I understand. Thank you. I see that torture occurs in order to motivate a person to move toward his soul and its goals by transcending his level of consciousness.

MASTER AKIVA: Lovely. You have figured out the association between the two terms. Torture certainly stimulates change. This also holds true for situations of ill health, infirmity, pain, dire economic situations, lack of security, dismal personal circumstances and so on. When a person is in a state of pleasure he certainly wants to maintain it. Only during hardship and difficult conditions does he turn toward change and even faith if it was formerly lacking. This is perfectly logical. Why would a person who feels healthy and enjoys his current existence desire change in his life? On the other hand it is clear and natural that a person who is experiencing hardship would do his utmost to change his circumstances.

The soul facilitates challenges in the form of crises, whose purpose is to replace the status quo with a state of affairs designed for the evolution of the soul. The change in the existing state of affairs is aimed at old patterns imprinted in beliefs, customs, thoughts, emotions and deeds. One does not choose to take apart a fine and well-made object. You break and discard that which is superfluous, obsolete, damaging and painful, that which no longer serves you well.

ILANA: Dear Master Akiva. I am thinking about the information that everything perpetually is and remains in existence in countless dimensions, influencing the timeframe, referred to as the present, in which our awareness is focused. I am considering the ramifications for the People of Israel, free here in their land, as our focal point.

Yet, in parallel, we were enslaved in Egypt, we suffered the destruction of the Second Temple, the expulsion of the Jews from Spain, we are undergoing the Inquisition, the Holocaust and all the wars. This is where slave mentality established itself, since slaves do not assume responsibility for their circumstances, they do not sense their power and their freedom of choice is taken from them. This is the origin of beliefs of insecurity, of belligerence, of defensiveness, of knowing that, "In every generation they come to annihilate us and the Lord saves us from their hands." (Even though it cannot be said that God saved the six million who perished during the Holocaust.) All the pain and trauma of the nation still affect us in the present, especially during the days of commemoration, designed to eternally engrave the underlying events in our memory. I understand that these are important days, but perhaps we should strive to heal the pain that envelops us on memorial days, instead of perpetuating it. What do you think? **How could we heal the People of Israel of past traumas? Is it at all possible? Is it part of a cosmic tapestry?**

MASTER AKIVA: Well said. You are receiving these thoughts and insights as the fruit of our link, for you are working with and stimulated by a constellation of enlightened guides. You are not apart from us, but a part of our physical being. Your biological brain receives and processes the relay of data. All your vocabulary is harnessed for this mission. This holds true to for anyone who is in tune with us, whether he is a chandler or a social, military or spiritual leader.

All timeframes exist here and now! That is a scientific fact which your science could verify, if not now then in the near future, through quantum physics: **All timeframes affect you here and now.** Correspondingly, since everything affects everything else and your empowerment is in the timeframe you are focused at, your point of power is in the present!

When you understand this, you are able to heal your entire past, both of the individual and the nation and even all of humanity. This can be clearly recognised through comprehension of the mechanics of past–life regression: Consciously, a person decides to heal his past in the present. He enters a state of relaxation. He closes his eyes and focuses on a period in his past, in other incarnations, which still affects him in the present. He does this by looking at something like a TV or a movie screen. He knows he is in the present, but he is focused in the past. After going through the therapeutic procedure he feels the change, the healing and the effect of the process.

ILANA: Yes, I see all this. **How is it possible, if at all, to heal the People of Israel?** The sin of the Golden Calf still weighs on our conscience together with the loss of the original Tablets. I have this interesting idea rising in my awareness: Is it possible that these guilt feelings guide our trials and tribulations: wars, disasters, the Holocaust? Do guilt feelings create crises and diseases for the individual? Certainly they affect the trials of the whole nation. Is it not so?

MASTER AKIVA: Dear Ilana, you have, with insight, solved a very deep layer that has been hidden from most of the unaware. As we discussed in our book, "The Dawn of Consciousness – Evolution of Awareness" (and indeed I was the guide who dictated the material there that relates to what is being discussed), guilt feelings have existed since the time of Adam and Eve. The sin of Cain who murdered Abel out of jealousy and a feeling of want; the sin of Adam and Eve, who tasted the fruit of the Tree of Knowledge of Good and Evil, thus sentencing themselves to the duality world of good and evil, reward and punishment, light and darkness. Evasion of responsibility and casting blame on another: Adam blames Eve who tempted him, while she casts the guilt on the serpent. **All these guilt feelings, to this very day, are affecting all of humanity. As was written, "...the fathers have eaten sour grapes and the children's teeth are set on edge."** (Jeremiah 31:29.)

ILANA: The sacred knowledge of light which is the Commandment beginning, "Thou shalt love!" was given to Moses by God. However, since mass consciousness was unable to accommodate it because the People had sinned with the Golden Calf, Moses was infuriated and shattered the original tablets. The Tablets with the Ten Commandments as we know them were not handed down until later. It would be interesting to know whether you agree that the sins of humanity, i.e., its transgressions and accompanying feelings of guilt, were the cause of all humanity's karma, especially that of the People of Israel?

MASTER AKIVA: Indeed it is so. Thus you see and through you our aware and deep–delving readers, that there is a narrative tying all past events to events occurring in the present. They are interwoven in the delicate tapestry of time, through karmic bonds which mutually affect all that transpires and all that exists. It is so on the individual as well as the collective level for humanity as a whole.

Can you see the beauty and importance of the cleansing that occurs on *Yom Kippur* by all the souls participating in the stage–play? Can you now understand the importance of atonement, absolution and complete forgiveness of yourselves, between you and your fellow–human and certainly between you and the hallowed place of divinity? This is why so many souls undertake to fast on *Yom Kippur*, even if they are not practicing Jews, even if they are secular in their beliefs. People think they fast on *Yom Kippur* for mundane reasons: To prove the strength of their willpower, to lose weight, out of fear and respect, out of a desire to conform with their social environment or for health reasons. As a matter of fact, these are interpretations of the personality, so they will undertake the commandment of abstention, atonement and amending. It is the soul that spurs them to fast and the personality that rationalizes it for them. Precisely for these reasons, it is very important to fast on *Yom Kippur*.

ILANA: I am thrilled by your reply. Now I understand myself better: Why does the personality find all kinds of excuses why or why not, to fast. On the one hand I find it unconvincing but on the other hand, I recognise a soul urge to observe the fast, which actually makes me happy. Apparently I did not comprehend the meaning until now. I like doing things whose significance I understand, rather than being imitative like a monkey or a parrot (with all due respect to these loveable animals, of course). I think there are many others like me, who rebel against the *Yom Kippur* fast because they are not observant.

I think I have a religious soul. For as long as I can remember, I have been attracted to religious and spiritual matters. On the other hand, I was born into a secular family and choose to lead a secular lifestyle. However, since nothing is random and there are no errors in creation, it appears that I was meant to experience my life this way, to get close to faith and the love of God, out of secular experience. Had I been born observant, I would not have learned all that I have attained: my training as a therapist. I would not have been able to think for myself and certainly, I would not have been channelling you. If so, then it is all for the best and all from God. I have always believed that the essence is what's important and the essence is to love God and to uphold, "Love thy neighbour as thyself." And that I have always done; so I am an observant soul immersed in a secular lifestyle. So be it. It is all for the best.

MASTER AKIVA: God scatters seeds of light all over the world, according to the needs of the souls. There is no coincidence as to whether one is born into an observant environment or not; whether one is born into one region or another, in a particular country, to certain parents. All is planned and there is no room for agents of the random. It is the hand of destiny that has woven it all. Everything is as it should be and it is all for the best. You are unable to grasp the greatness in the process and only when you are in-tune with faith can you make the necessary leap of consciousness, which the human mind and its intellectual patterns left unto their own devices are incapable of grasping.

Dear Ilana, you should rest now and release the energy that has accumulated in your brain due to excessive expansion and accommodation. We will carry on presently. This also applies to our distinguished and illustrious readers. You need to internalize what has been said and let the frequency establish itself while you ask for the facility to accommodate it. Blessed be in your eternal, pure and enlightened being, which is journeying back unto itself and its source.

Here I Am, Master Akiva, the bearer of the message of good tiding, unity and salvation to the whole House of Israel, herald of the coming of the Messiah and source of the seeds of consciousness of "Love thy neighbour as thyself, [is] 'a great commandment of the Torah.' "

And thank you dear, Ilana, my blessed messenger, who, with your purity, enables accommodation of holy expression and knowledge so that such can be transmitted through the channell that you are, to secular individuals whose soul guides them to the light and to dedication to God.

ILANA: (Proceeding after a break.) Dear and beloved Master Akiva, is there a process by which humanity's karma may be healed? As I am asking, it comes to me that the process was already provided in our book, "The Dawn of Consciousness – Evolution of Awareness." Well, **is there a process by which the individual can heal and repair the sum total of his incarnations? What is the recommended method? To my mind, if one can see the whole picture, everything is possible.**

MASTER AKIVA: Here I am dear and beloved Ilana. Your thought is highly compassionate and merciful. As I have already said, the moment of power is in the present. This moment is a gigantic portal through which it is possible to reach and affect all incarnations of the entity in this and other dimensions. Every particle of existence contains all of its parts. With focused and correct intention it is possible to avail oneself of the healing, which would consist of several stages:

a. One may ask for **healing for the entire entity,** in all bodies, layers, dimensions, incarnations, here and now and in the entire being.

b. One may ask for **a comprehensive process of forgiveness,** which would include: Asking forgiveness from anyone one has hurt, whether by speech, thought, deed or inactivity; choosing to forgive anyone who has inflicted hurt in such manner. Forgiveness for oneself, for all that has been done by speech or thought or deed or by inactivity. This will release the karma between the individual and all those who are tied to him and to whom he is tied.

This would be a good place to seek **release from guilt feelings** in all bodies, layers, dimensions, incarnations, here and now and in one's entire being.

c. Say with total intention: "Create in me a clean heart, O God and renew a right spirit within me." (Psalms 51:10.) It should be said three times. Take a deep breath each time, exhaling through the mouth in order to internalize the request in all bodies and to feel the fusion. Repeat three times for all the processes delineated above.

ILANA: I have had the thought that, possibly, when one reaches total, final enlightenment, all his incarnations will join together and receive healing and oneness. Is it true? And, will it not happen as long as a person does not become enlightened? Please focus on the question and clarify the matter for me.

MASTER AKIVA: Dear and beloved Ilana, the enlightenment you are referring to is a final purification, a coming together of all the layers and incarnations of the personality, a clean union with God. The awareness of the oneness of creation pulsates in you. It is be the most influential aspect of your activity. All your personal desires will be annulled and you will be in communion with the divine will. The ego is very fearful of this. Therefore, some people never approach enlightenment and even seek to distance themselves therefrom. The longer they remain focused in the material, the further they will be from enlightenment, which demands that they forego such attitudes.

ILANA: If it is so, then, once more, you are dividing spirit from matter which is a manifestation of the consciousness of separation. Moreover, justification for vows of abstention and material abstemiousness now become clear. Is there no way to merge the two?

MASTER AKIVA: Nicely stated. It is a very important question. I am speaking of a list of priorities, about placing material subjects at the top of the list. Hoarding money and accumulating property, enslavement to the lusts of the physical body, all of these come at the expense of the spirit and the soul. The golden path which unites matter and spirit equally is best. There is no need to exaggerate either way, but you should strive to maintain balance.

You are affected by your disparate parts. One part is the "inner child," innocent and clear, connected to the soul in its purity. Another part is the higher self, old and wise, which advises you well.

You have other parts, the totality of which is your ego (body–personality). Each part seeks exclusivity and is driven to lead you. Each one feels separate and is disinclined to attain unity and thus lose its self–identity. Therefore, the ego is an obstacle on the path to enlightenment.

ILANA: We have already discussed the ego and how to refine it. Could you please briefly relate to it here?

MASTER AKIVA: Paradoxically, it is impossible to heal the ego by way of the ego. The ego cannot be negated through the ego. All methods conceived by the ego are conceptually limited. The correct and best course would be to call upon the soul and seek to be at one with it, to be placed under its overall guidance. From the connection with the soul, the requisite processes, which we will not specify here, would emerge. Love is required in order to achieve complete healing. Pure unconditional love, "Love the Lord thy God with all your soul and all your strength," "love thy neighbour like yourself."

When you judge and criticize yourself or your fellow man, you are immersed in a state of survival and defensiveness and you cannot attain inner integration. You cannot reach the desired enlightenment which is the goal of all souls. Only through the frequency of love, acceptance, accommodation and enabling, can you progress toward enlightenment. That is why the Ten Commandments were bestowed upon you, as a course of sanctification and enlightenment.

They were given in the form of positive and negative decrees in order to clarify and refine what is required of you. When you do not love yourself you cannot understand the verse, "Love thy neighbour as thyself." In other words, just as you do not like being criticized, do not be critical of others. Just as you dislike being hurt by others, do not inflict hurt on them and so on.

ILANA: I now understand *Yom Kippur* at a deeper level, as a vital way to reach enlightenment. You must release the past, cleanse all its residue and karmic effects, release all hurt from yourself and your fellow human beings and between you and God, to be rid of all feelings of guilt, to turn over a new leaf. This is why we wear white on *Yom Kippur,* as a symbol of the purity we seek to attain. It is the colour of the crown chakra, the gateway to higher worlds by way of unconditional faith!

MASTER AKIVA: I like that. You summarized well all that was said and brought it back to the holiness of *Yom Kippur*, the day on which we are writing this, our current lesson. You and the esteemed readers can observe how everything connects and ties in with everything else, how important love is in **every aspect of the whole**, how holy days are energy portals of great value in connecting with a particular frequency: "Love thy neighbour as thyself," which is a concise summary of the whole Torah.

"May goodness and grace be with you and you shall stay in

the House of the Lord forever." Here I Am, Master Akiva, the herald of the message of unity and salvation for the People of Israel and the nations of the world.

Thank you dear, Ilana, mouthpiece of creation and a true devoted and dedicated student. Blessed be, and, because of you, blessed will be all who cross your threshold. Amen.

Lesson 39

A Genuine Connection
Proactive or Reactive
A Paradigm for a Healthy and Creative Society

ILANA: Good morning dear and beloved guides, good and blessed morning to you, dear and beloved Master Akiva. I am in the final stages of our joint and enlightened book. I woke up early this morning or was it night? Honestly, I tried to get back to sleep. I so much like to dream, but when I realized I could sleep no more I resolved to rise. Maybe you wish to conclude our book later today. I am starting to get it ready for printing. Is the book complete and ready as it is or are there any additional materials forthcoming? No doubt it will be amazingly thick. It is astonishing that we started writing just three months ago. I would like to proceed with our discussion, if at all possible. Thank you.

MASTER AKIVA: A pleasant morning to you dear and beloved Ilana, beloved by me and all of creation. Your significance is very great for you are a mediator between heaven and earth, between the high and low worlds.

ILANA: Oh, I feel an energetic current under my ears, I sense a physical presence and it feels very pleasant. Yes, please continue (a smile).

MASTER AKIVA: This is not a coincidental distraction. It comes to show you, by way of a physical sensation, that you are indeed connected with us, the senior guides of humanity. You still harbour a portion of the old ego and it is time to relinquish it. This portion tends to humble you and your activity. Do not take it too seriously. Do let it lead you through the new plateaus of probable reality which are opening before you now. True, in previous incarnations you have known the sin of hubris, but then again, you made complete amends long ago in that respect.

You must be meticulous with your thoughts in all aspects of life. Self-appreciation is very important. There is no place for belittling yourself and your creative efforts. (It is clear to me that you value yourself and your creation, nevertheless, the emphasis is of consequence for the future.) Now and at later stages of your life you will be presented with a few choices. Notice the degree of difficulty and effort you invest. You do not need to make an effort; there is no longer any need for you to suffer. There is no need to experience anger, self-pity and other emotions. The time has come to release them.

Your inner content is clean, pure and strong. You are very powerful, Ilana and your degree of faith in the Creator of the universe, in yourself and in your mission is high and very clear. Now is the time to rest on the laurels you have acquired with the toil of your hands, the sweat of your brow, tears and blood in many incarnations, most significant ones. It is time to transcend. This transcendence includes a constant, static state of happiness, though nuances of feelings will still come into being, vibrating in the range of the rainbow. You will experience serene joy, pure bliss, primeval elation, gentle delight, effervescent ecstasy and uncontrolled happiness.

I have listened to your conversation with your friend, the one who believes that a primary teacher, which is how she defines an actor in the field of activity where linkage occurs between the worlds, who has to experience hardship, suffering and torment in order to learn. You heard her. At one level you tended to agree with her. Nevertheless and the senior management of the light and I emphatically applaud (smiles in the grandstands), you disagreed with her. Well done! Your experience is not like hers. You do not experience and *interpret,* with the emphasis on interpreting, as she does. She naturally creates for herself experiences and difficulties based on her beliefs. This is generally true for people who write life scripts for themselves, sinking neck–deep into the drama, forgetting that the source of the creation is they themselves, of course, at a higher level.

Did you Ilana or you, dear readers, notice that people often tend to agree with one another? They do so because they seek some sort of common denominator, a conduit for connection and communication. Some would consequently rescind, even unconsciously, their own true expectations and desires. There are people who have no real desire or genuine thought of their own. In any conversation they adopt the opinions of those closest to them. This is the reason for gossip – the need for common subjects of discussion.

Dear Ilana, you have forever avoided such conduct, always finding it distasteful. Your spiritual insight has elevated you to the level of an observer and a witness and this has prevented you from wading in this compressed energy (gossip). Every conversation you conduct is energy. Imagine a pool of water. A conversation is like wading in the pool. Sometimes you sense that the pool is rancid or filled with sharks and crocodiles. At other times, you experience clear, cool and refreshing water, that gives you a sense of joy and great pleasure.

Gossip lowers your frequencies and leads you to rejoice in gloating, a low level of the personality. Be aware, be alert, be selective about the subject of any conversation you choose to participate in. Ask yourself, what is the value in it? Does it contribute anything of significance to you or to your partner? Does it contain malice? Gossip? Gloating? Malevolence? Does it contain truth? If it were recorded and replayed to you, would you be pleased with your remarks? With your manner of conversation? Energetically, did you feel agreeable?

ILANA: Dear and so very beloved Master Akiva, people talk and weave all those elements you have mentioned into their conversations and seemingly they are very happy. What would really cause them to avoid it and why is it important that they do so? Could you please clarify the subject?

In addition, it now seems appropriate for me to ask you about the subject that came to light lately in an exchange with a friend. It is about youths who tag along with others, who are influenced by their peers, affected by others due to their need to be like everybody else. This phenomenon causes them to start smoking, to drink liquor and to commence sexual activity too early. To my great delight, I am not personally acquainted with the phenomenon but I know of it. Please explain this and tie it to the need to find a common denominator.

MASTER AKIVA: Dear and beloved Ilana, your question is very pleasing to me. Indeed, the subject of our conversation is: Focusing on your inner truth, placing internal and external limits on your connection to your high desire, in your connection with your true inner identity. This is the last chapter in our book and this particular issue will seal my message (do not worry, very temporarily).

As to your question about avoiding hurting another person, that came up during a conversation at which I was present (as a matter of fact, you should, at a more advanced stage, take responsibility for your thoughts). Ask yourselves this question and answer sincerely: was the conversation held in the spirit of "love thy neighbour as thyself? Or was it in the spirit of isolation and hurting your fellow human being? Always remember: "That which is hated by you, do not do unto another." When you hurt another, you are hurting yourselves; you become disconnected from complete union with the light of the soul and with God.

Humans seek to be like everyone else. They tag along and are affected by the prevailing mood of those around them. The purpose of society is to form associations of individuals, to create bridges between human beings, to unite them. Theoretically and conceptually, spiritually and practically, it is a wonderful and blessed idea. Societies are based on mutual interests and needs, as well as divergent interests which form a stimulating and competitive factor that aims to encourage individual thinking.

You have a fierce urge to belong. You have a great desire to be accepted as you are, to receive love, appreciation and attention. Why is that? It is because you have an inner call to belong to yourselves, to be connected with the source of light and love, guidance and acceptance. That is the source of inner power and truth, coming from the high echelons of the soul: the truth of the One. The truth, that you are all one; the truth that you are one with your soul and its desire; one with the Creator of the world.

When you fail to comprehend this, you search for the

connection in human company, for belonging with another, instead of with your essence. That is a necessary stage in the process of learning the truth. Trial, through direct experience, within your belief system is very significant for sake of your growth, development and spiritual evolution as a chosen and preferred species in all of creation.

However, you may choose to be a follower, the object of others' influence, helpless and disconnected from your pure and personal source of power, the truth within you. Or you can choose to be in it. When you are in tune with your inner truth, you know your true desire. You become aware of your limits. You are true to yourself. You are attentive to the guidance of your soul and through it to the Creator of the world, to God. Is there a greater source of power?

With your indulgence, I will bring a parable. A nomad roves the desert sands. He is thirsty and hungry. The blazing sun overhead scorches his skin, leaving its mark. Then he is caught in a ferocious sandstorm that threatens to bury him under heaps of sand. Seeking shelter, he clutches a reed to save himself from being carried away.

What do you think will happen?

Surely you will reply that the reed would be torn from the ground and carried away with him. That is how you get carried away, lacking control, lacking true will, with societal conventions, when you are ruled by the need to be like everyone else.

Adolescents search for meaning. They need self–definition; they want to understand who they are. They are no longer children; their bodies are maturing, they are becoming young adults. The body has needs of its own, which are new and unfamiliar to them. Exciting and titillating on the one hand and frightening and threatening, on the other. It is easier for a young person to define himself when he has before him a model for imitation with whom he can identify. When you are afraid of being unpopular you give up your personal self–definition. It is the atavistic fear, dating from the days of prehistoric man who lived in caves or as nomadic tribes, of being rejected by the clan, of abandonment, of being cast off and dying alone. The survival instinct leaves its mark. You adopt tribal norms, those of your society, a prehistoric, ancient society where might is right, while the individual trails behind, influenced and maneuvered by others.

When it occurs among adolescents, it is easy for you to observe the phenomenon with detachment and even be infuriated by it. However, it reflects what takes place in the adult world. You replace social leaders and a social agenda with mass media opinion leaders. You religiously and faithfully read newspapers, listen to the radio, watch television and accept the biased commentary that is fed to you. You are stuffed with commentary and you soak it up, you store it in your body, you tune in to it as a gauge of absolute truth. You become dependent on what you are told. You think the way the headlines suggest you should. You adopt a party and follow it come what may. You imitate the leaders that rose through the ranks.

You are highly suggestible creatures. You are followers "to the max." You toe the line. You do not break conventions and most of you do not even doubt their validity and legality, the legality of your laws. You have forgotten who you are. You have, at times, been detached from the true will of your soul. You do things because you must, there is no other way, there is no choice. This is not about paying taxes, which is essential. This is not about military service, which is vital. This is about the fact that sometimes you do things that contradict your inner intuition, out of fear of hurting someone else's feelings, which is in fact a fear of getting hurt yourself. Or out of a desire for appreciation, admiration and attention, even the negative kind, even if it is a rebuke or pity.

I would like to summarize all this, in clear and simple terms:

As a follower you are weak.

When you are influenced contrary to your real desire, you are weakened.

When you seek to be empowered at the expense of others,

you are in fact impotent. You are very weak.

When you are angry and behave violently and you forcibly try to take love, you are extremely weak. You are dependent on the external response of energy sources – other people.

When you get dragged into taking drugs, smoking cigarettes or drinking alcoholic beverages in order to be like everybody else, you are weakened, you become cut off from yourself. You become detached from your power. You may become like everyone else, but alas, you will not be like yourself, not like your soul.

When you are severed from your soul, from your true desired, you feel lonely, you feel bored, you sometime feel you have lost your way. At times you feel that the taste of life has faded. You need to fill up the resulting void. You need external support.

There is only one way to feel real happiness, the meaning of life, beauty, gratitude and joy, which is simple and accessible to whoever would choose it: **The path of total connection!** Through complete connection to all bodies: the physical, emotional, mental and spiritual. It is vitally important to connect with your spiritual body, from which you will receive the full guidance of your soul. This includes unconditional love, compassion, wisdom and great intelligence and it links you with the most sublime source in creation: God Almighty, the Creator of the universe.

Form the connection as follows:
Take a deep breath, as always, through the nose. Breathe slowly and hold your breath, as your attention goes to your chest – the heart chakra – and briefly remains there. Exhale slowly through the mouth. This breath activates and catalyzes the energy centres. Since you create your own reality, you can make declarations and regard them as a clear and quick creation that has its own true will.

Declare:
"I choose a total connection - physical, emotional, mental and spiritual.
"I choose to be in the complete light and guidance of my soul.
"I choose to be in tune with my high truth.
"I am synchronized in all my bodies, here and now with all my strength!
"Thank you for all possible assistance."

Take a deep breath and merge imagination with creativity. Feel and see in your mind's eye energies being streamed to you through the crown, entering your body, cleansing, purifying, enlarging you aura (the energetic envelope that surrounds you).

You can call upon your spiritual guides, even if you are not acquainted with them. They know you and are eagerly awaiting your call and acknowledgment. Naturally, it is important that you should be in tune with light and love before you make the call! If you are not sure which frequencies you are connected to, choose first to connect to the light, to love, as described above.

I recommend the use of energy processes by way of guided imagery. This could be conducted in schools to provide practical tools for adolescents, helping them search for themselves and get in tune.

I recommend introducing meditation into all educational institutions, workplaces and even the government and parliaments (such as the Senate and House of Representatives in the U.S.) This course of action could be part of a healthy, orderly, correct and fit way of life.

Aware society is an evolved society! Conscious and serene society is a harmonious, just, wise society. An aware society is a society of abundance and prosperity. A conscious society is highly creative and productive.

Please, dear and beloved people, do not harm yourselves. Do not cut yourselves off from your true connection with the source of your truth and power. Do not belittle your own value. Do not forget that you create your lives, your society and your world.

Honor every single individual. honour yourselves in particular. Do not cut yourselves off from spirit or from the material aspect of being. Do not label people "spiritual" and then treat them with disregard, arrogantly and maybe with envy, **for all of you, in actual reality, are spiritual beings manifested in matter and connected to spirit.**

Be patient, it will bring satisfaction to you and lift your mood.

Total connection with the spirit, raising consciousness of every individual in your society – that is the ultimate solution to all of society's ills.

Your path may be short or long, easy or hard. It is you who choose the kind of trials and experiences you shall have. Be careful with your thoughts and discerning in your interpretations, whether personal or the ones you absorb from without, from society and from the world.

It is time for you to become a light unto the nations of the world.

"For the law shall go forth from Zion and the word of the Lord from Jerusalem." (Micah 4:2.)

It is all truly very simple, you just have to ask to internalize, accommodate and implement the message of the whole Torah, "love thy neighbour as thyself," and "thou salt love the Lord thy God with all your soul and all your might."

That is all, truly **All!**

I Am Master Akiva, herald of the message of unity and of the salvation of Israel, the harbinger of the path in the spirit of Holy God for the People of Israel and for all the nations of the world. All are my children, remember that well. (God's words.)

Thank you dear and so very beloved Ilana. Thank you for being creation's mouthpiece, a pure channell for the knowledge of the most sublime truth of unity, bearing in your codes and frequencies the **Consciousness of the One**.

Blessed be in your eternal being. Blessed be those who come under your roof, the inhabitants of your city, your beloved homeland, Israel, all of whom are the children of Abraham – Arab and Jews alike; all the nations of the world and all of creation.

Remember, all is one! All is love.

"In the beginning God created the heaven and the earth." You were created by God to connect heaven and earth. You are composed of the heaven and the earth. And that is the subject of our next book.

"Blessed be the Lord God, the God of Israel, who only doeth wondrous things and blessed [be] his glorious name forever: and let the whole earth be filled with his glory; Amen and Amen." (Psalms 72:18–19.)

"Love thy neighbour as thyself."